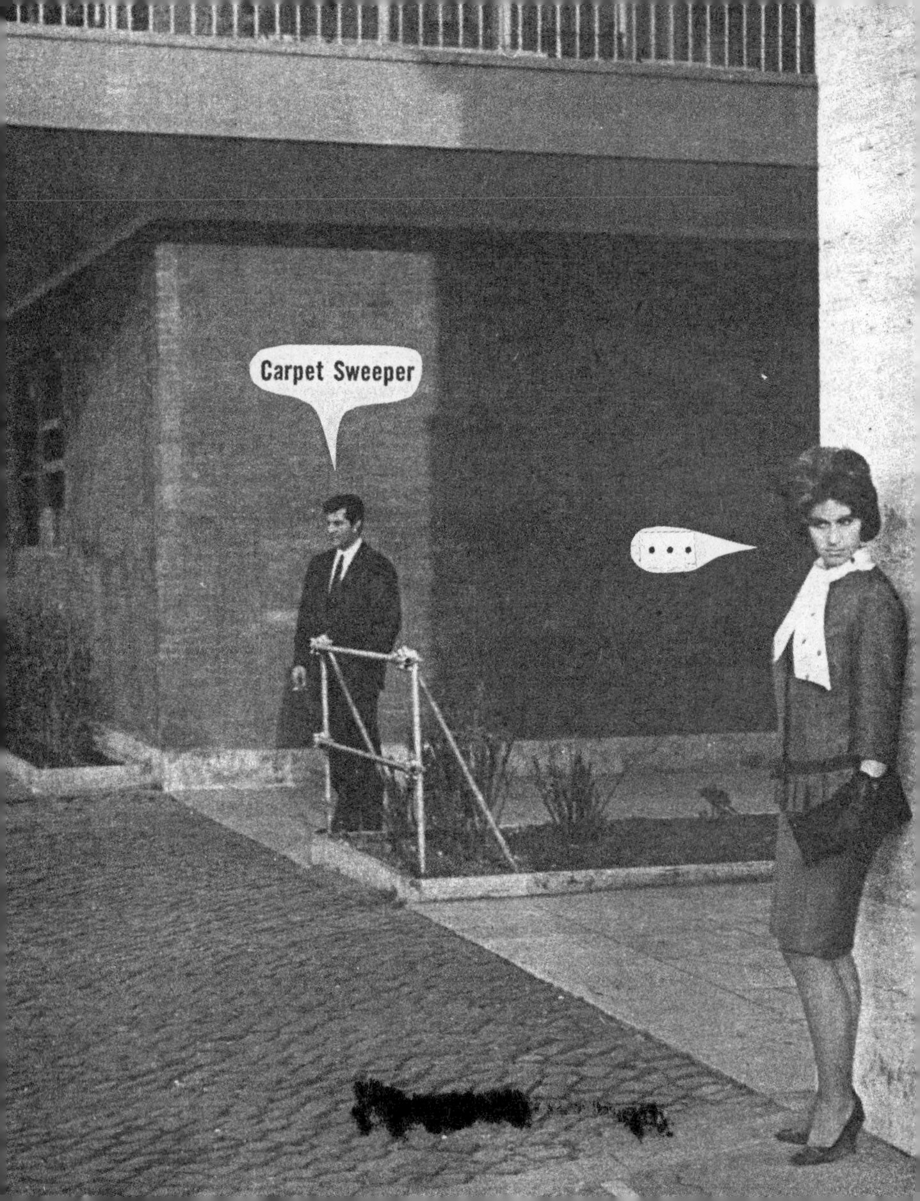
Carpet Sweeper
• • •

Julie Doucet

CARPET SWEEPER TALES

Drawn & Quarterly

This book is made of a collection of old Italian fumetti:
The Knocked over Flower (1962)
Young People Can Love Too (1965)
I Was Helpless (1966)
Jennifer Top Secret (1971)
And of a selection of even older everyday-life American magazines:
Better Homes and Gardens (1948–1958)
Good Housekeeping (1954–1959)
Mechanix Illustrated (1963 and 1964)
Needlework & Crafts (1968–1970)

drawnandquarterly.com

First edition: March 2016. Printed in Canada. 10 9 8 7 6 5 4 3 2 1

Library and Archives Canada Cataloguing in Publication:
Doucet, Julie, 1965–, author, illustrator. *Carpet Sweeper Tales* / Julie Doucet.
ISBN 978-1-77046-239-7 (paperback). 1. Graphic novels. I. Title. PN6733.D68C37
2016 741.5'971 C2015-906024-9

Published in the USA by Drawn & Quarterly, a client publisher of Farrar, Straus and Giroux. Orders: 888.330.8477. Published in Canada by Drawn & Quarterly, a client publisher of Raincoast Books. Orders: 800.663.5714. Published in the United Kingdom by Drawn & Quarterly, a client publisher of Publishers Group UK. Orders: info@pguk.co.uk

Canada Drawn & Quarterly reconnaît l'appui du gouvernement du Canada/Drawn & Quarterly acknowledges the support of the Government of Canada and the Canada Council for the Arts for our publishing program.

Drawn & Quarterly reconnaît l'aide financière du gouvernement du Québec par l'entremise de la Société de développement des entreprises culturelles (SODEC) pour nos activités d'édition. Gouvernement du Québec—Programme de crédit d'impôt pour l'édition de livres—Gestion SODEC.

CONTENTS

Read it out loud

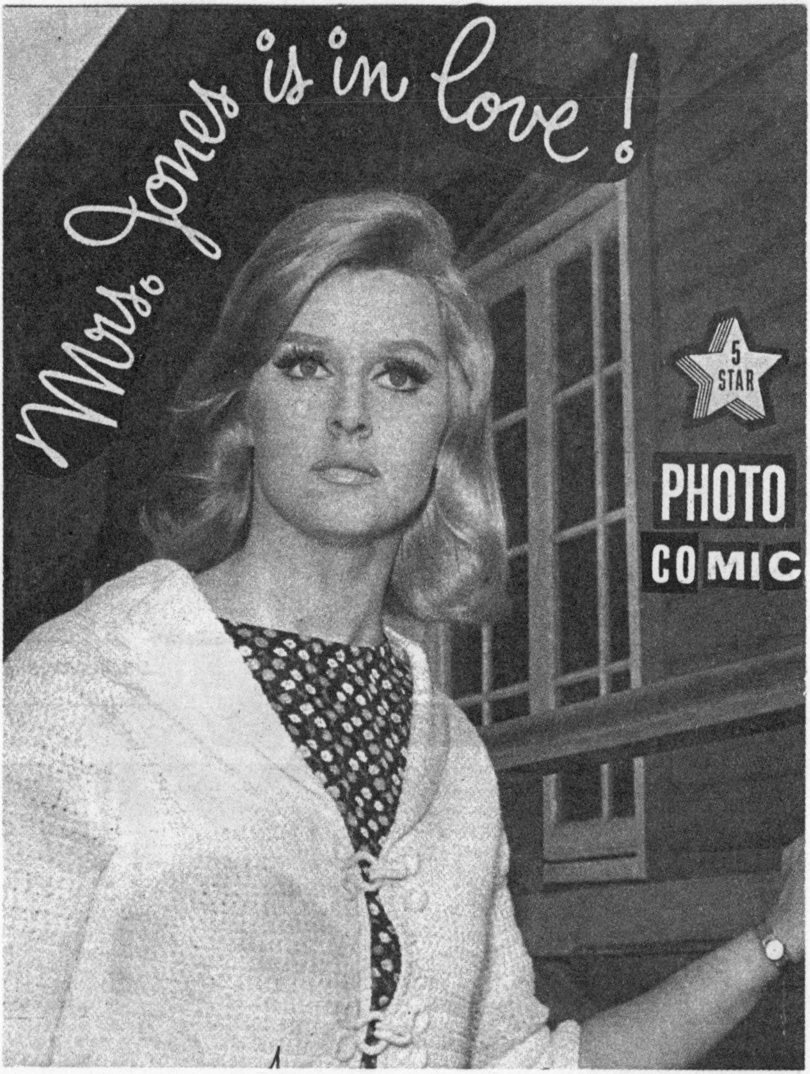
Mrs. Jones is in love!
5 STAR
PHOTO
COMIC

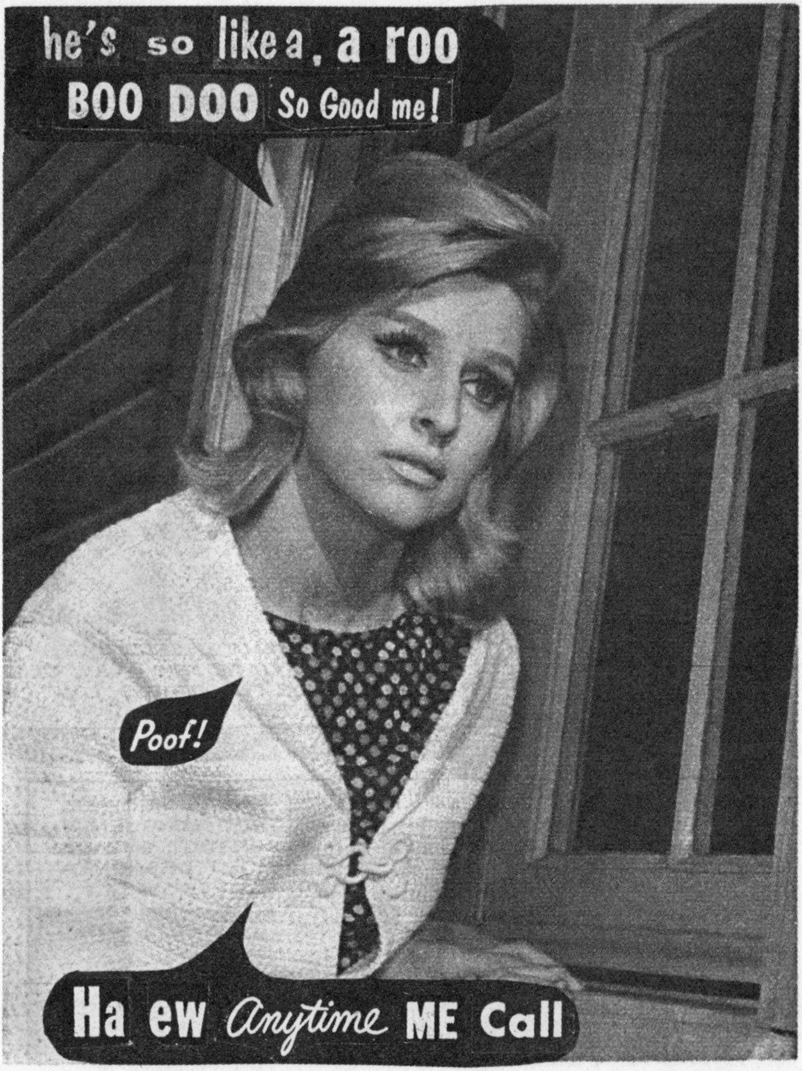
he's so like a, a roo BOO DOO So Good me!
Poof!
Ha ew Anytime ME Call

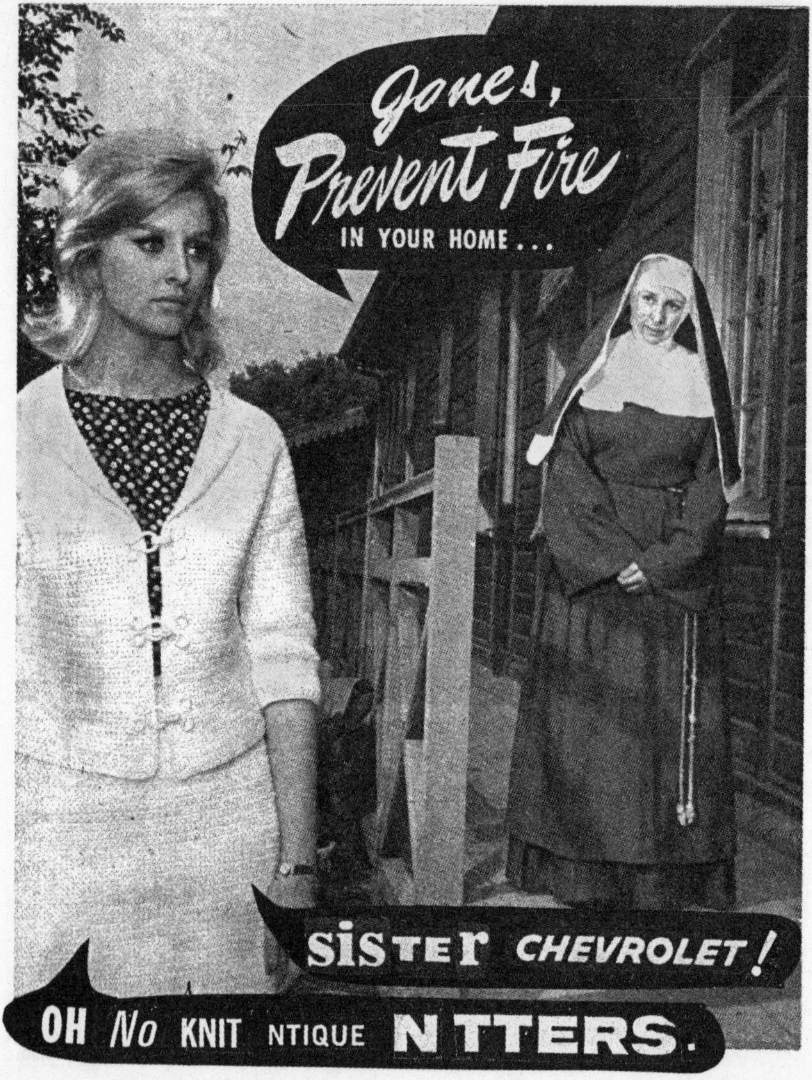

Jones,
Prevent Fire
IN YOUR HOME...
SISTER CHEVROLET!
OH No KNIT NTIQUE NTTERS.

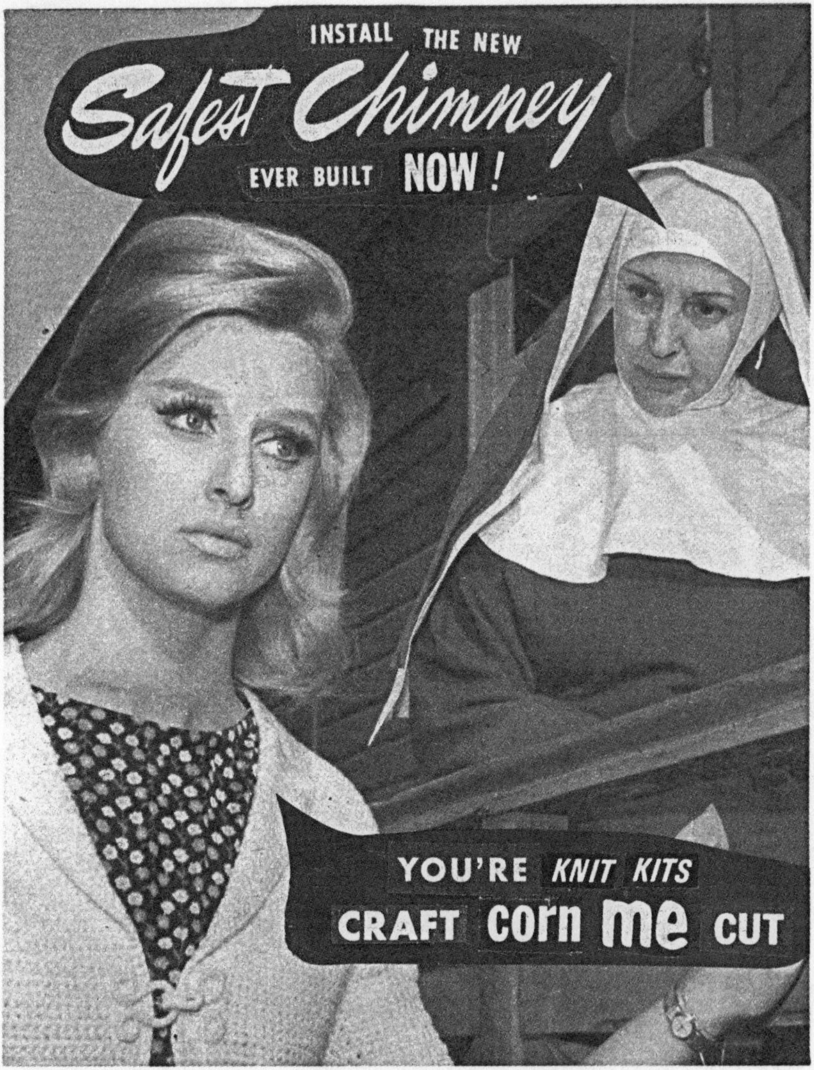
INSTALL THE NEW
Safest Chimney
EVER BUILT NOW!
YOU'RE KNIT KITS
CRAFT corn me CUT

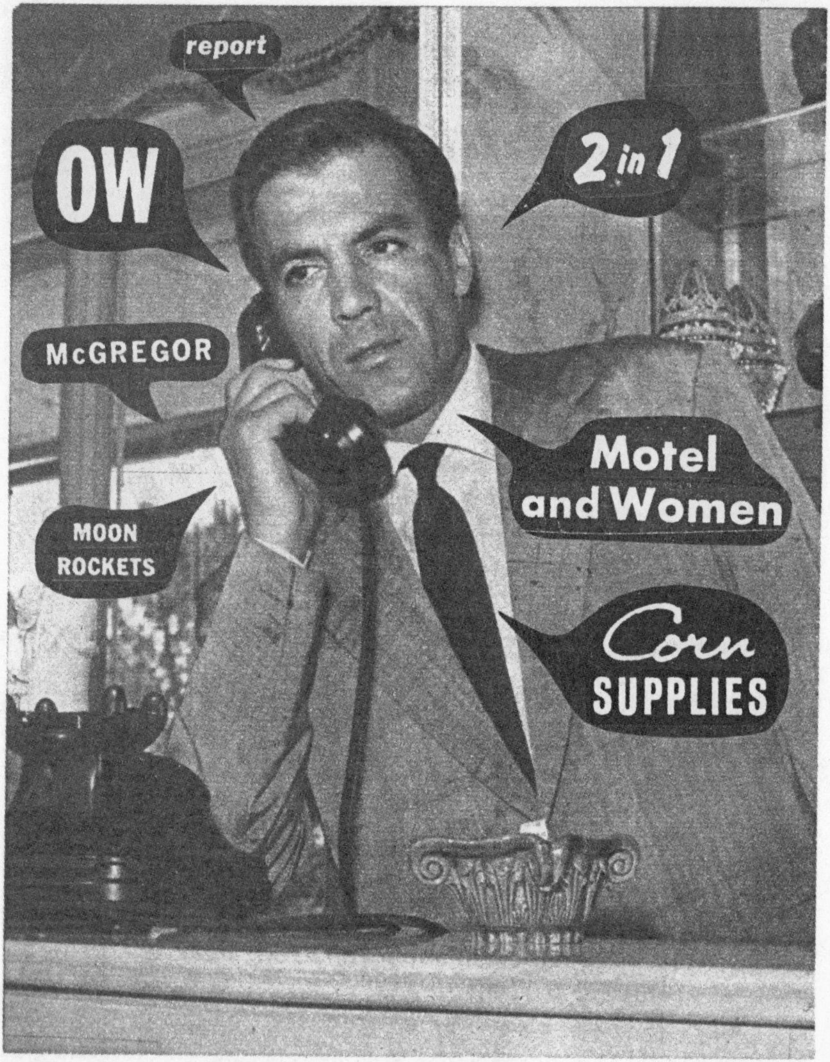
report
OW
2 in 1
McGREGOR
Motel and Women
MOON ROCKETS
Corn SUPPLIES

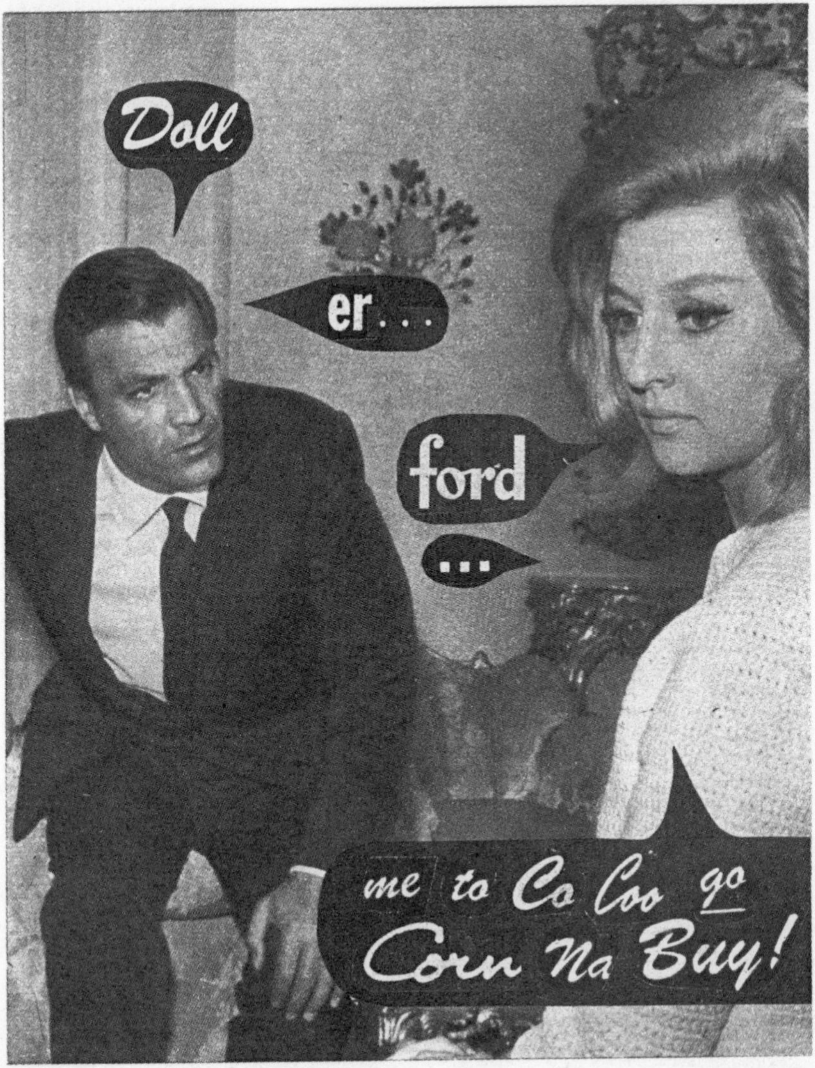
Doll
er...
ford
...
me to Co Coo go
Corn Na Buy!

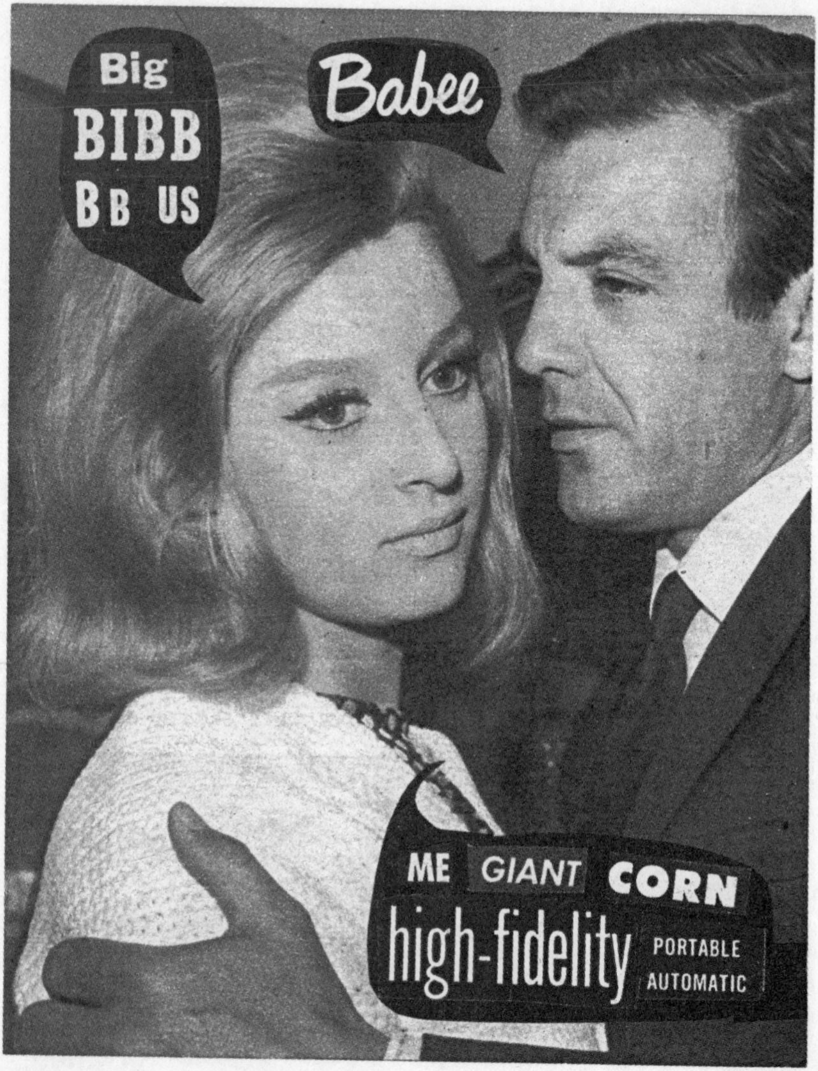
Big BIBB BB US
Babee
ME GIANT CORN
high-fidelity PORTABLE AUTOMATIC

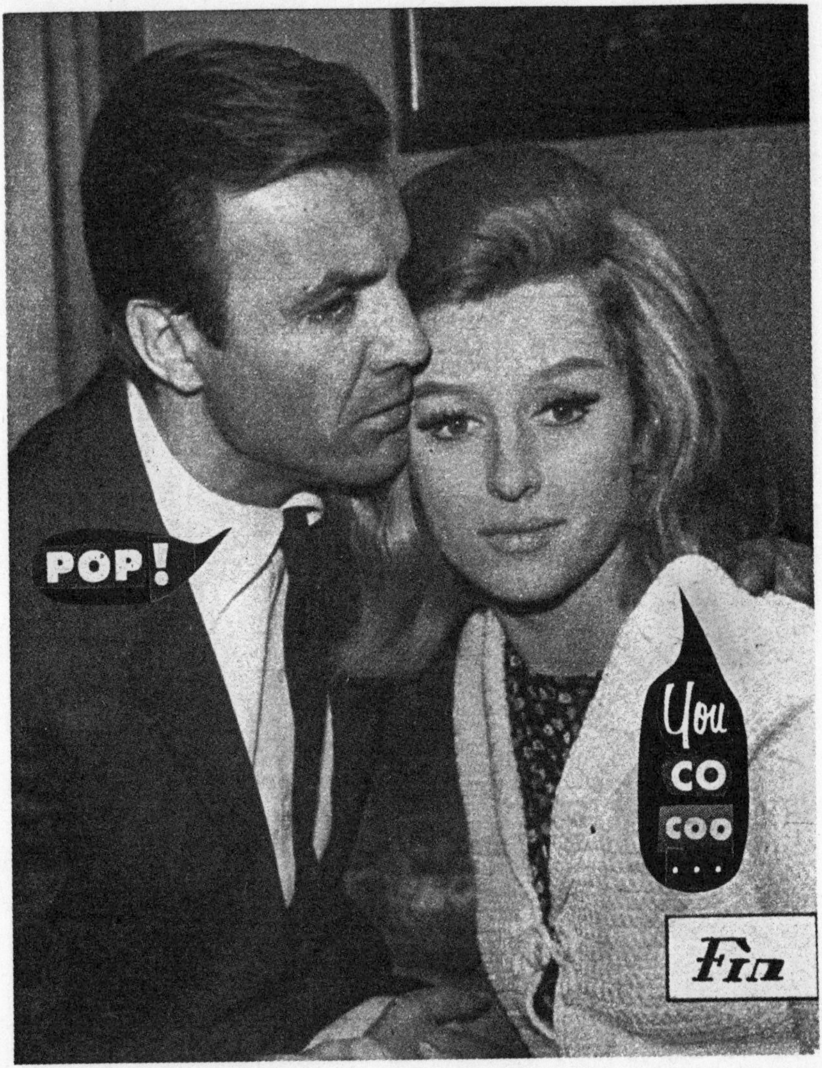
POP!
You
CO
COO
...
Fin

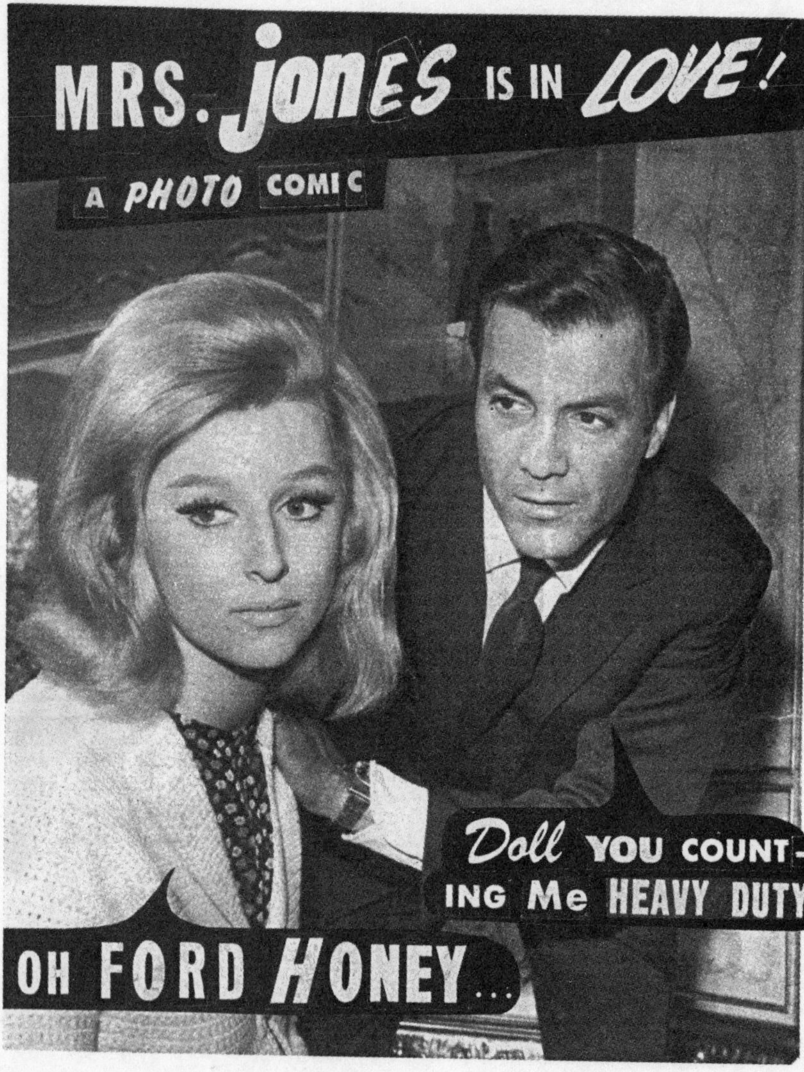
MRS. jones IS IN LOVE!
A PHOTO COMIC
Doll YOU COUNT-ING Me HEAVY DUTY
OH FORD HONEY...

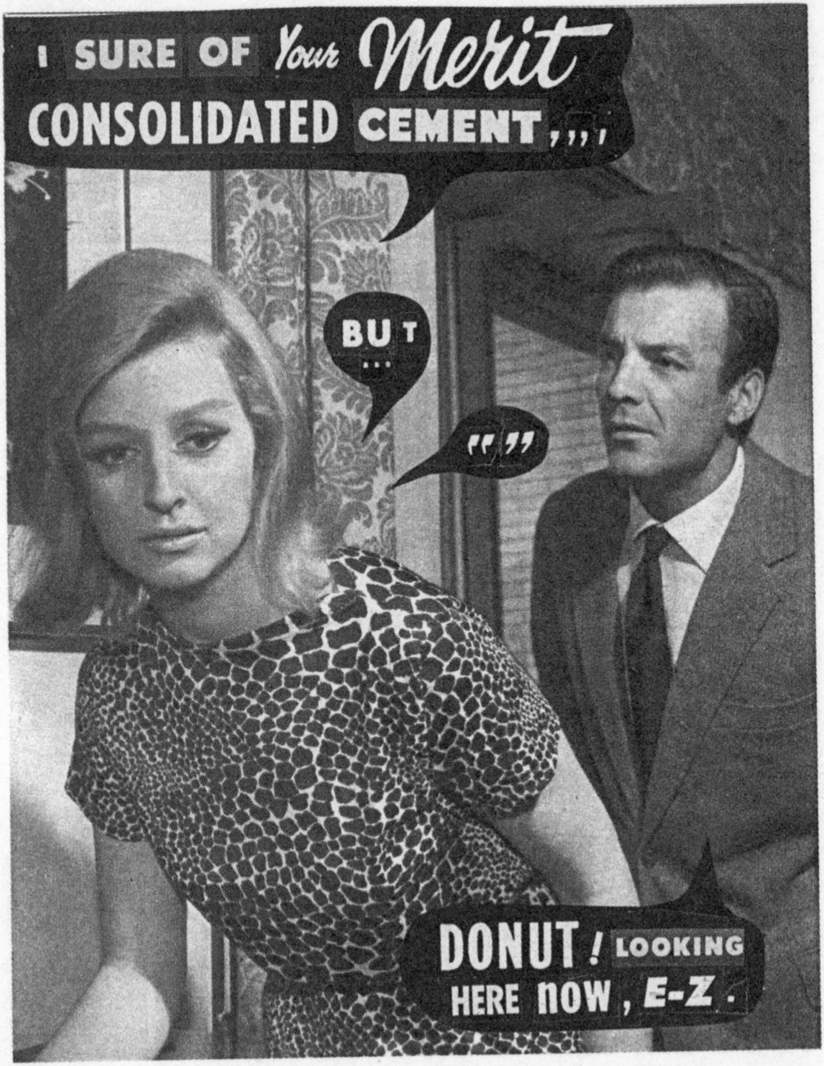
I SURE OF Your Merit
CONSOLIDATED CEMENT,,,,
BUT ...
" "
DONUT! LOOKING
HERE now, E-Z.

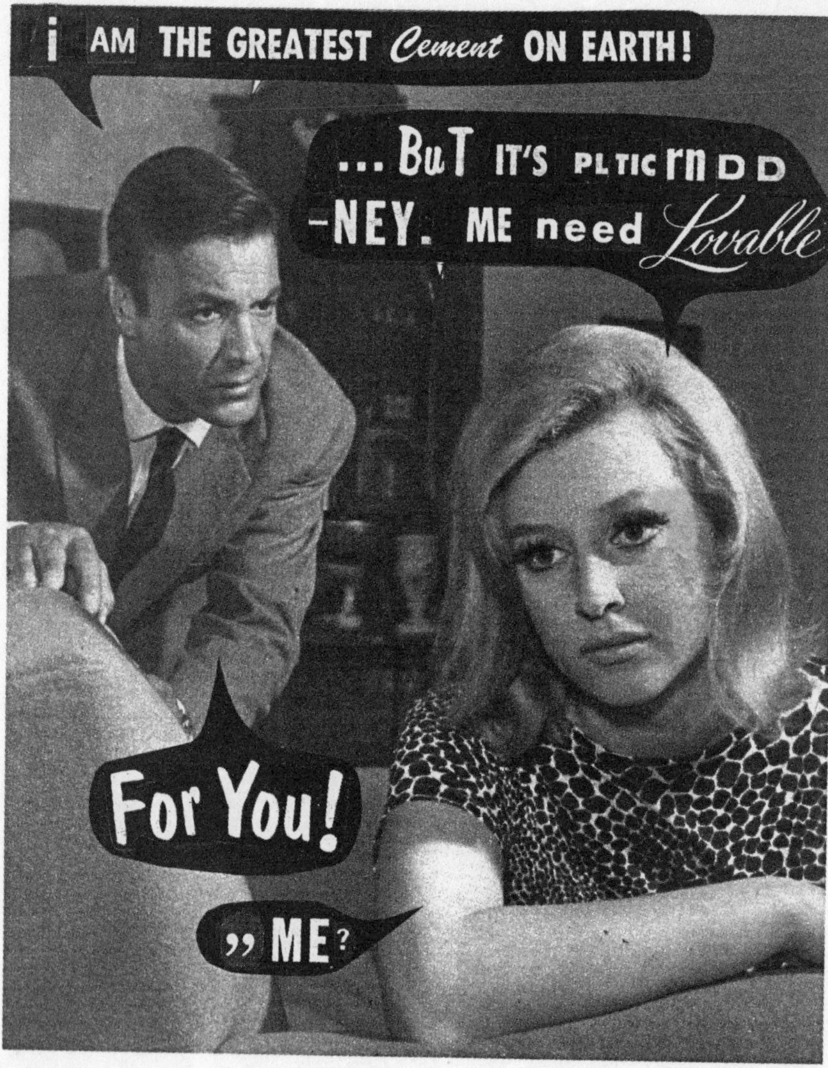
i AM THE GREATEST Cement ON EARTH!
...BuT IT'S PLTICrnDD -NEY. ME need Lovable
For You!
,, ME?

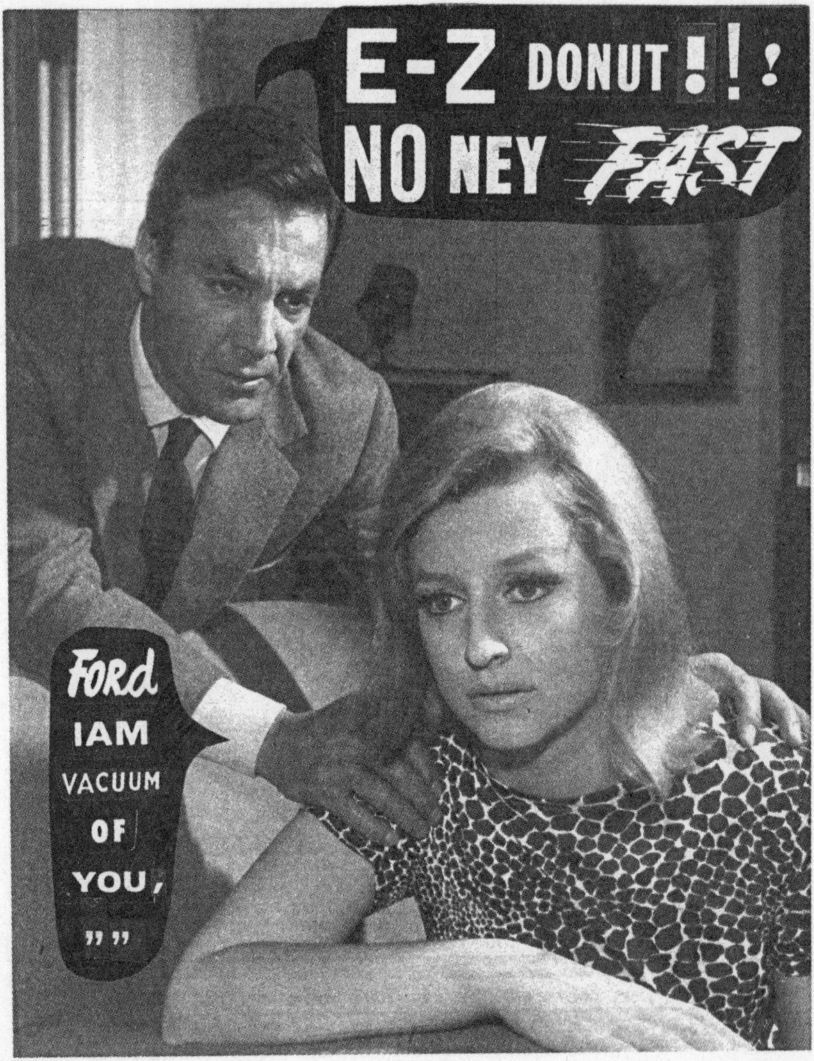
E-Z DONUT!!!
NO NEY FAST
Ford
IAM
VACUUM
OF
YOU,
"""

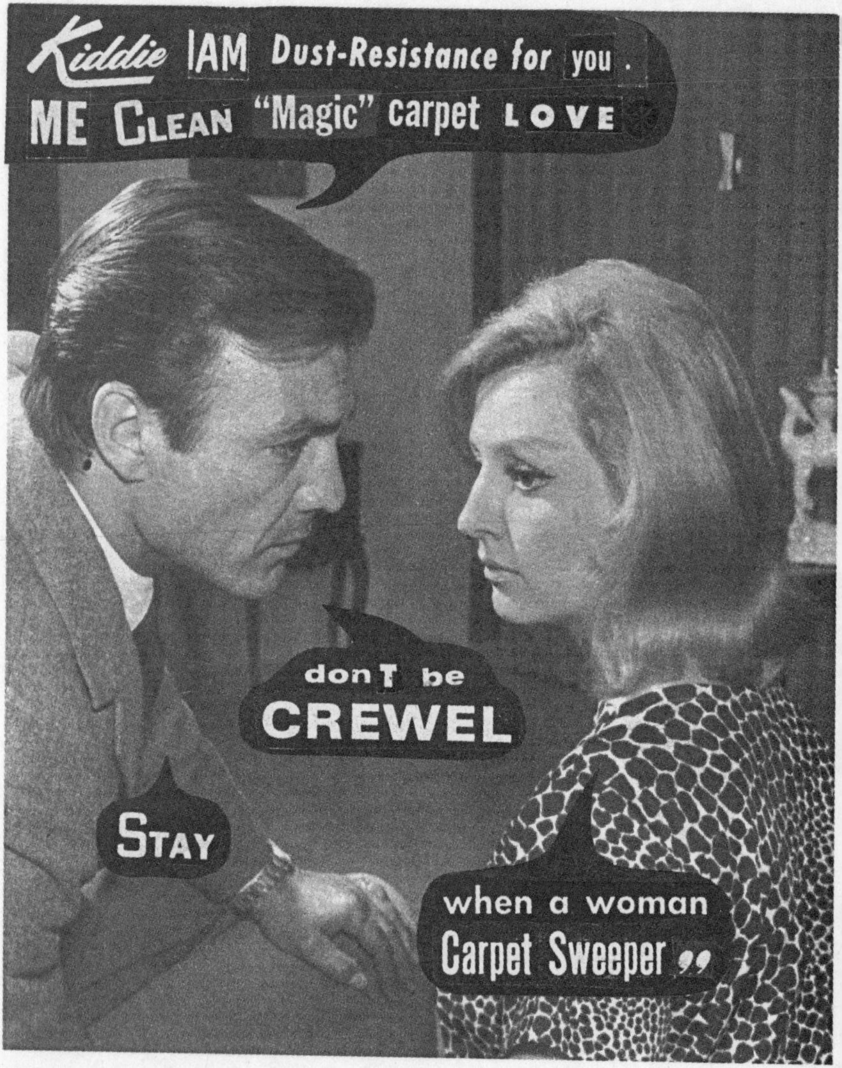
Kiddie I AM Dust-Resistance for you.
ME CLEAN "Magic" carpet LOVE
don T be
CREWEL
STAY
when a woman
Carpet Sweeper ,,

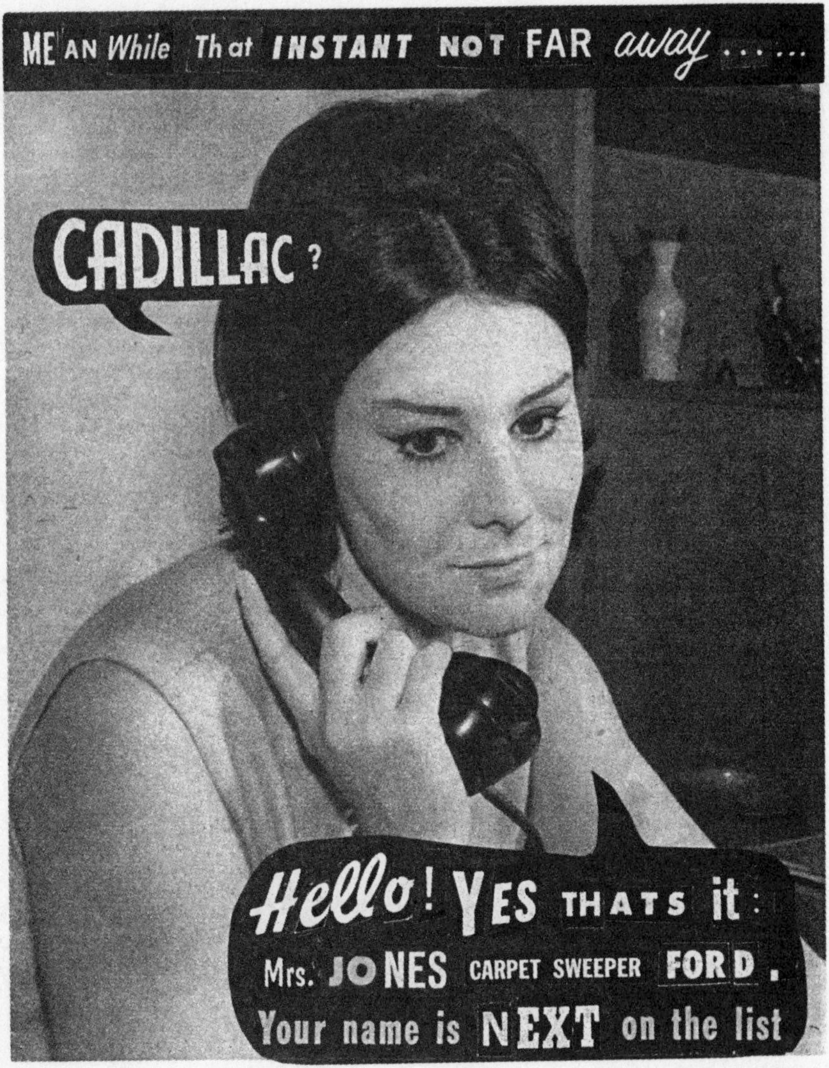
ME AN While That INSTANT NOT FAR away......
CADILLAC ?
Hello! YES THATS it:
Mrs. JONES CARPET SWEEPER FORD.
Your name is NEXT on the list

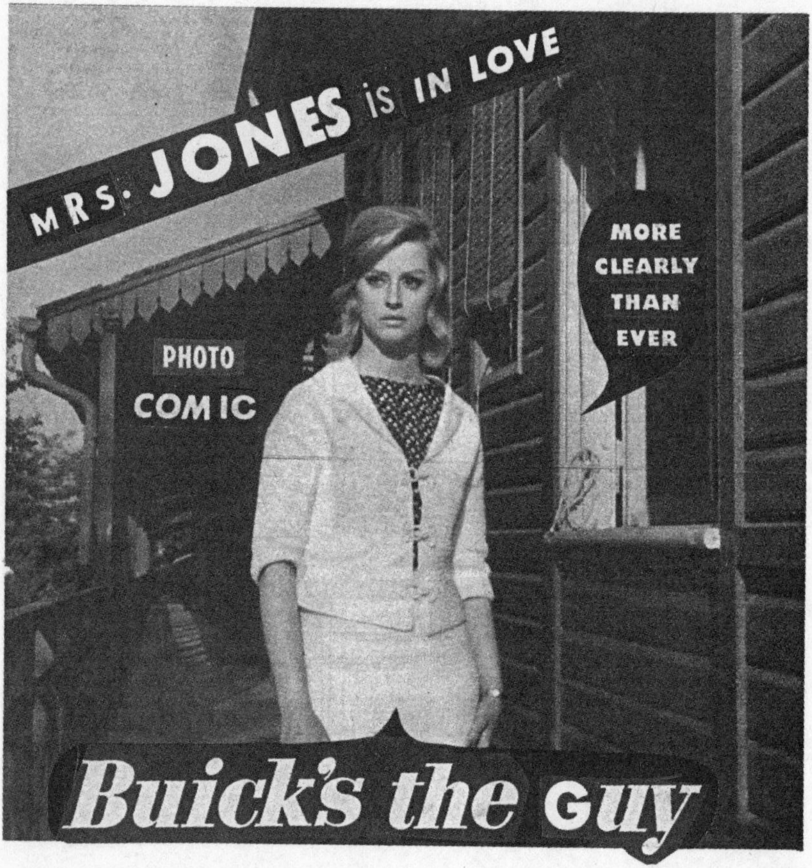
MRS. JONES is IN LOVE
MORE CLEARLY THAN EVER
PHOTO
COM IC
Buick's the GUY

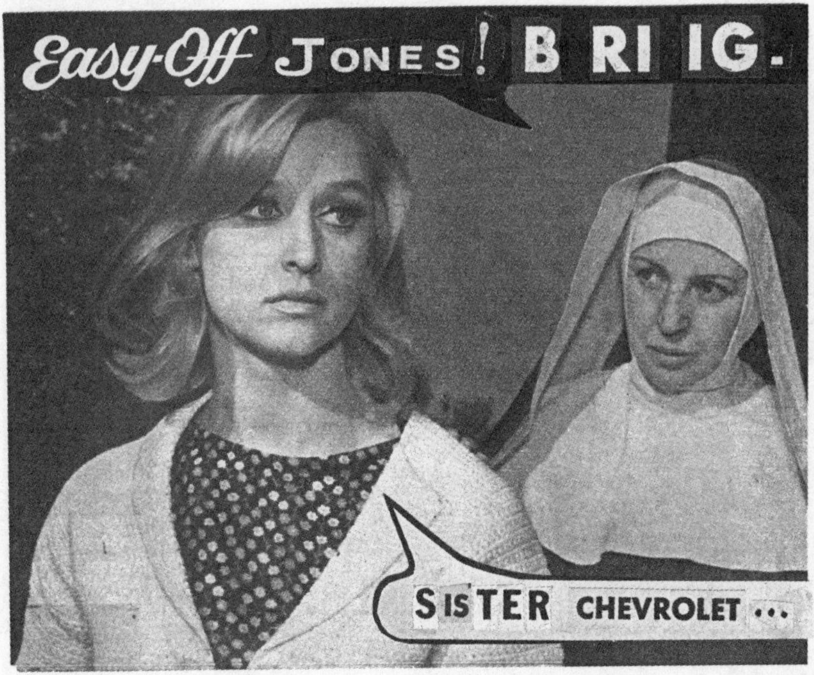
Easy-Off JONES! B RI IG.
SisTER CHEVROLET ...

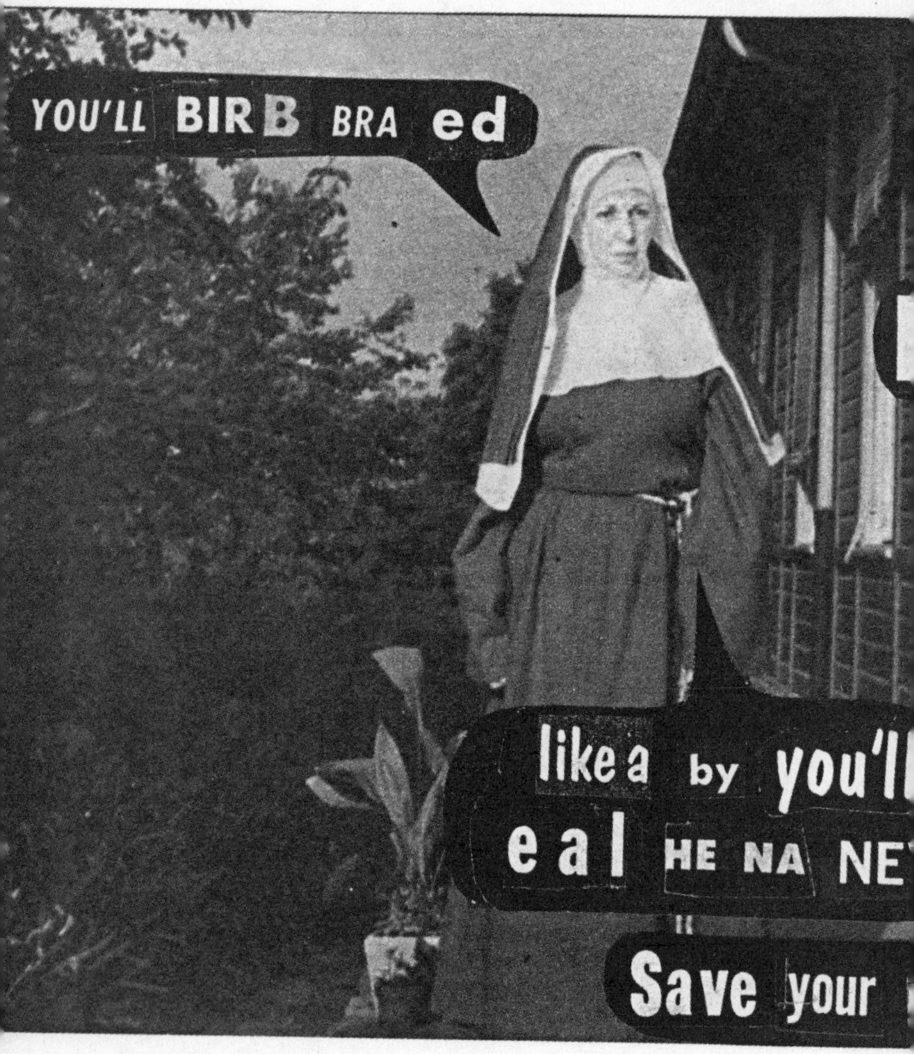
YOU'LL BIRB BRA ed
like a by you'l
e a l HE NA NE
Save your

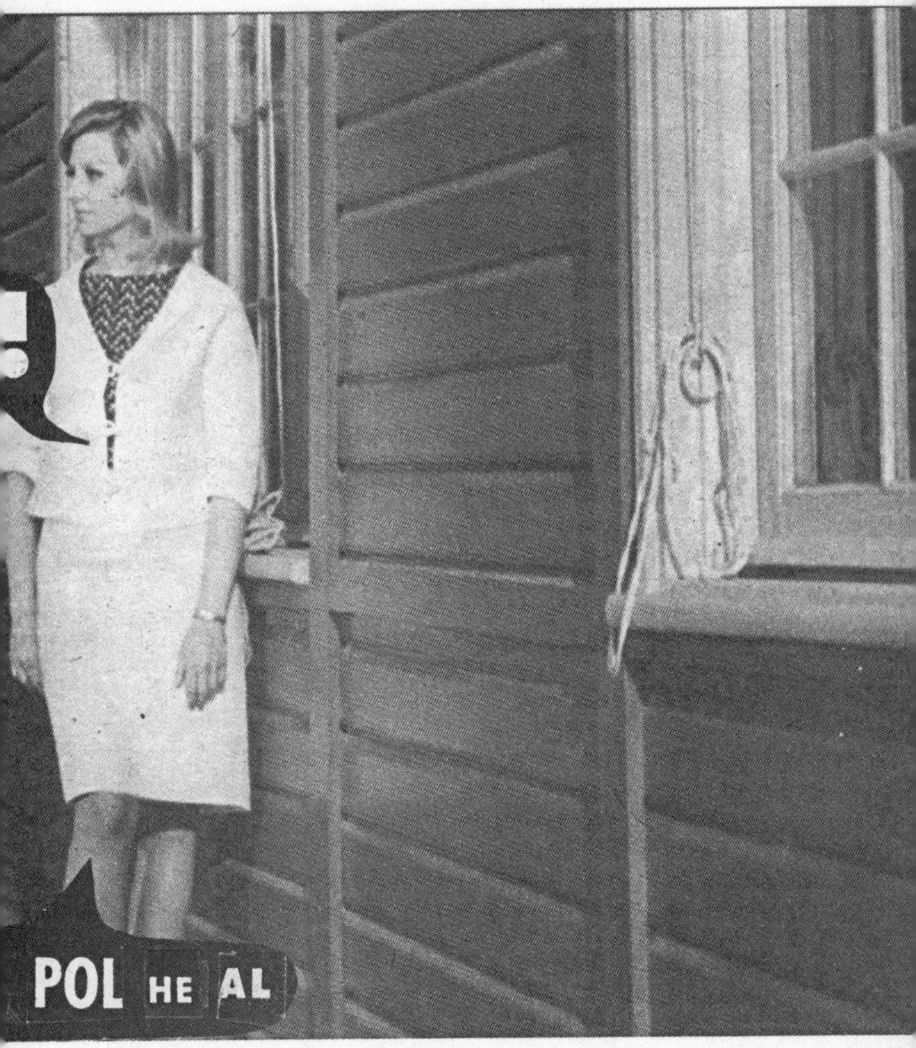
POL HE AL

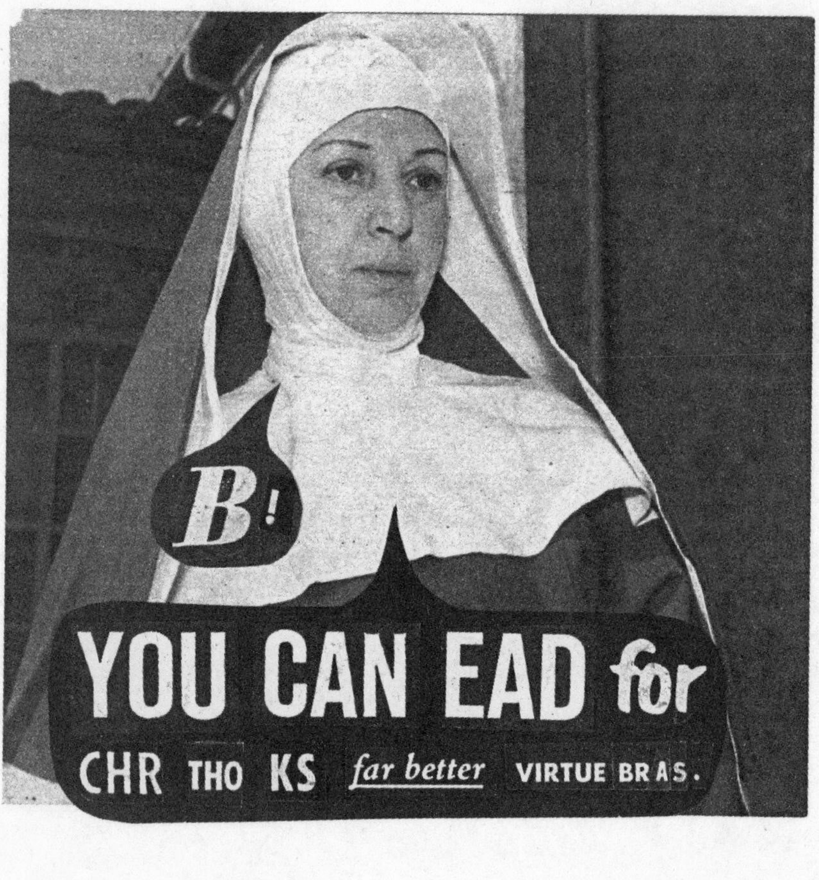
B!
YOU CAN EAD for
CHR THO KS far better VIRTUE BRAS.

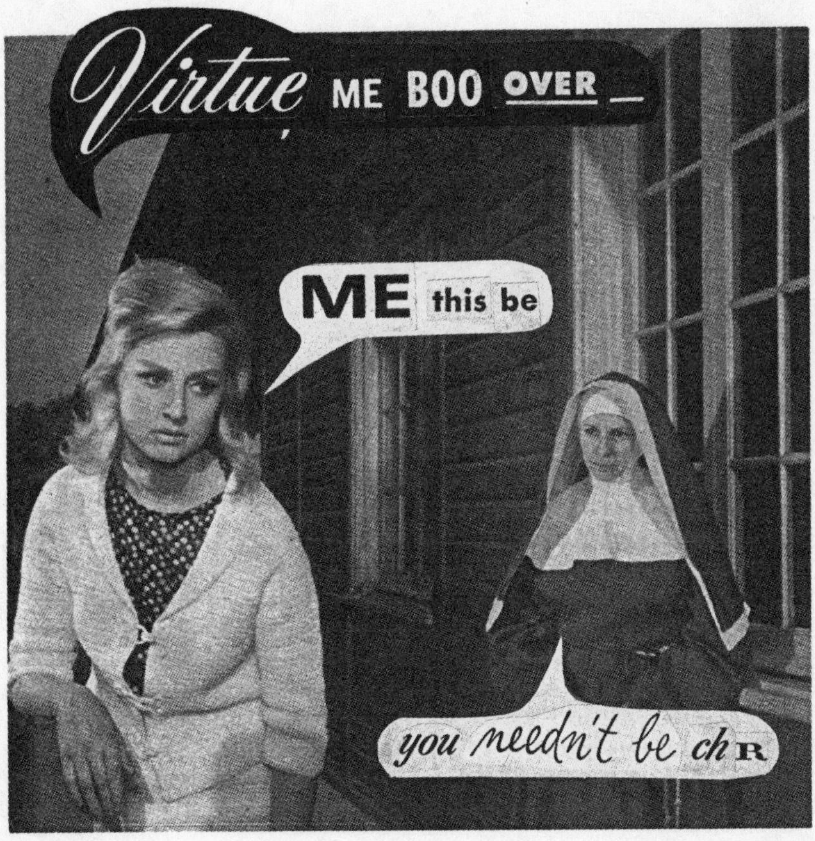

Virtue ME BOO OVER _
ME this be
you needn't be chR

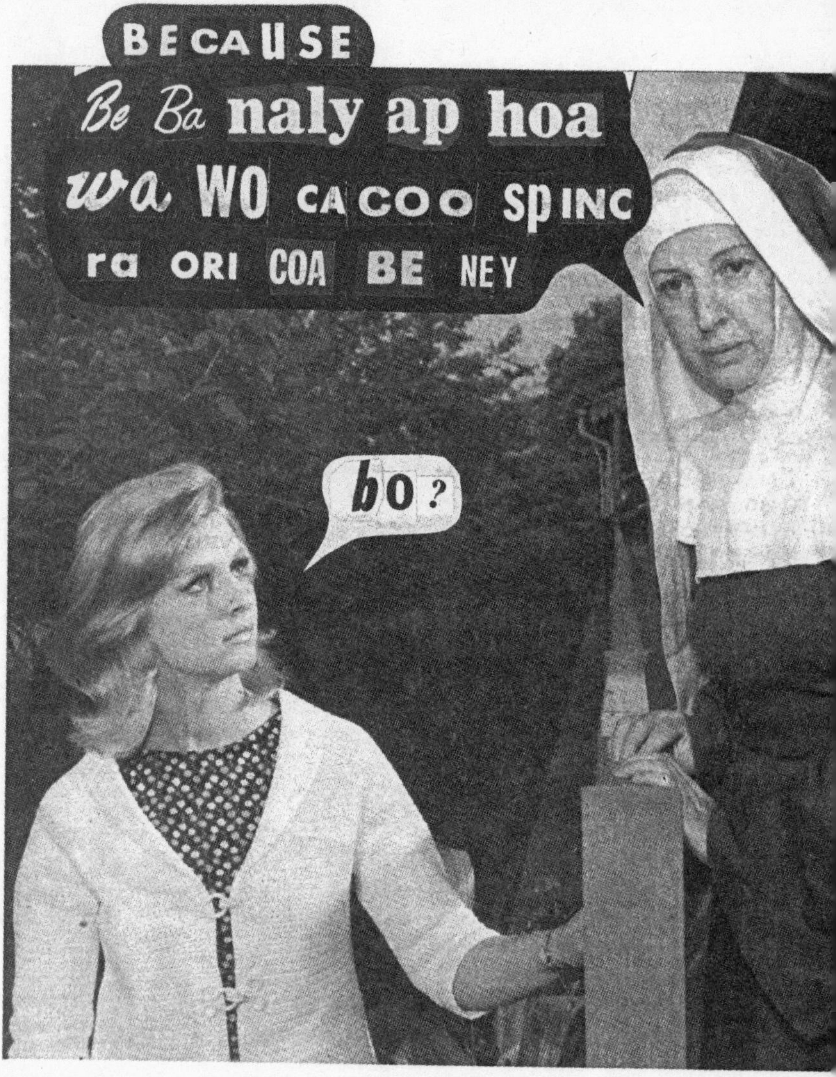
BECAUSE
Be Ba naly ap hoa wa WO CACOO SPINC ra ORI COA BE NEY
bo?

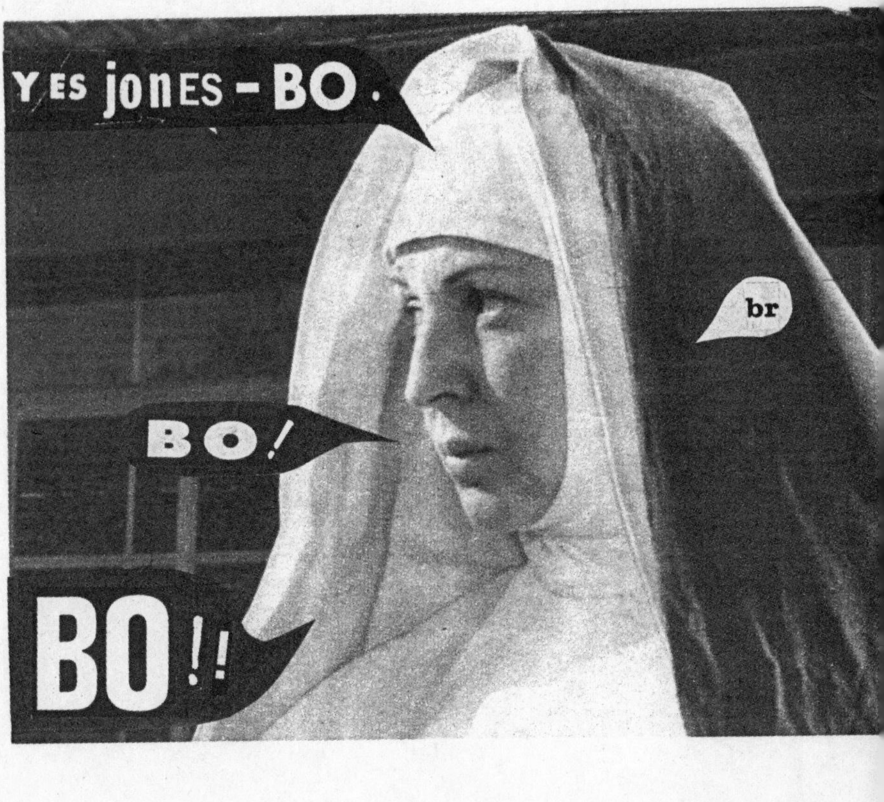
YES jonES - BO.
br
BO!
BO!!

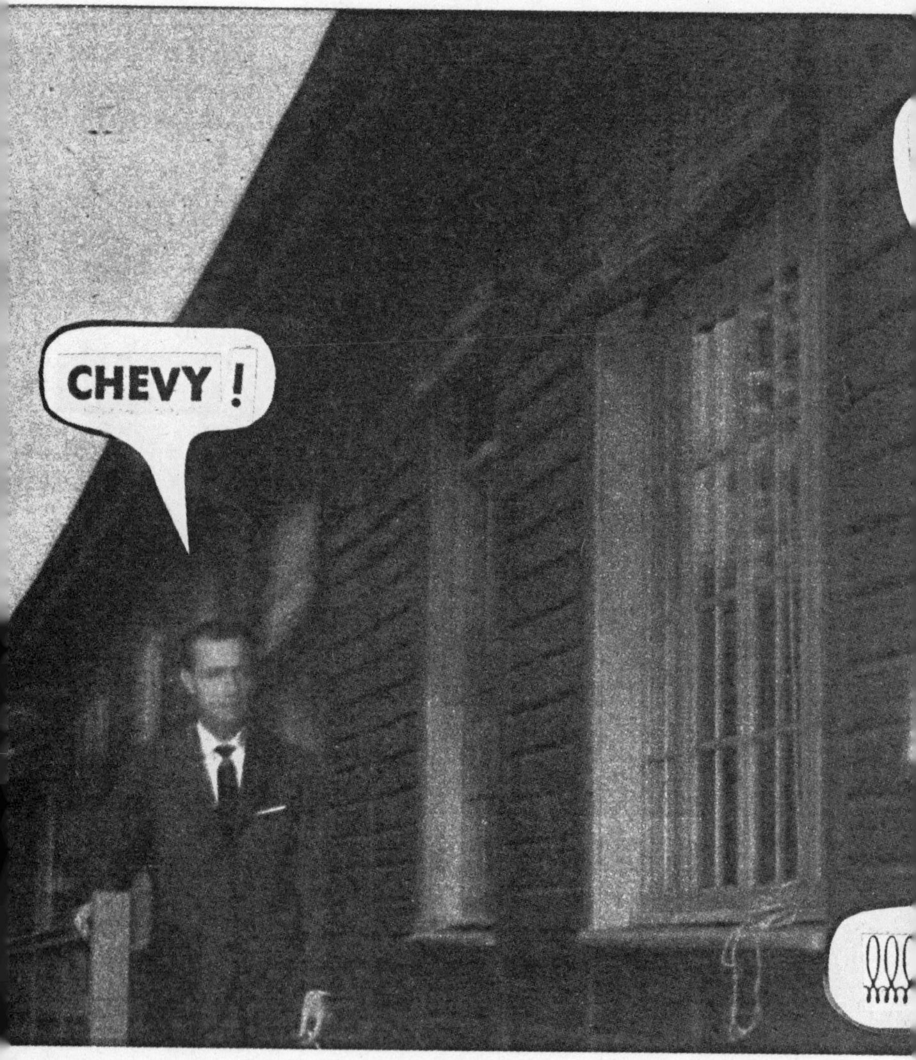
CHEVY !

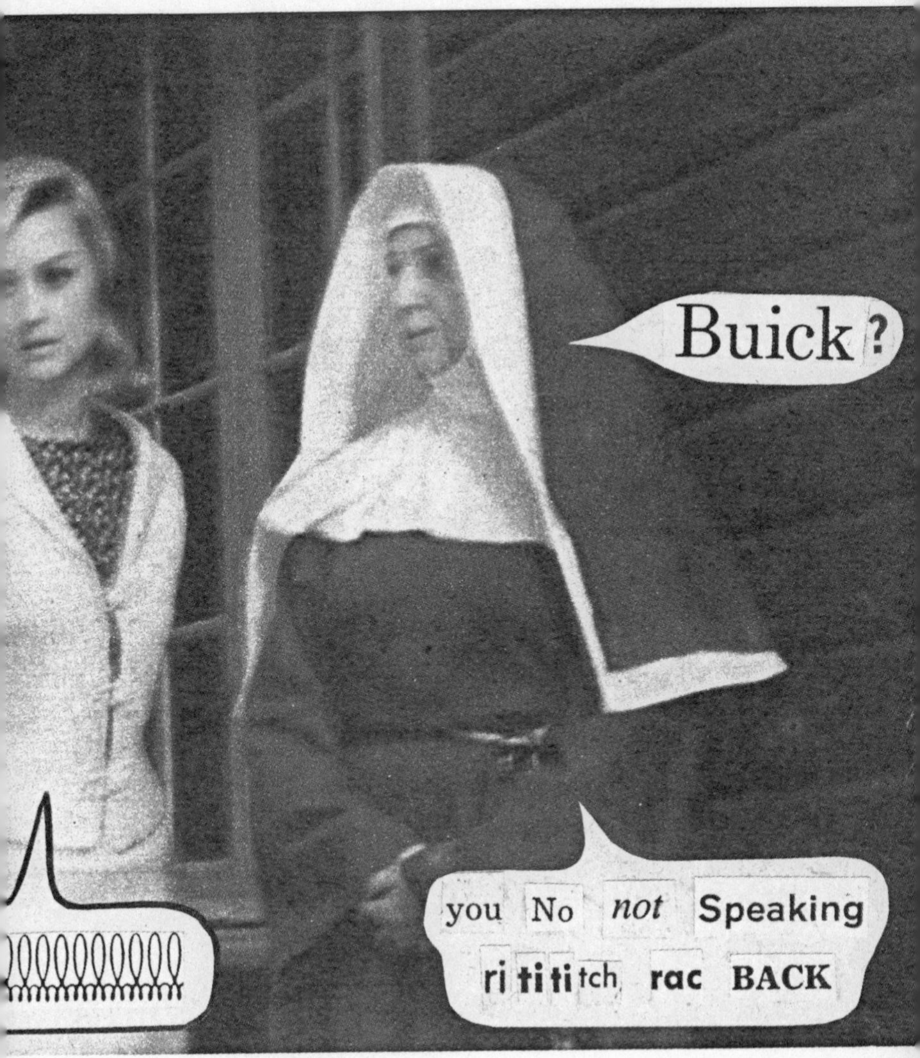

Buick?
you No not Speaking ri ti ti tch rac BACK

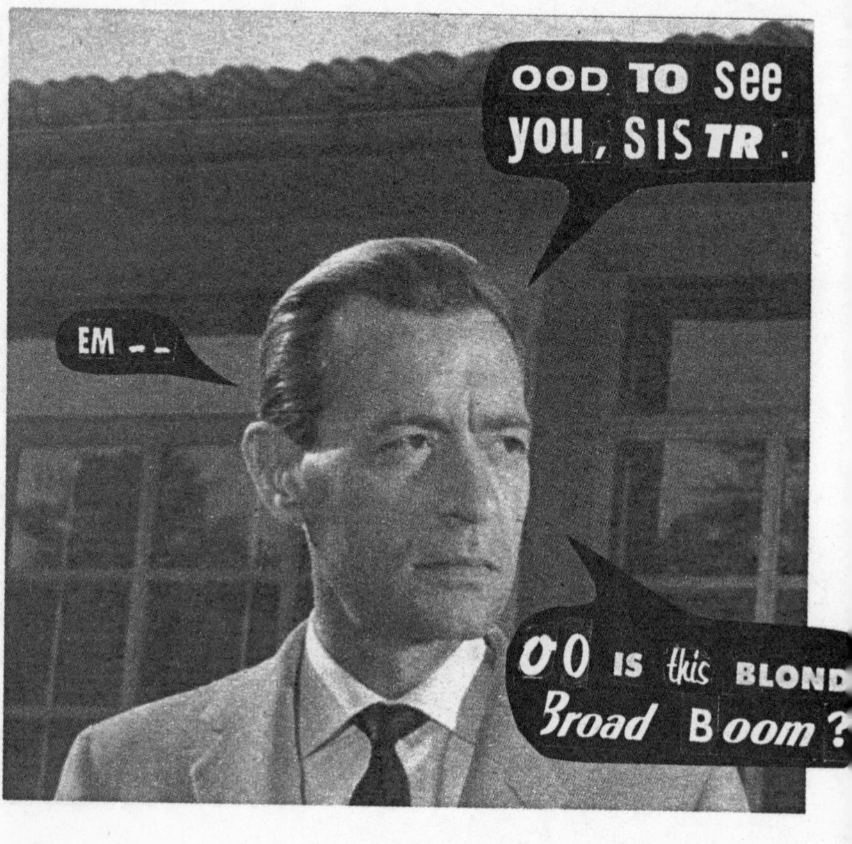
OOD TO See you, SISTR.
EM --
OO IS this BLOND Broad Boom?

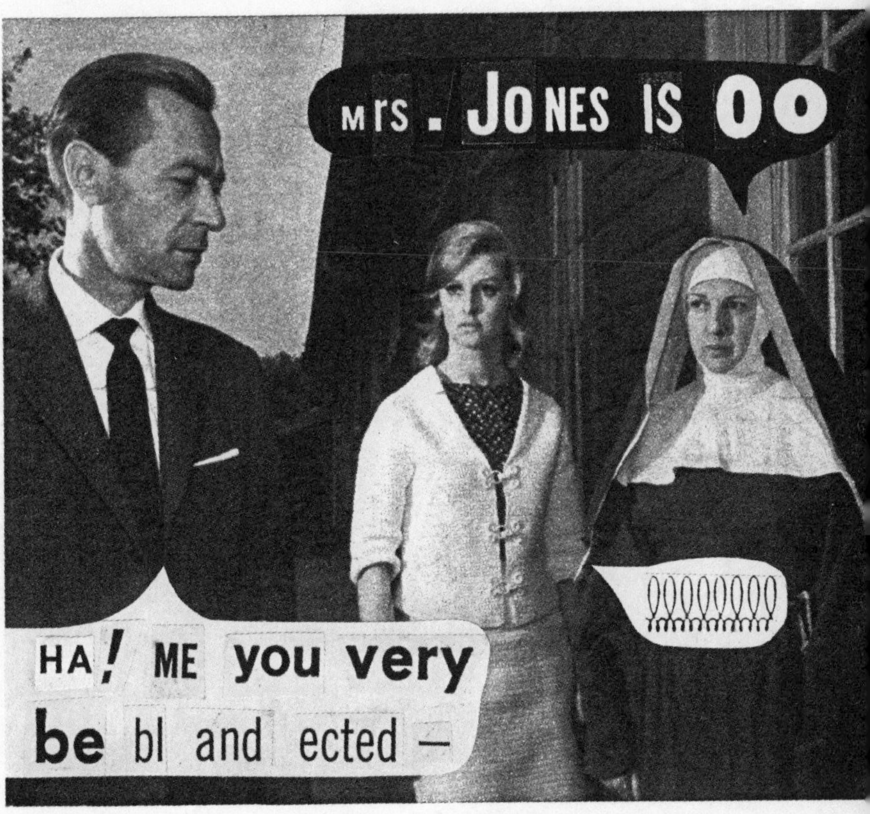
MrS. JONES IS OO
HA! ME you very
be bl and ected –

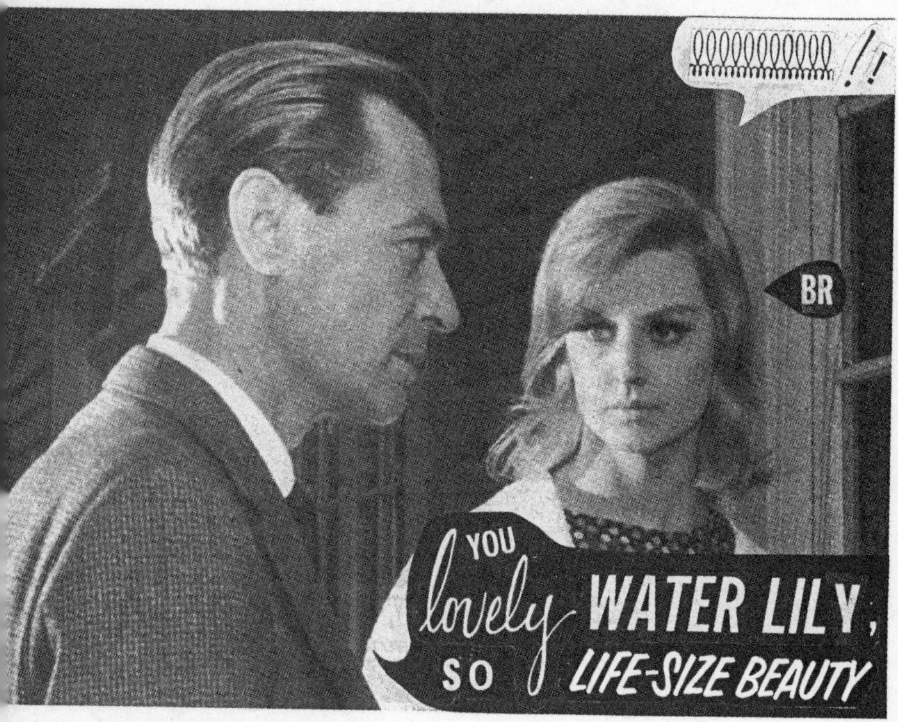
!!
BR
YOU lovely WATER LILY,
SO LIFE-SIZE BEAUTY

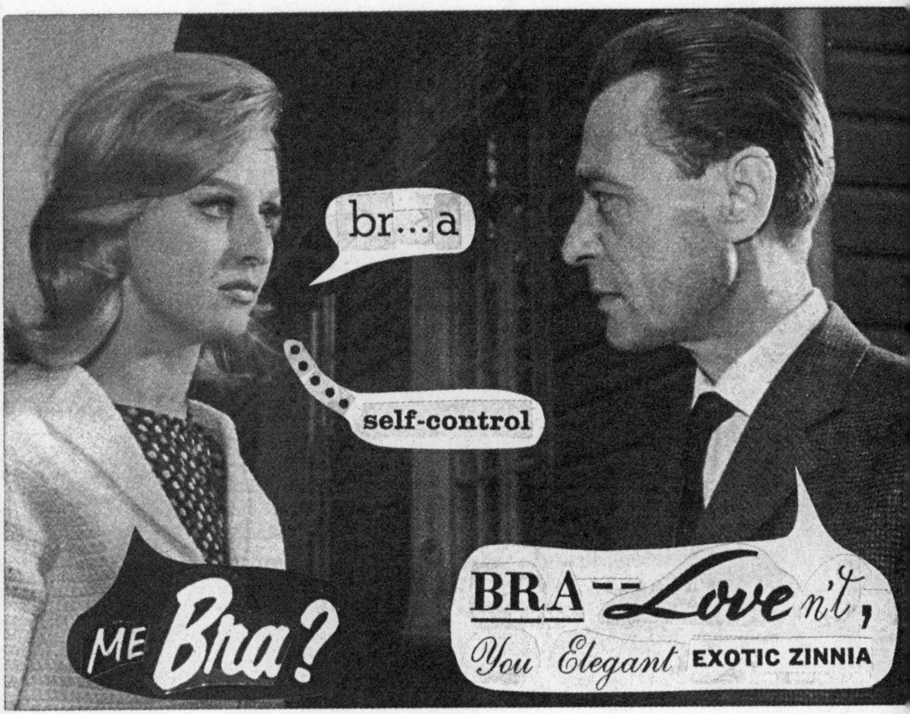
br...a
self-control
ME Bra?
BRA--Love n't,
You Elegant EXOTIC ZINNIA

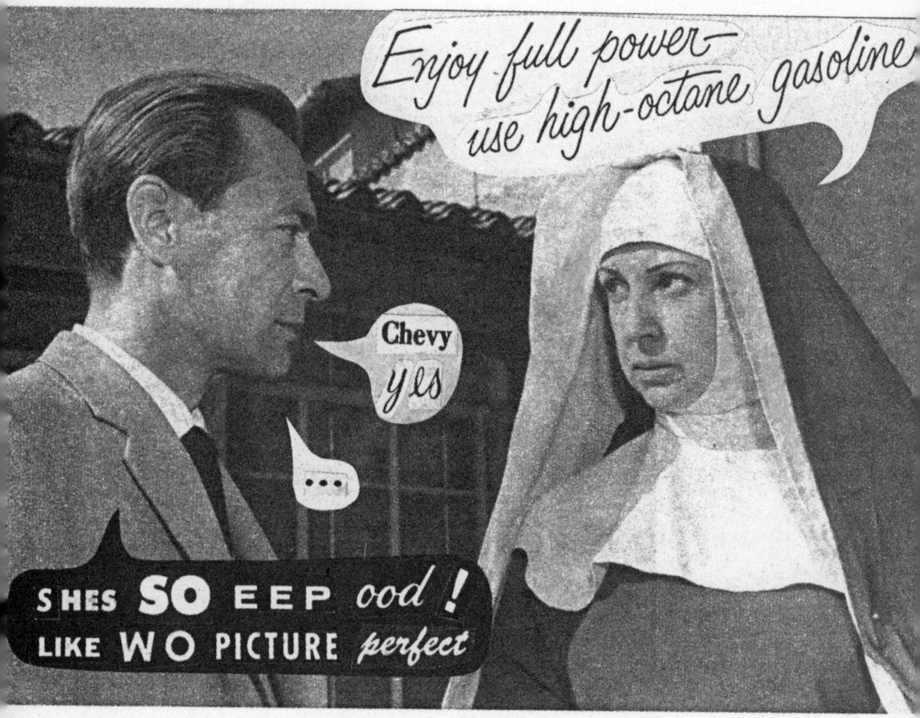
Enjoy full power—
use high-octane gasoline
Chevy
yes
...
SHES SO EEP ood !
LIKE WO PICTURE perfect

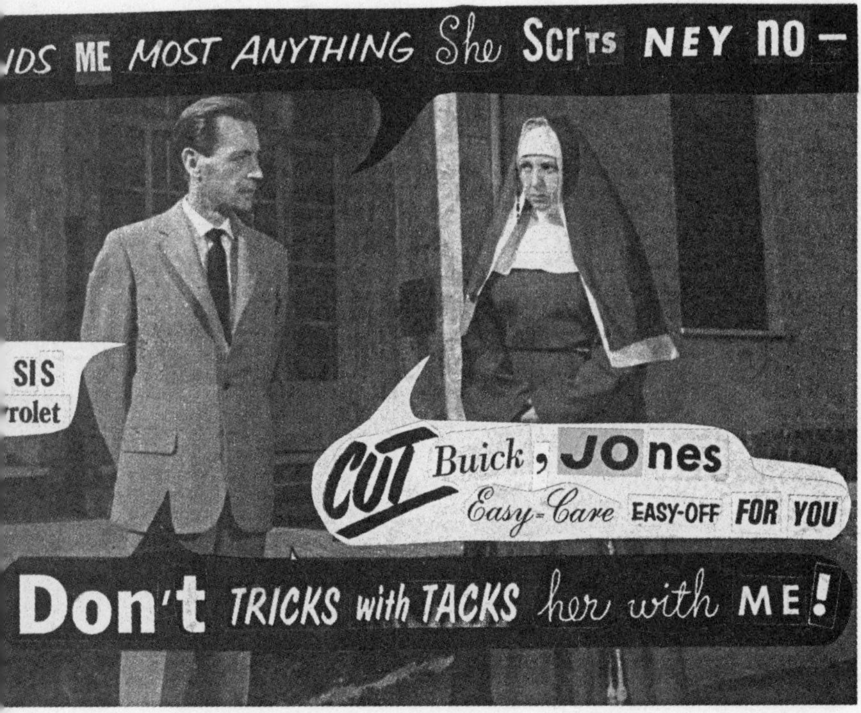
IDS ME MOST ANYTHING She Scrts NEY no—
SIS
rolet
CUT Buick, JOnes
Easy-Care EASY-OFF FOR YOU
Don't TRICKS with TACKS her with ME!

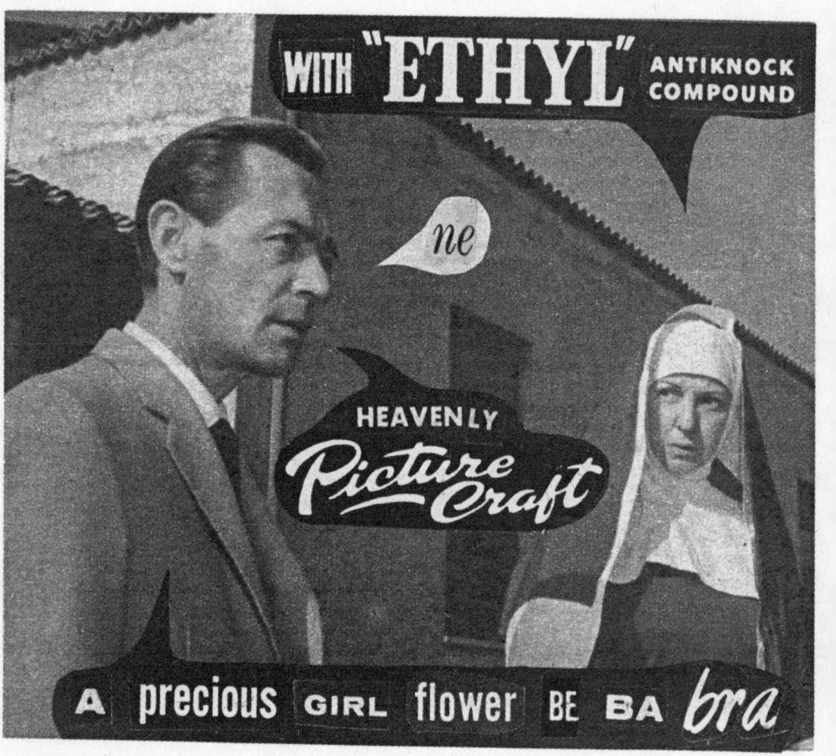
WITH "ETHYL" ANTIKNOCK COMPOUND
ne
HEAVENLY
Picture Craft
A precious GIRL flower BE BA bra

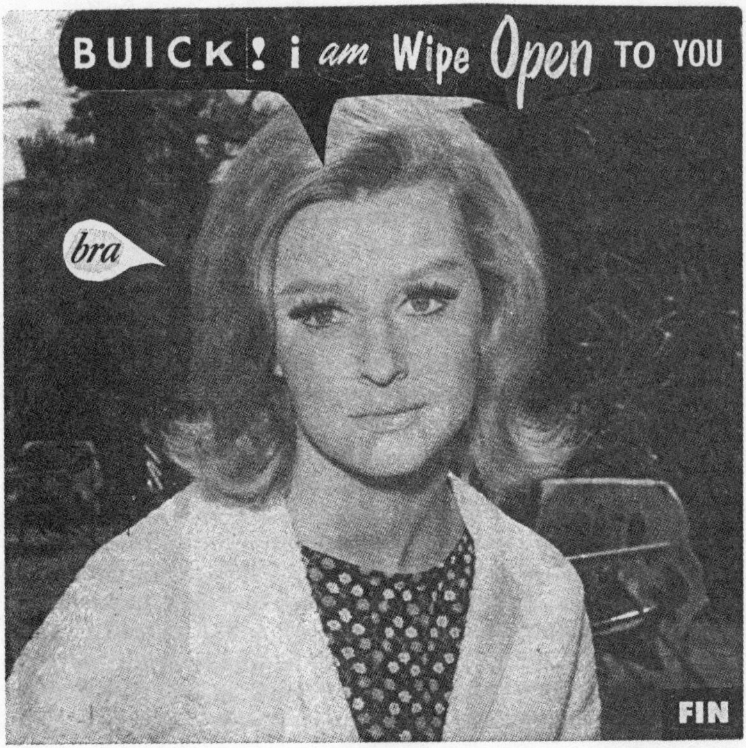
BUICK! i am Wipe Open TO YOU
bra
FIN

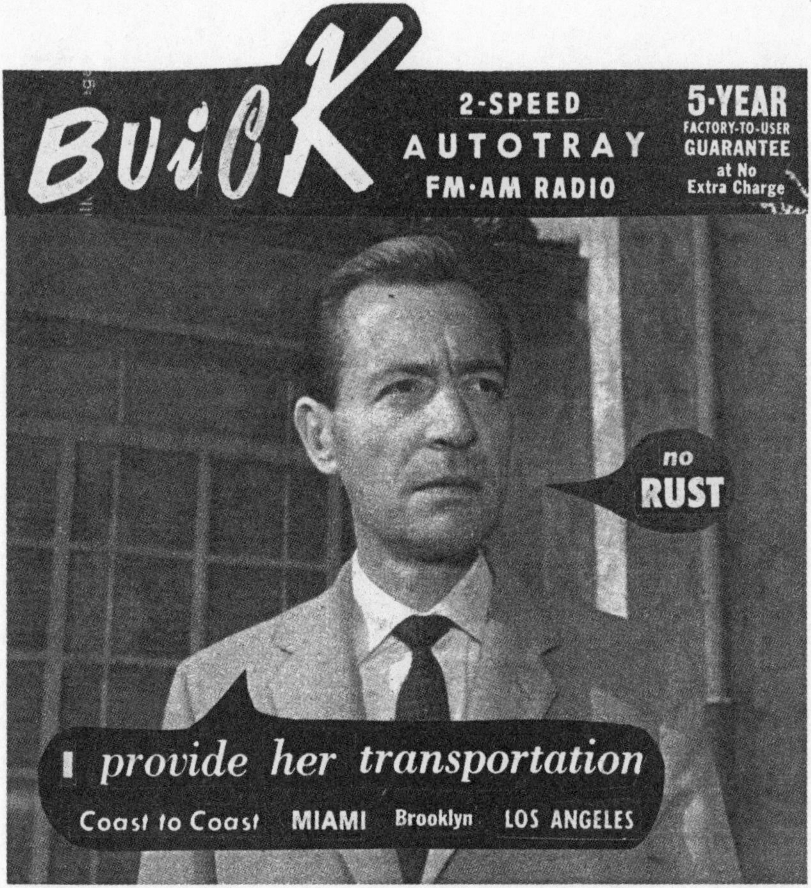
BuicK
2-SPEED
AUTOTRAY
FM·AM RADIO
5·YEAR
FACTORY-TO-USER
GUARANTEE
at No
Extra Charge
no
RUST
I provide her transportation
Coast to Coast MIAMI Brooklyn LOS ANGELES

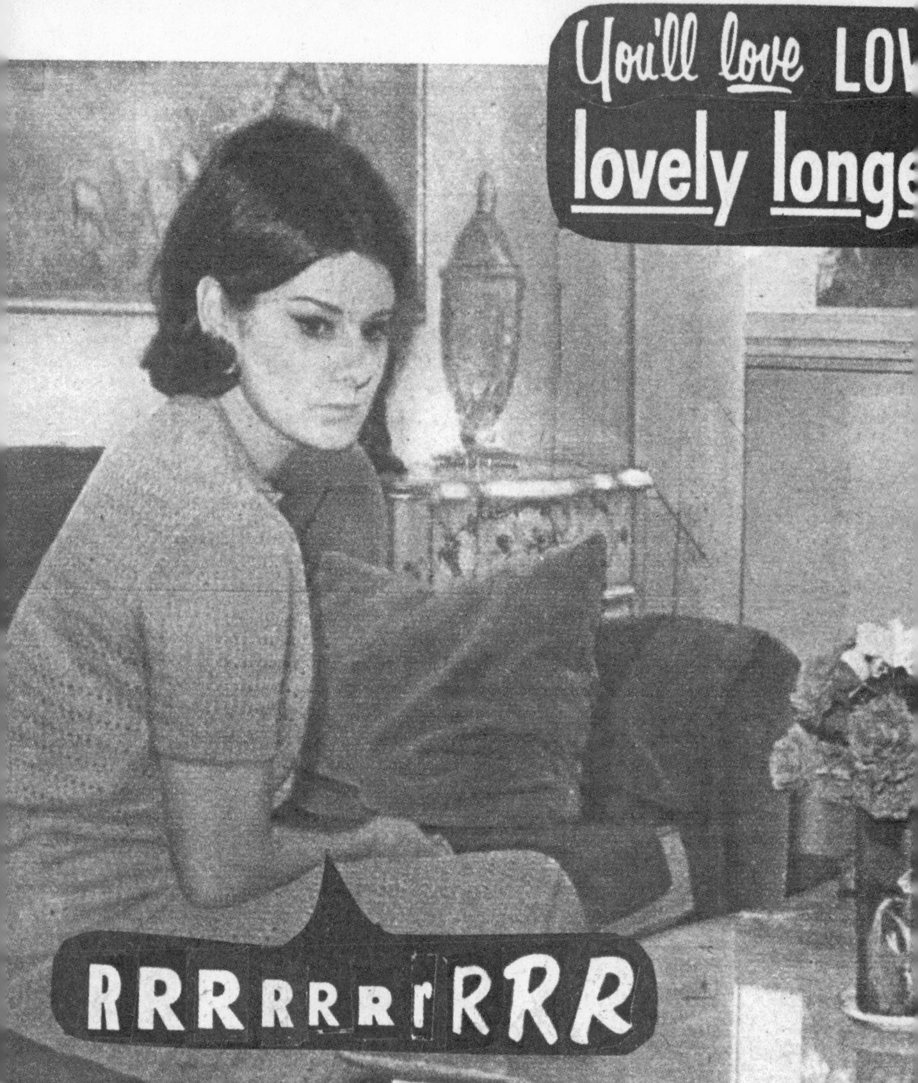
You'll love LOV
lovely longe
RRRRRRrRRR

LLY *So lovely,*
ly LOVE SEAT

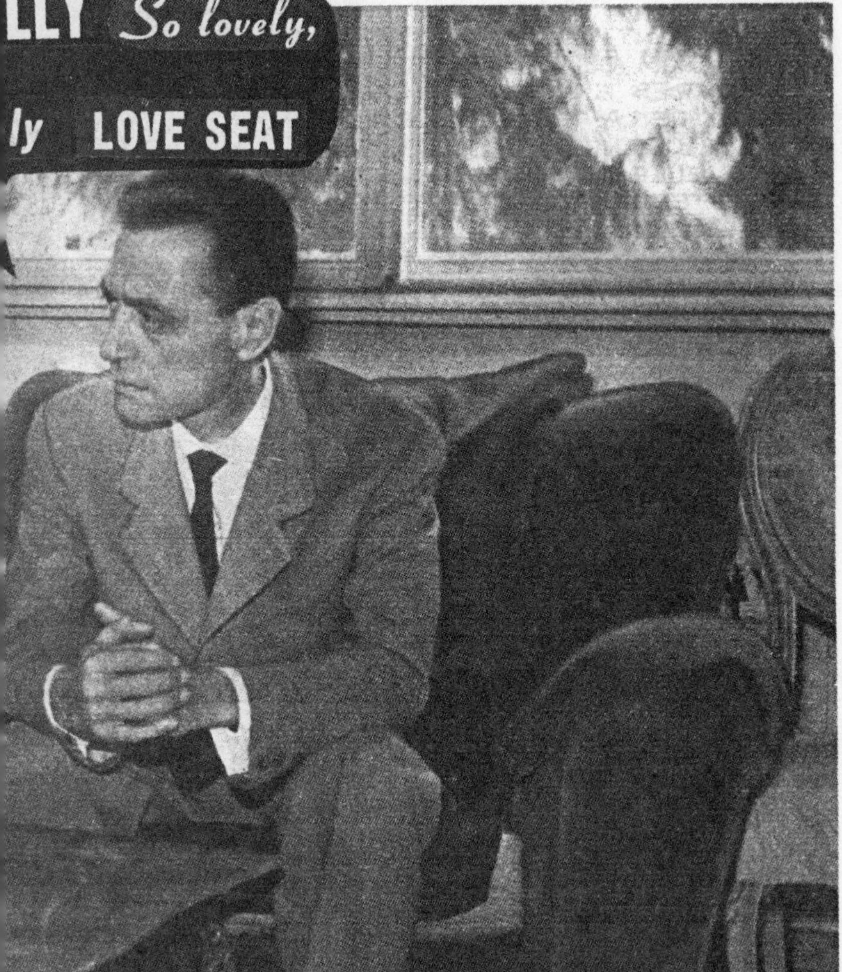

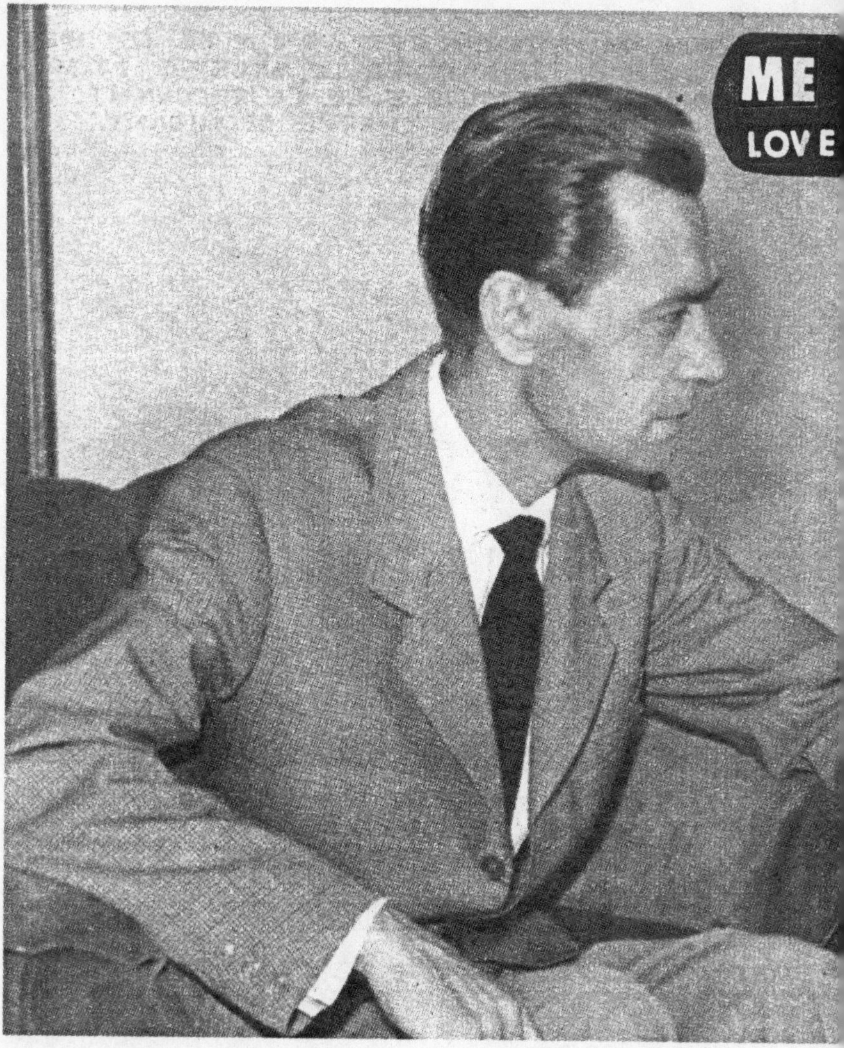
ME
LOV E

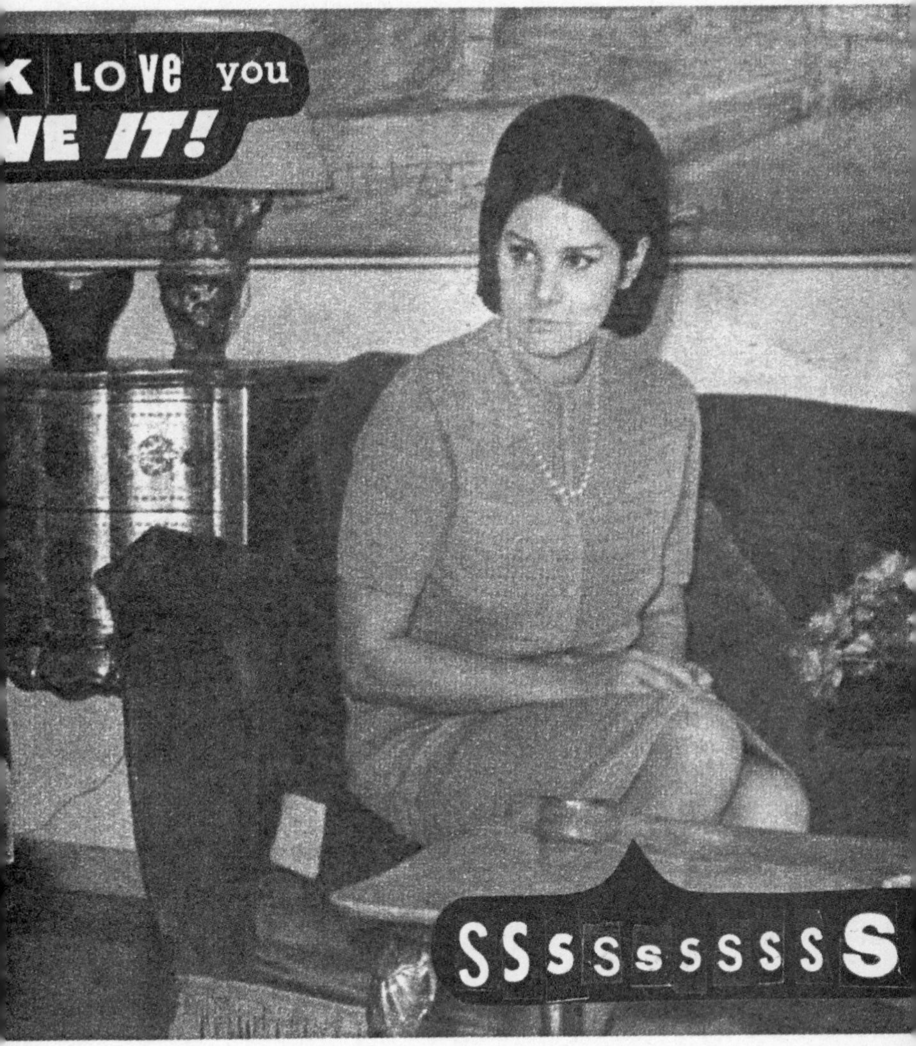
K LOVE you
VE IT!
SSSSSSSSSS

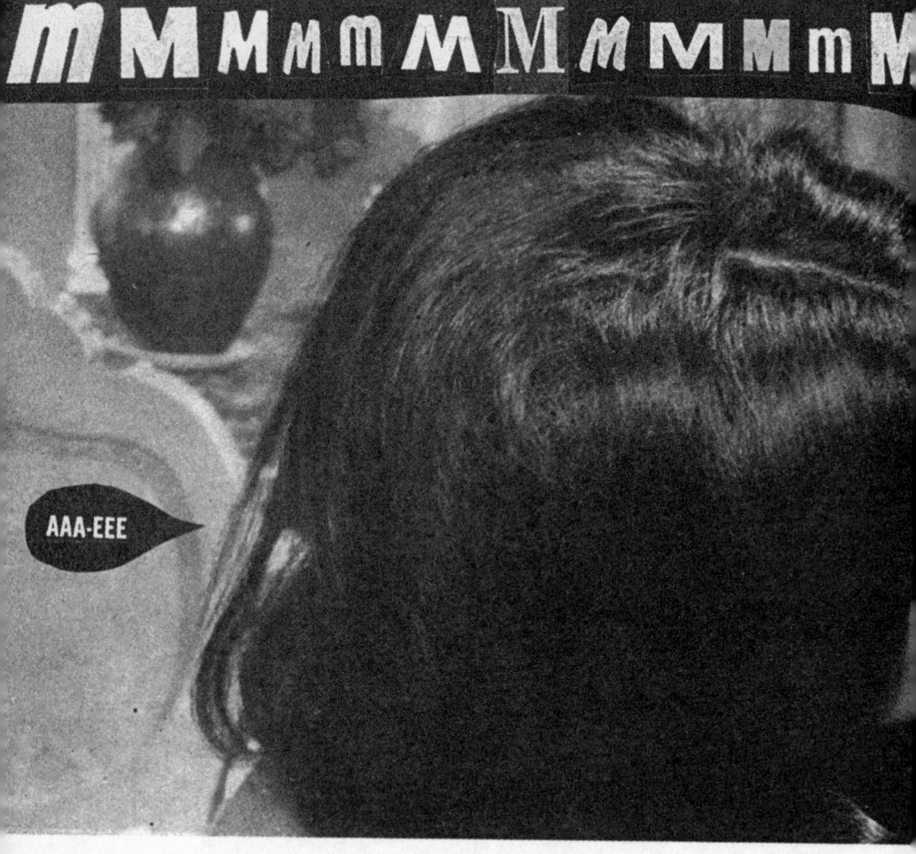
mMMmmMMmMMmM
AAA-EEE

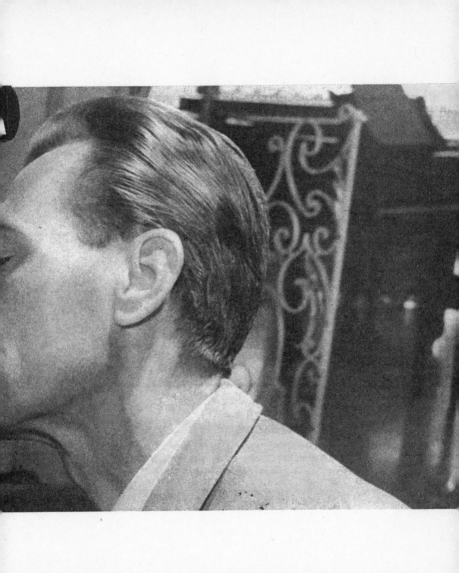

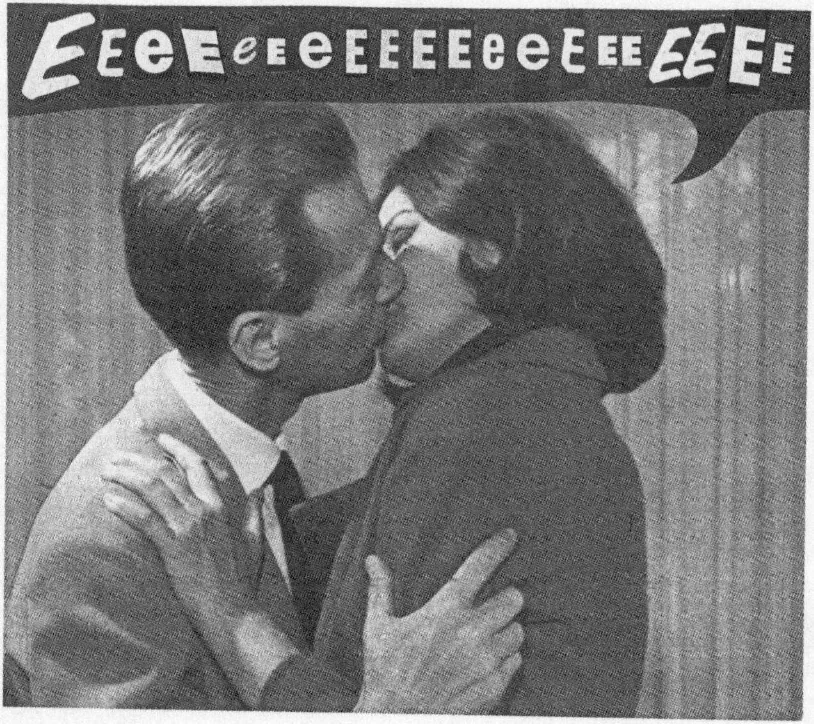
EEeEeEeEEEEeeEEEEEEe

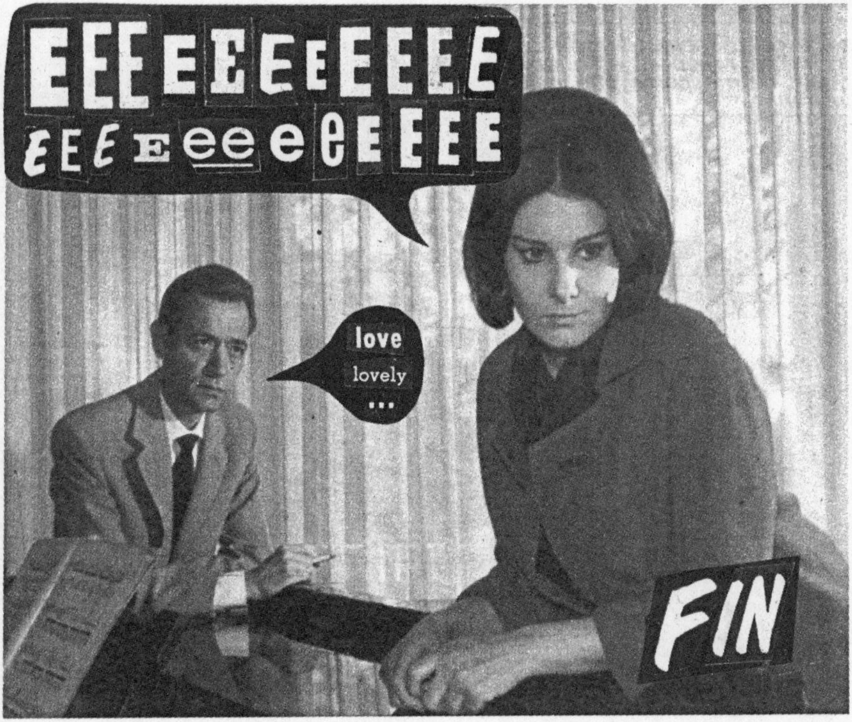
EEEEEEEEEEE
EEEEeeeeEEEE
love
lovely
...
FIN

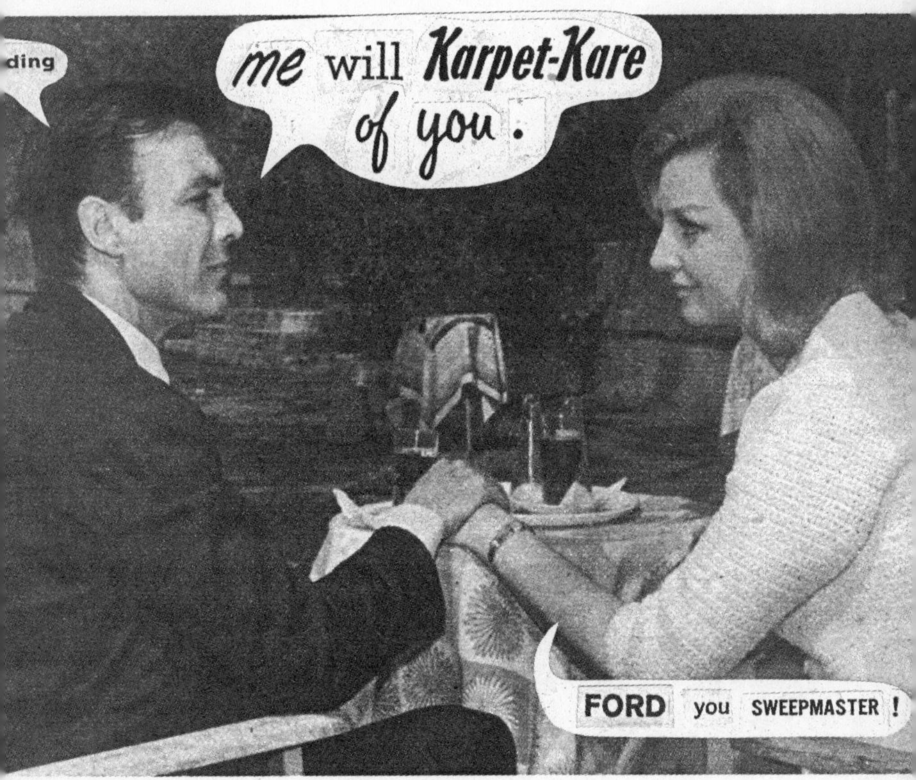
ding
me will Karpet-Kare of you.
FORD you SWEEPMASTER !

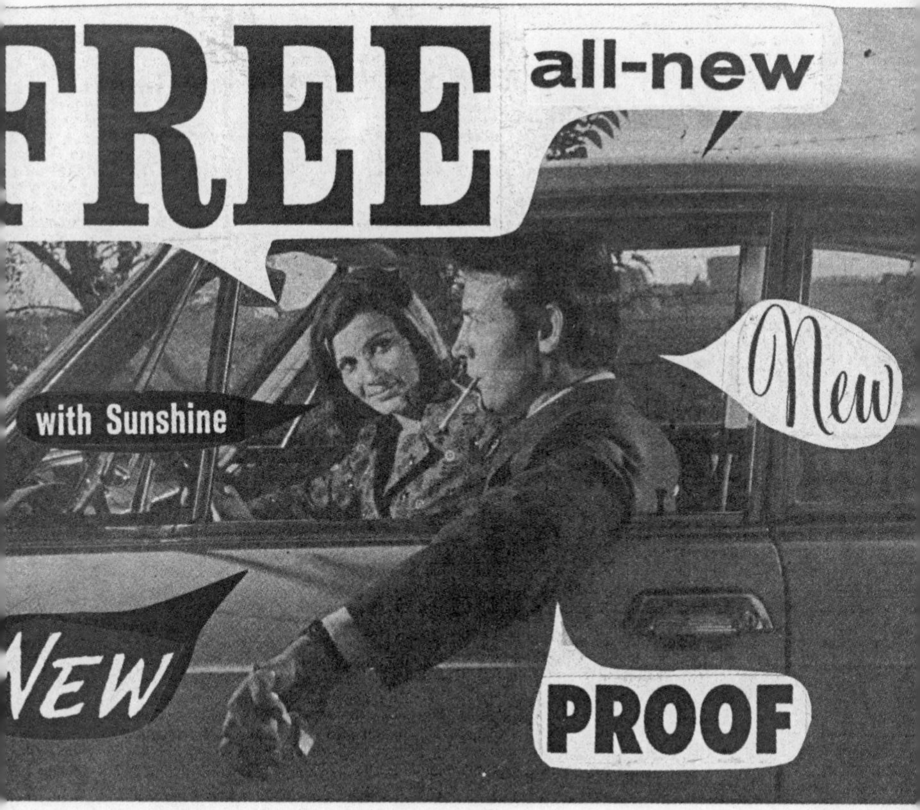
FREE
all-new
New
with Sunshine
NEW
PROOF

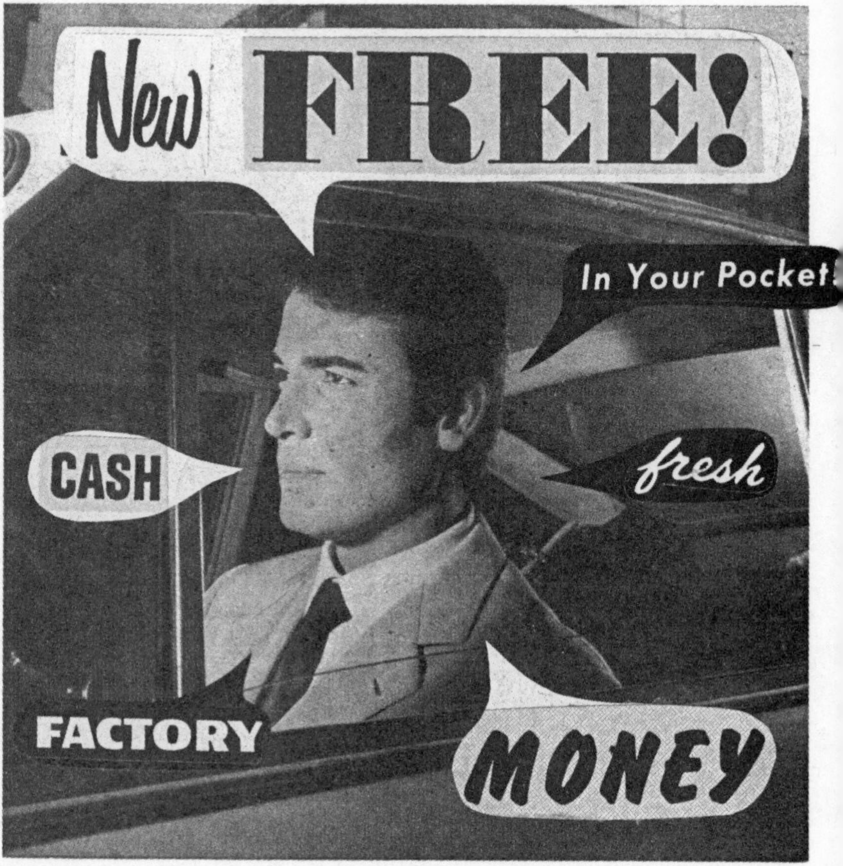
New
FREE!
In Your Pocket!
CASH
fresh
FACTORY
MONEY

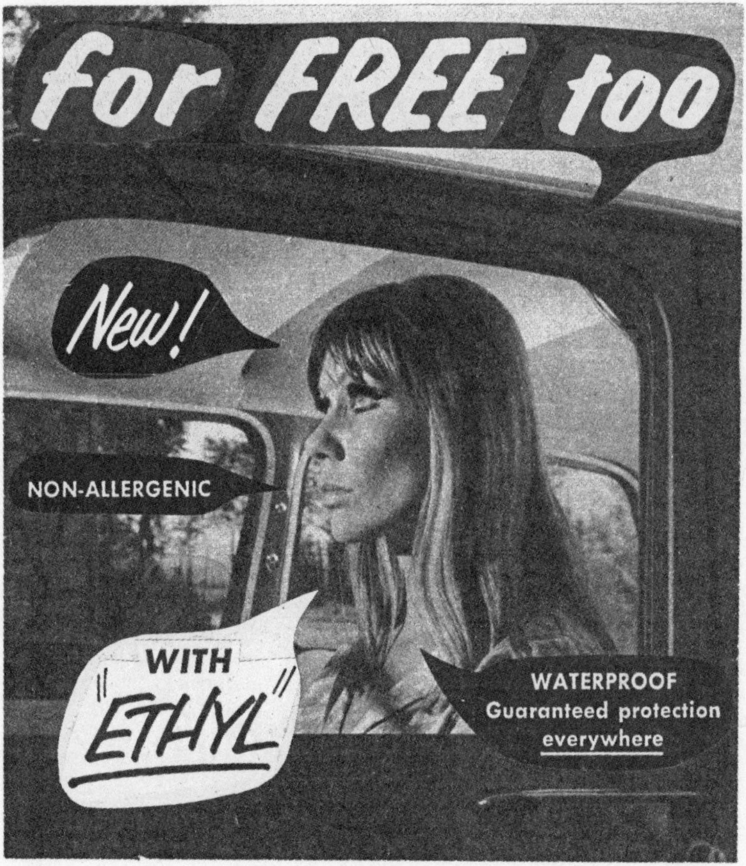
for FREE too
New!
NON-ALLERGENIC
WITH "ETHYL"
WATERPROOF
Guaranteed protection everywhere

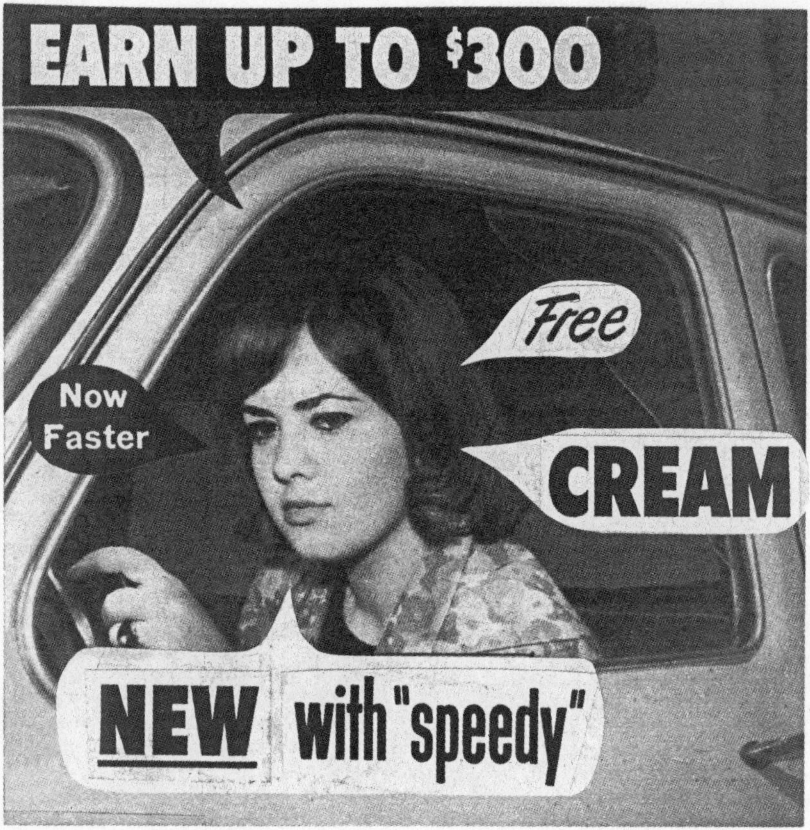
EARN UP TO $300
Free
Now Faster
CREAM
NEW with "speedy"

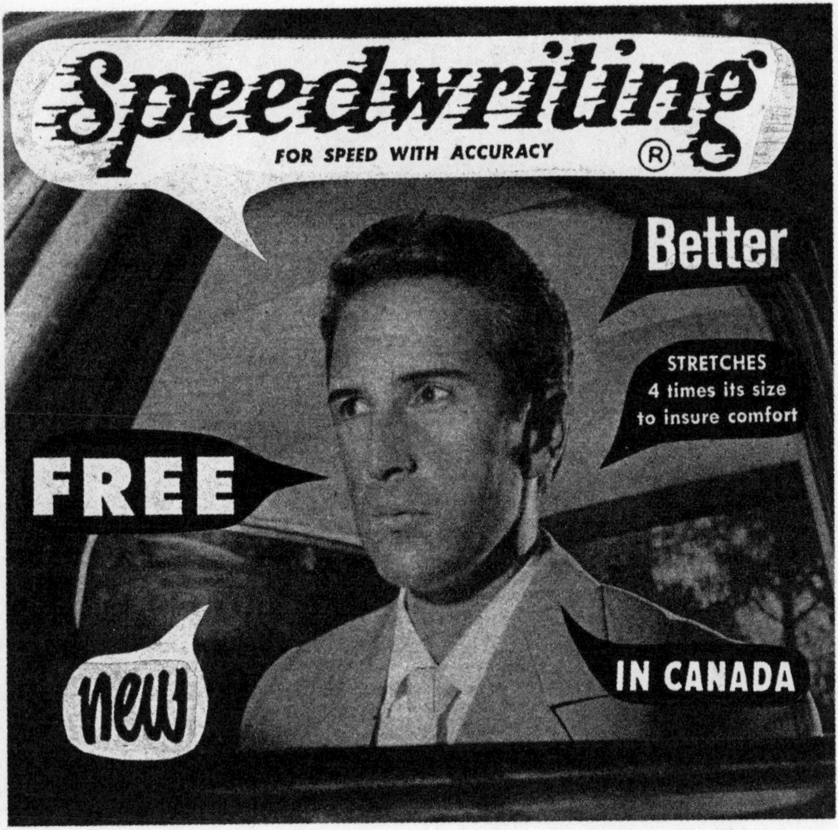
Speedwriting
FOR SPEED WITH ACCURACY
®
Better
STRETCHES
4 times its size
to insure comfort
FREE
IN CANADA
new

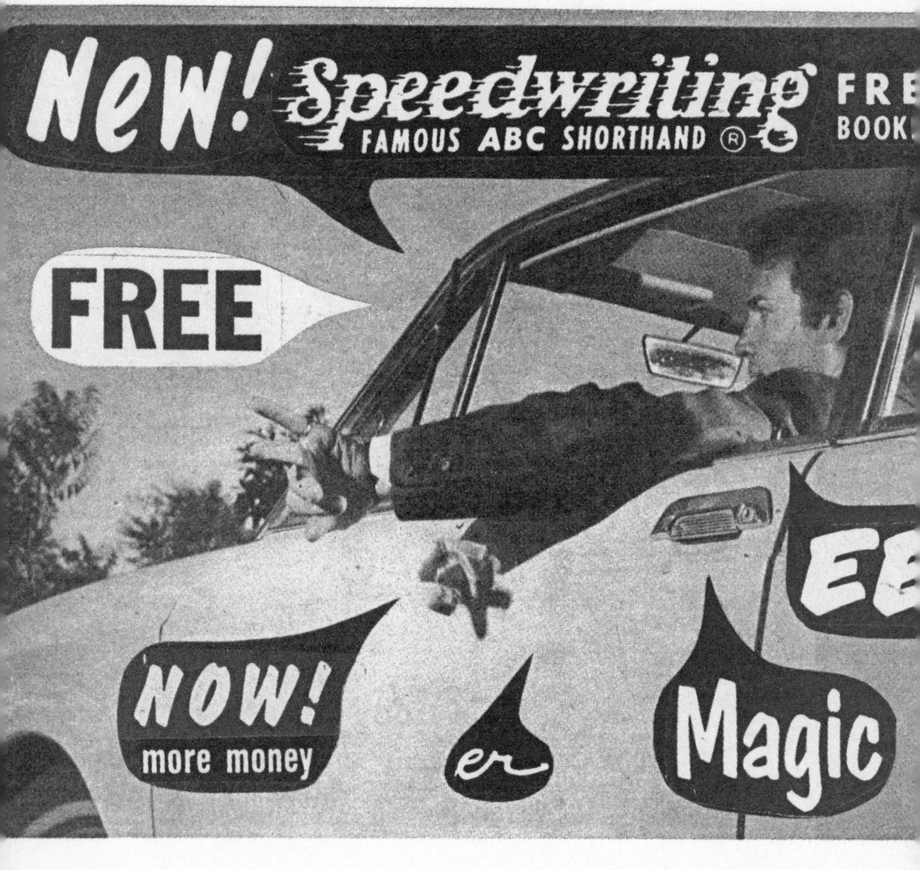
New!
Speedwriting
FAMOUS ABC SHORTHAND ®
FRE
BOOK
FREE
NOW!
more money
er
Magic

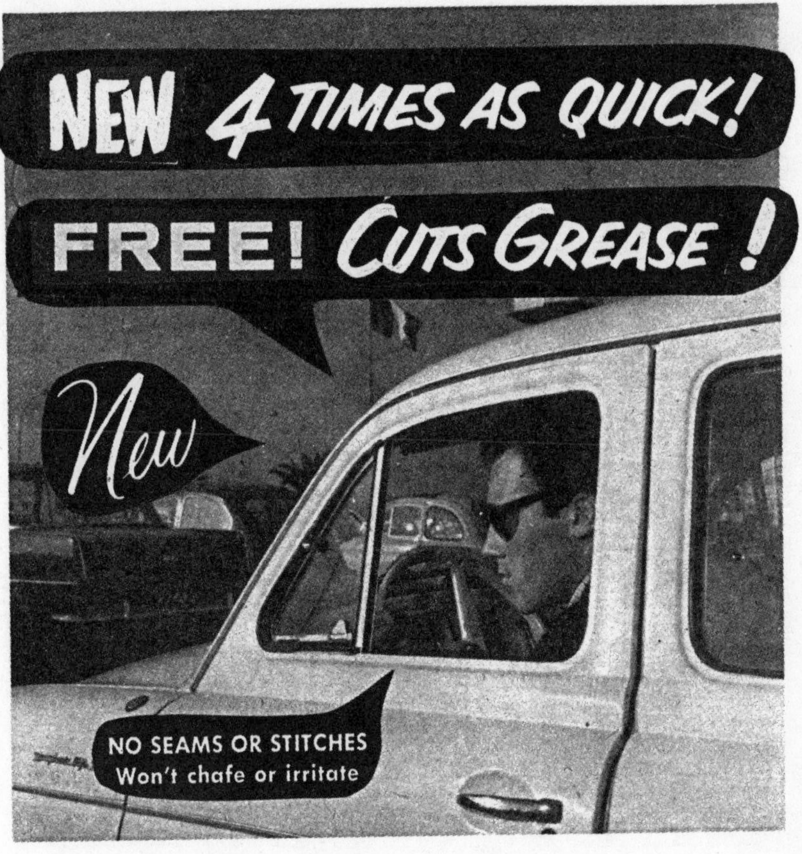
NEW 4 TIMES AS QUICK!
FREE! CUTS GREASE!
New
NO SEAMS OR STITCHES
Won't chafe or irritate

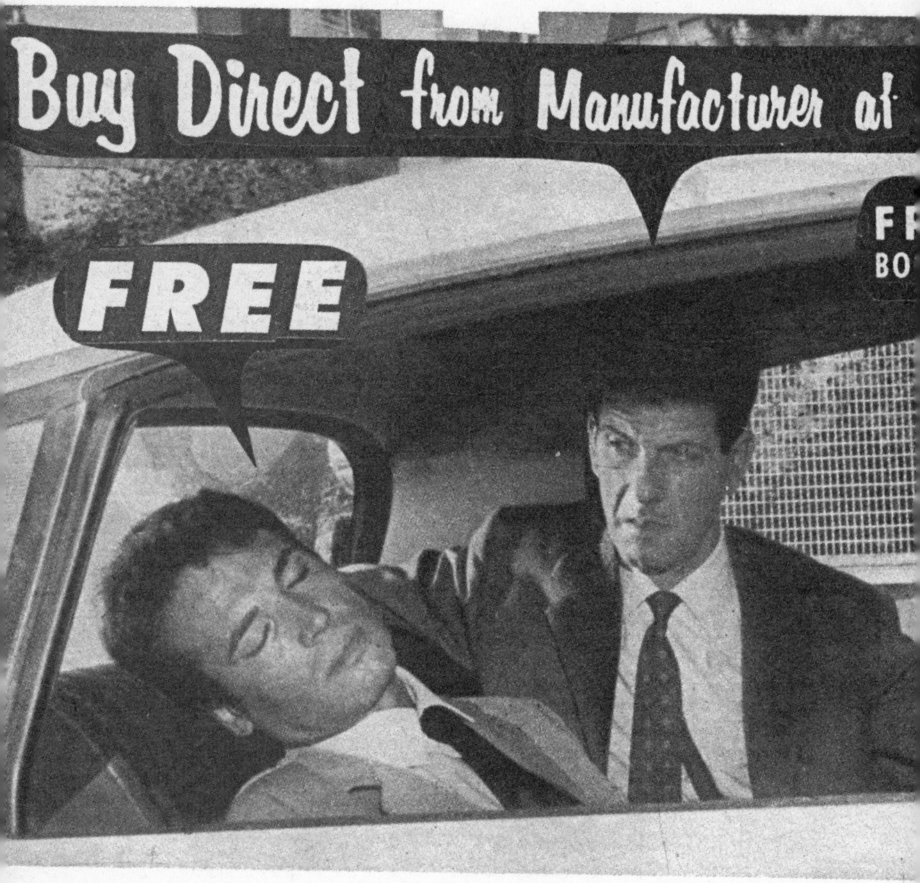
Buy Direct from Manufacturer at
FREE
FR
BO

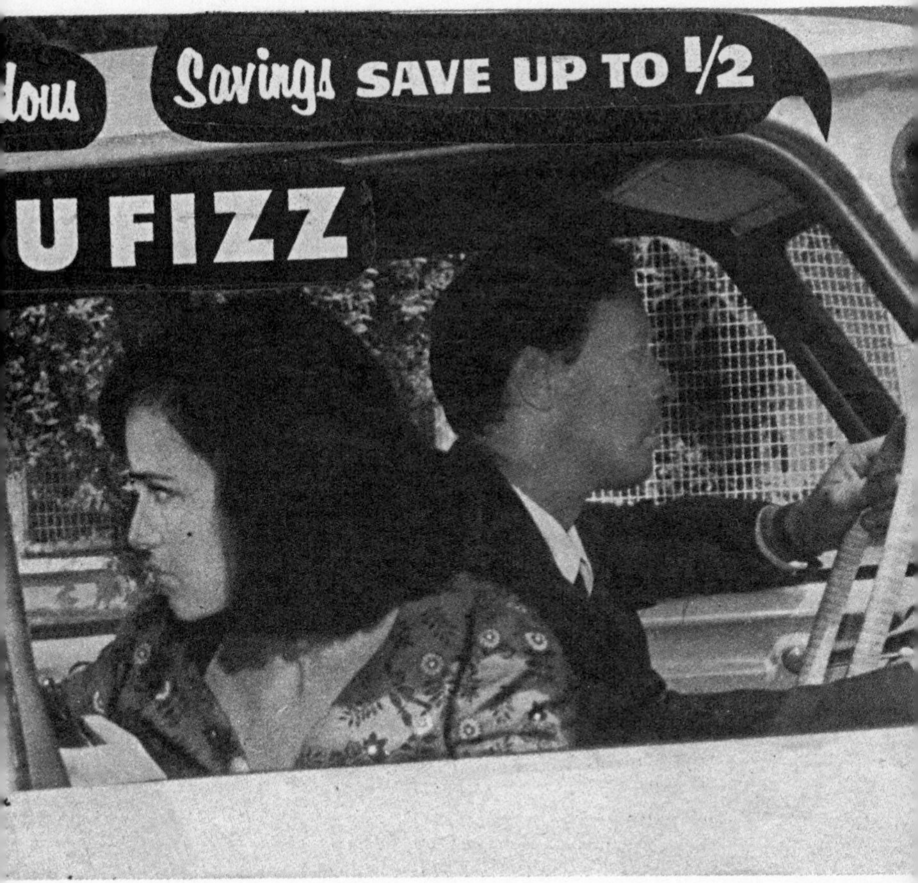

lous
Savings SAVE UP TO 1/2
U FIZZ

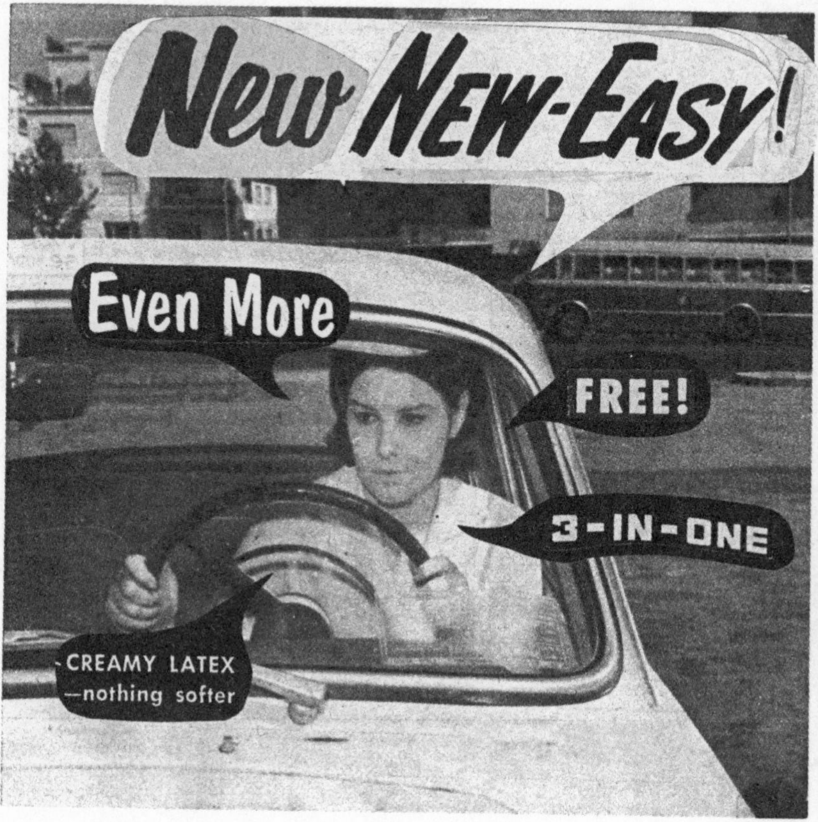
New New-Easy!
Even More
FREE!
3-IN-ONE
CREAMY LATEX
—nothing softer

New Style for Less Money
Luxury
New
FREE
HUNDREDS OF EXTRA DOLLARS

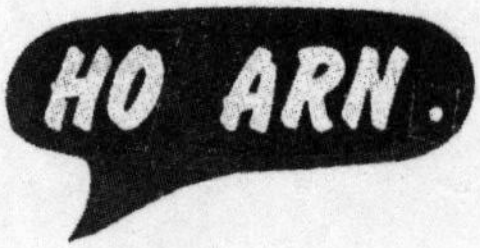
HO ARN.

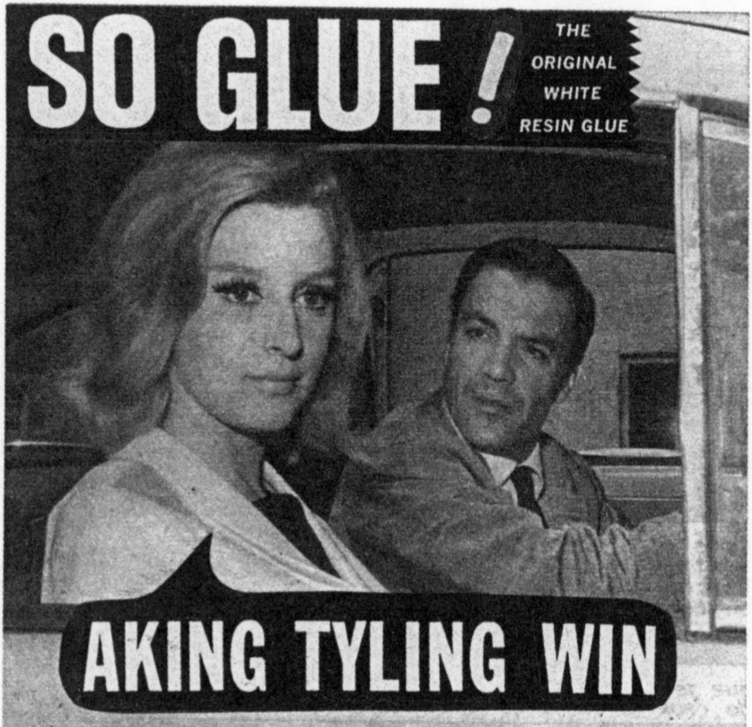
SO GLUE!
THE ORIGINAL WHITE RESIN GLUE
AKING TYLING WIN

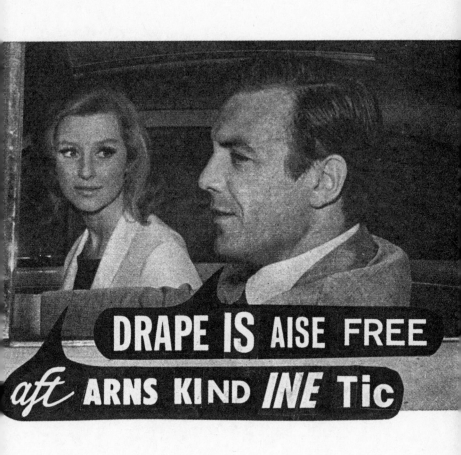

DRAPE IS AISE FREE
aft **ARNS KIND** *INE* Tic

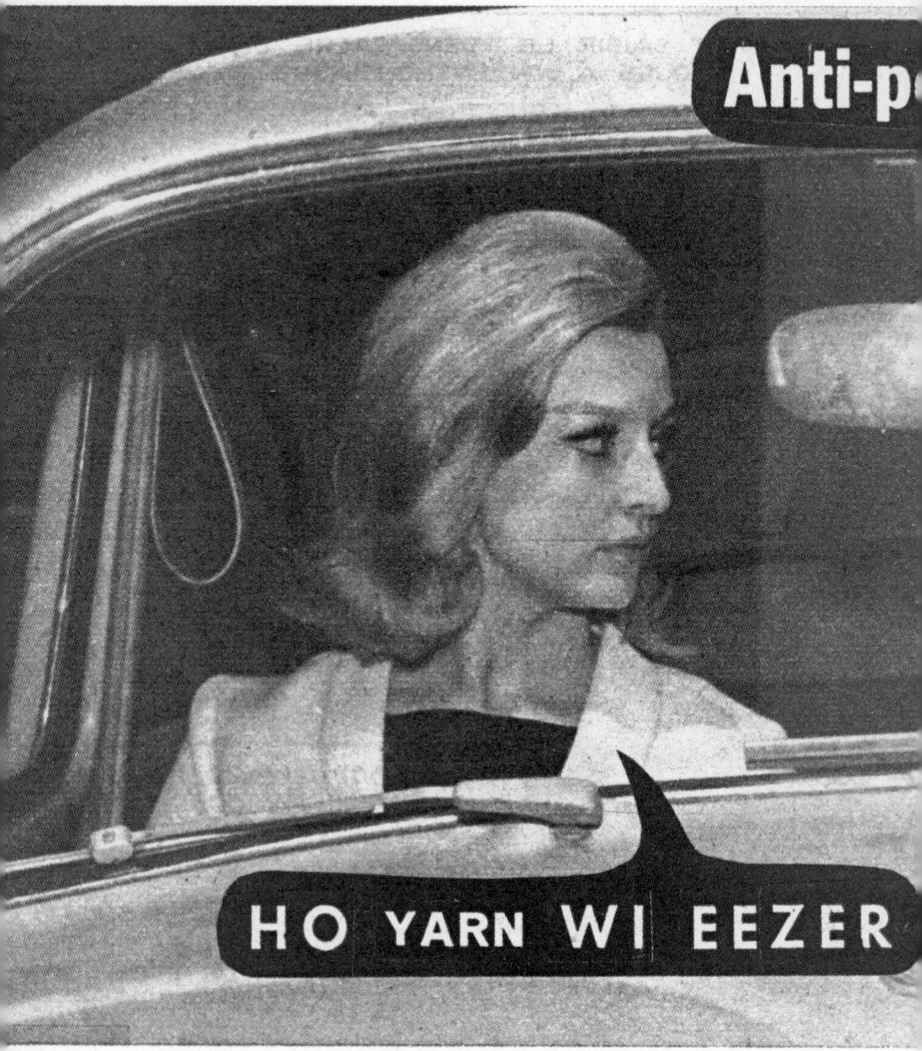
Anti-p
HO YARN WI EEZER

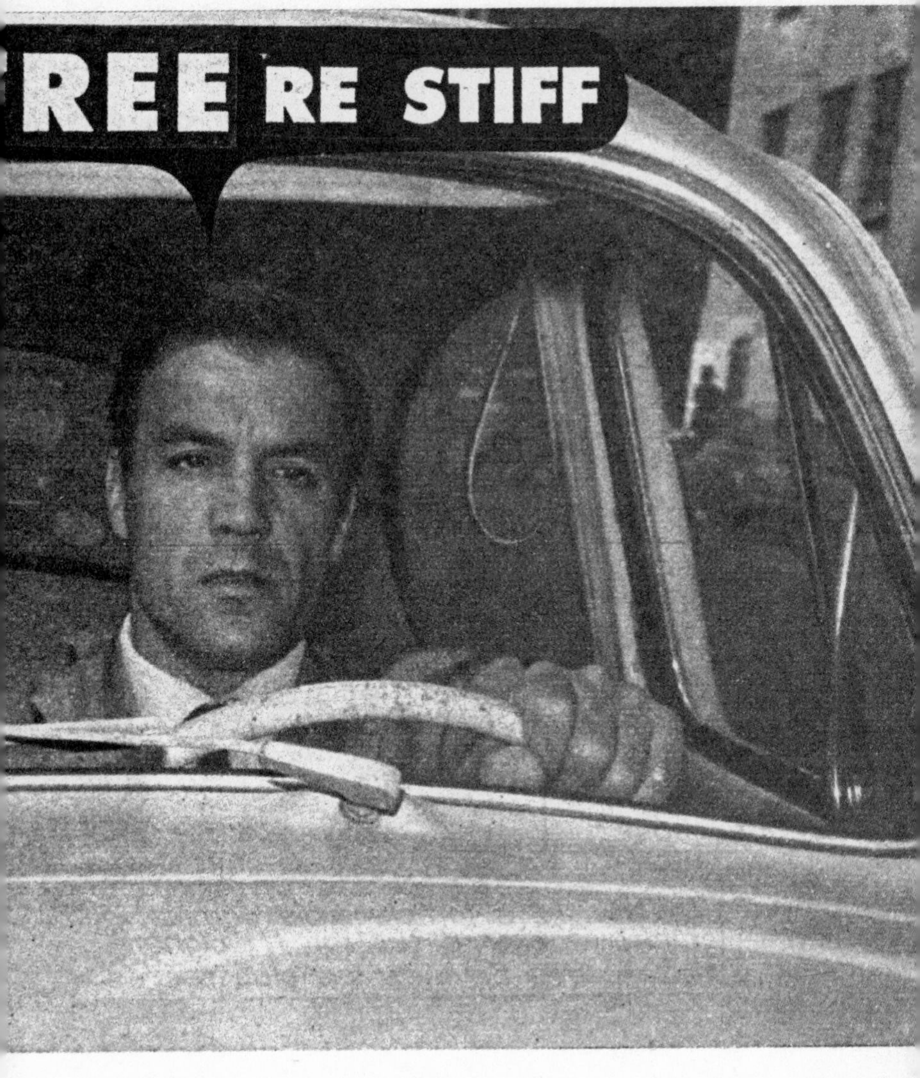
REE RE STIFF

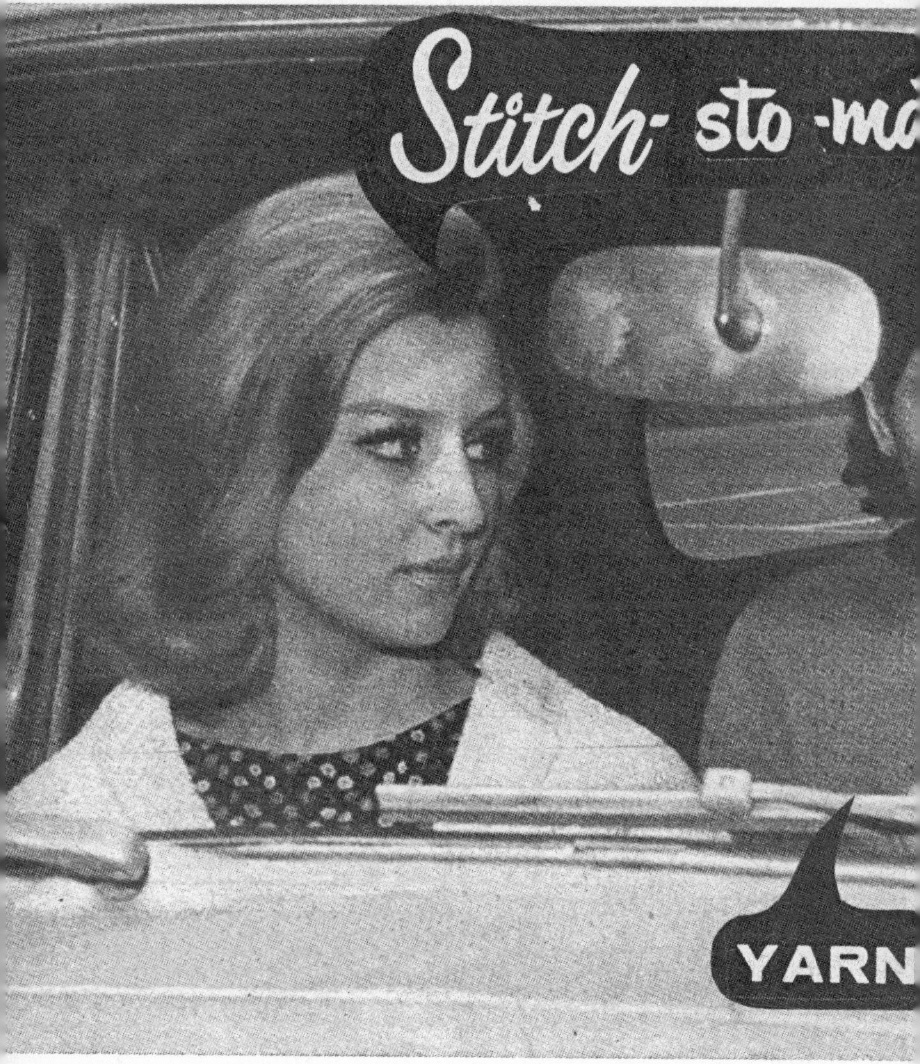
Stitch- sto -ma
YARN

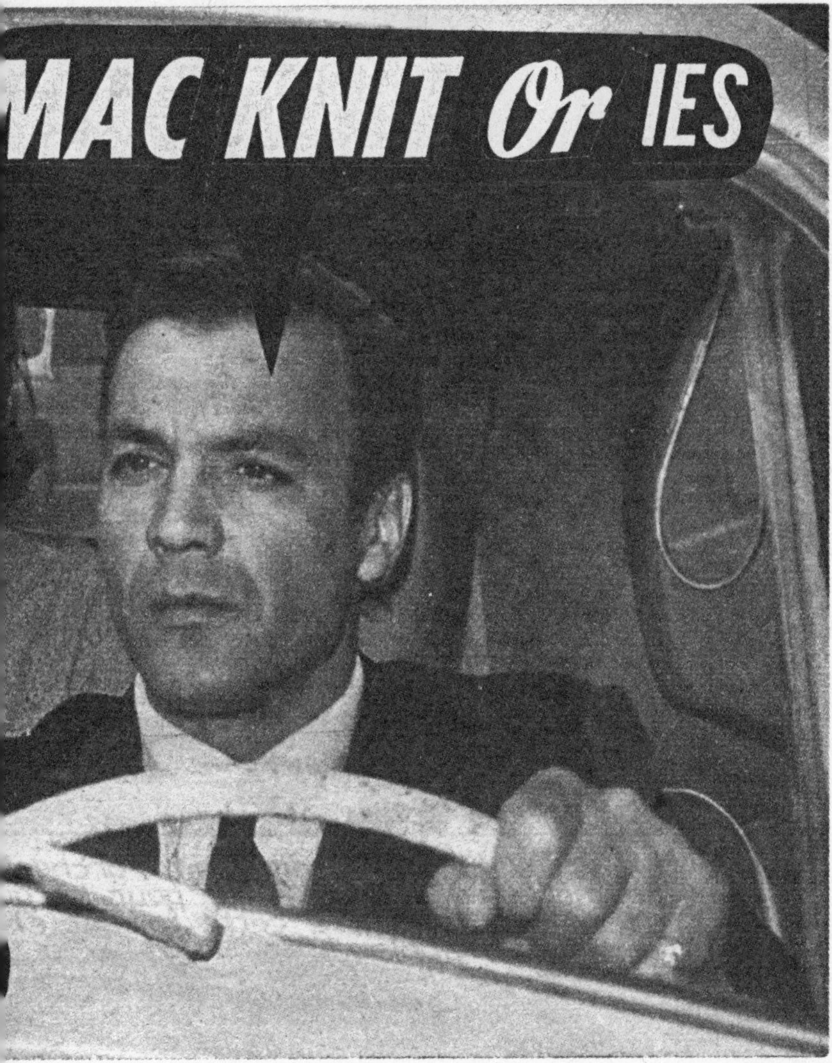
MAC KNIT Or IES

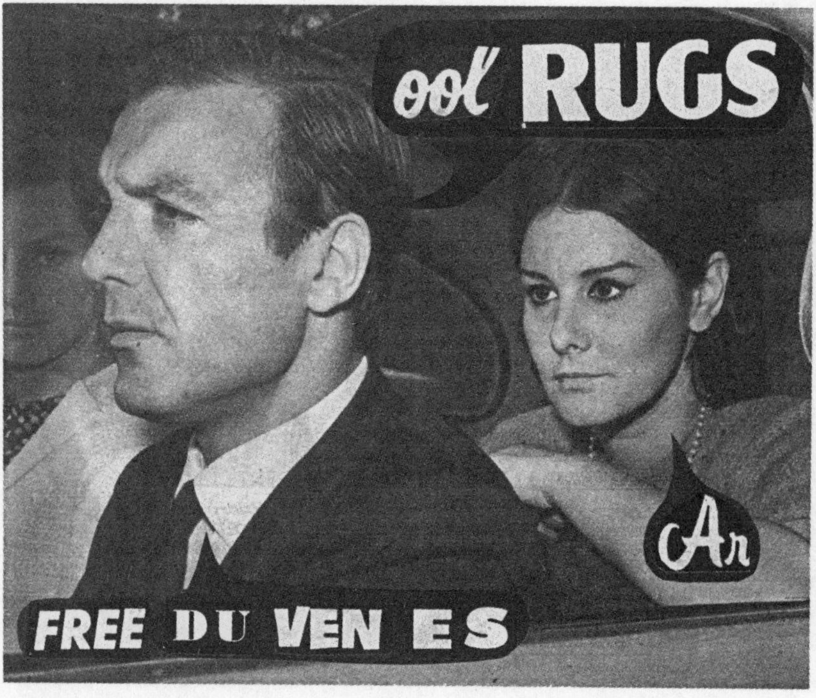
ool' RUGS
Ar
FREE DU VEN ES

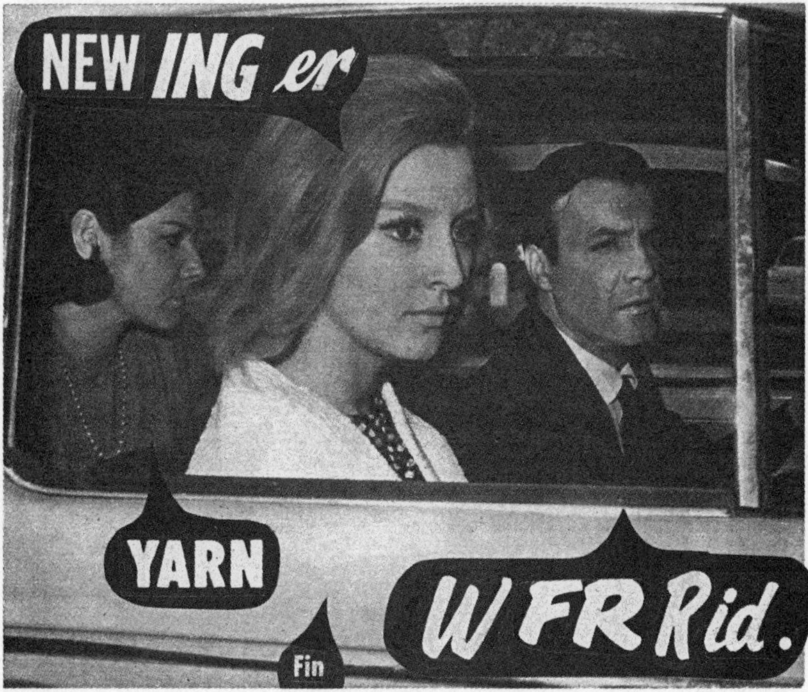
NEW ING er
YARN
Fin
W FR Rid.

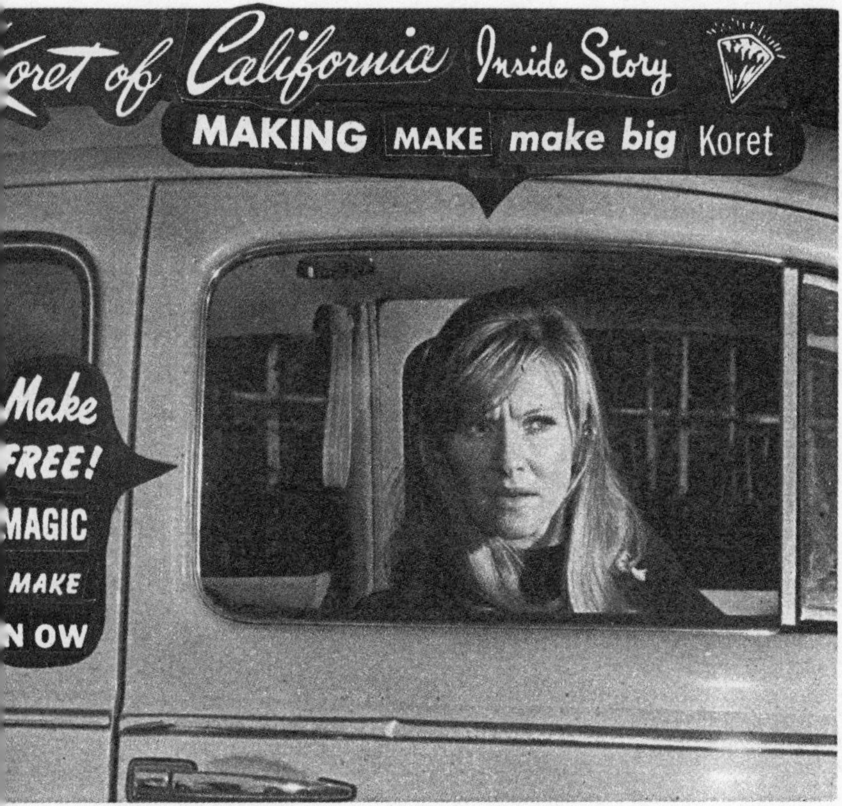
Koret of California Inside Story
MAKING MAKE make big Koret
Make
FREE!
MAGIC
MAKE
N OW

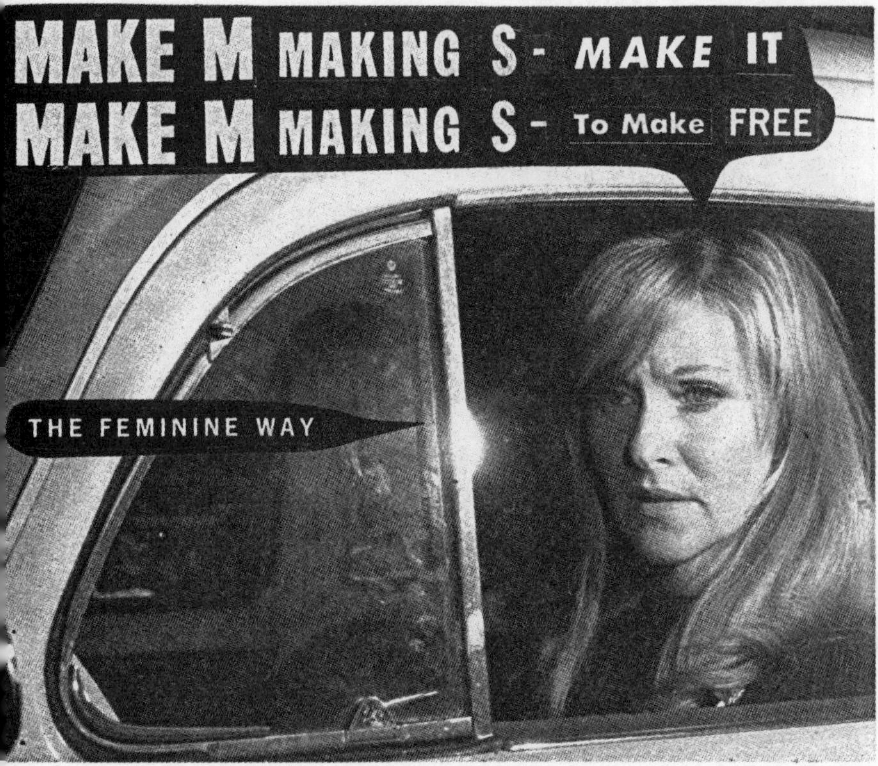

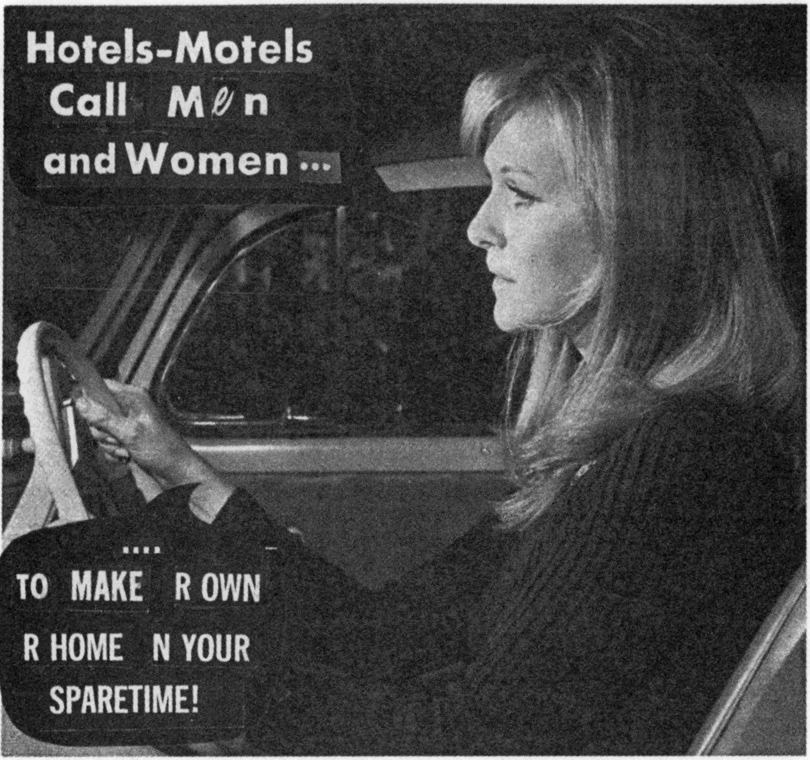
Hotels-Motels
Call Men
and Women ...
....
TO MAKE R OWN
R HOME N YOUR
SPARETIME!

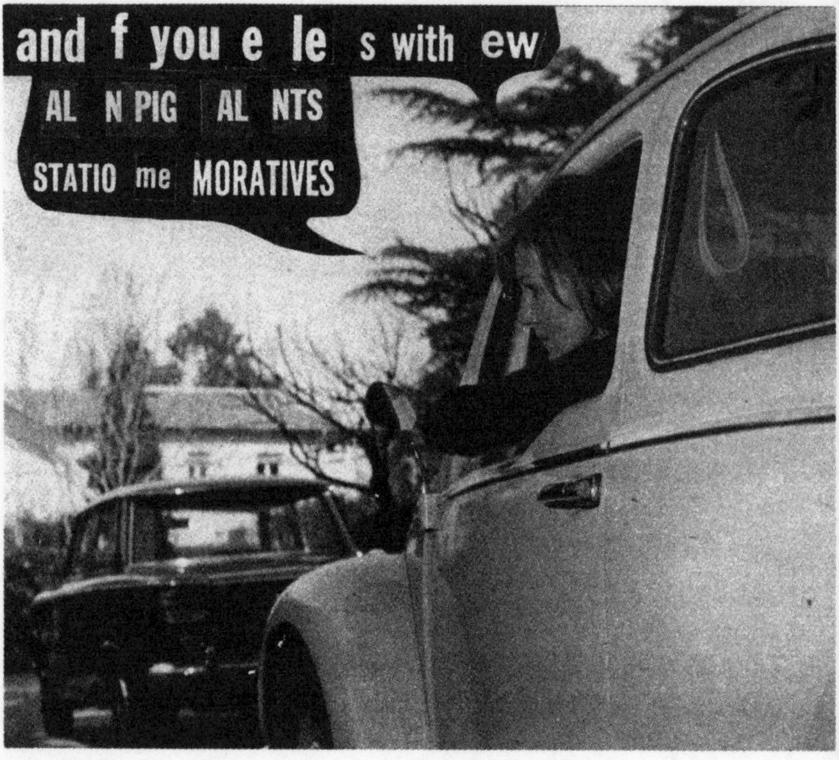
and f you e le s with ew
AL N PIG AL NTS
STATIO me MORATIVES

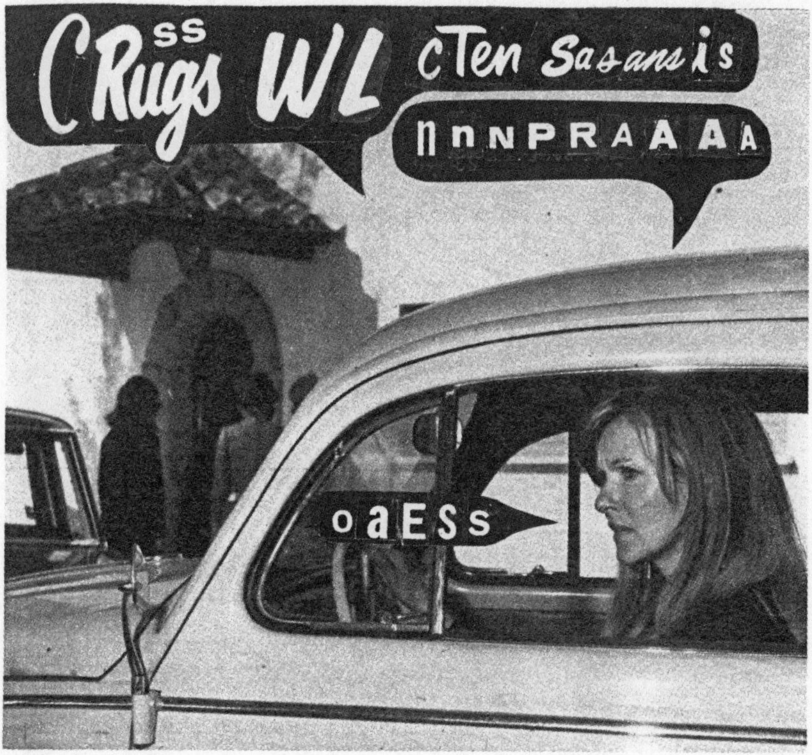
CRugs WL
cTen Sasansis
nnNPRAAAA
oaESs

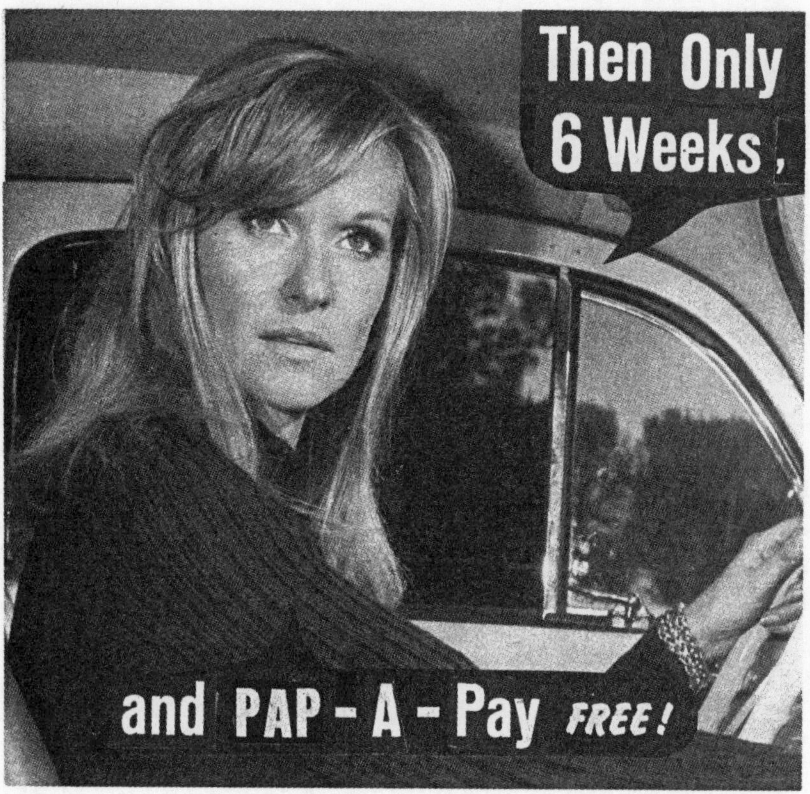
Then Only
6 Weeks,
and PAP-A-Pay FREE!

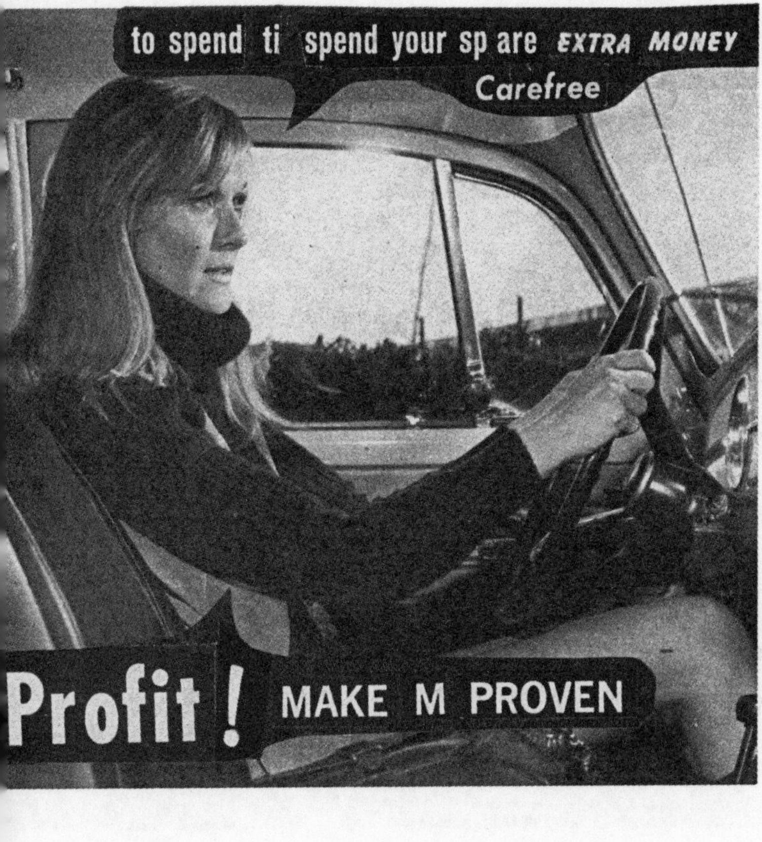
to spend ti spend your sp are EXTRA MONEY
Carefree
Profit!
MAKE M PROVEN

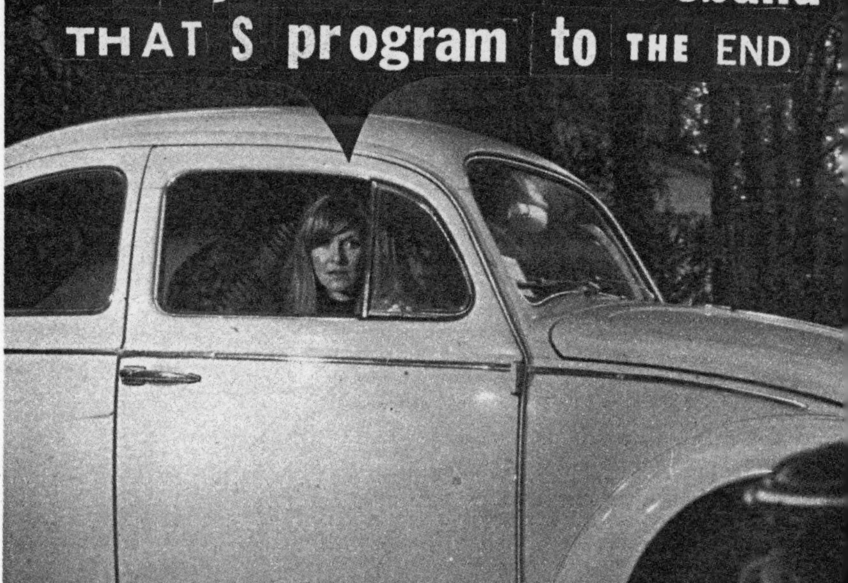
PROFIT PORT IN M The long Way
sted your own Life and sband
THAT S program to THE END

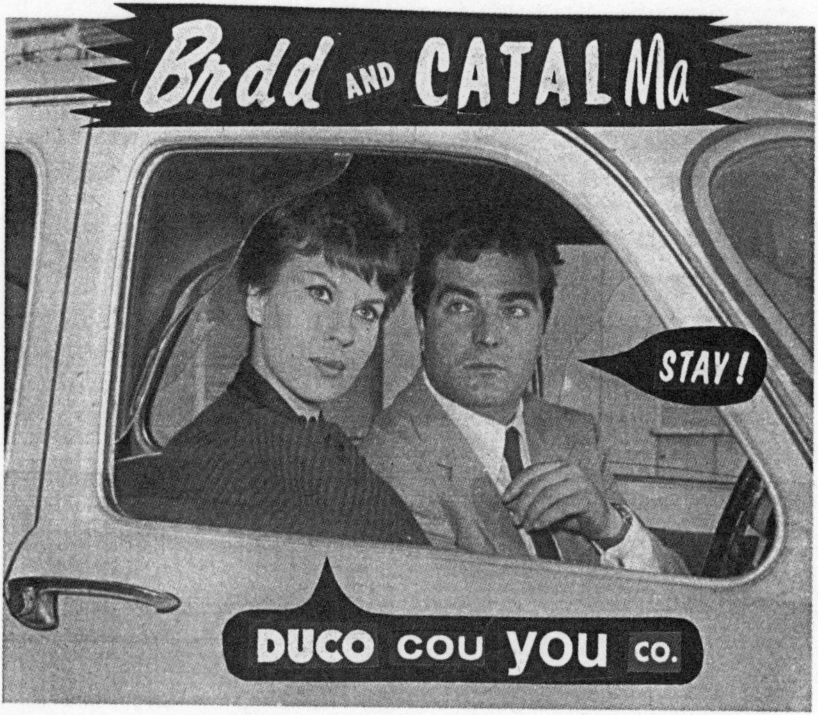
Brdd AND CATALMa
STAY!
DUCO COU YOU CO.

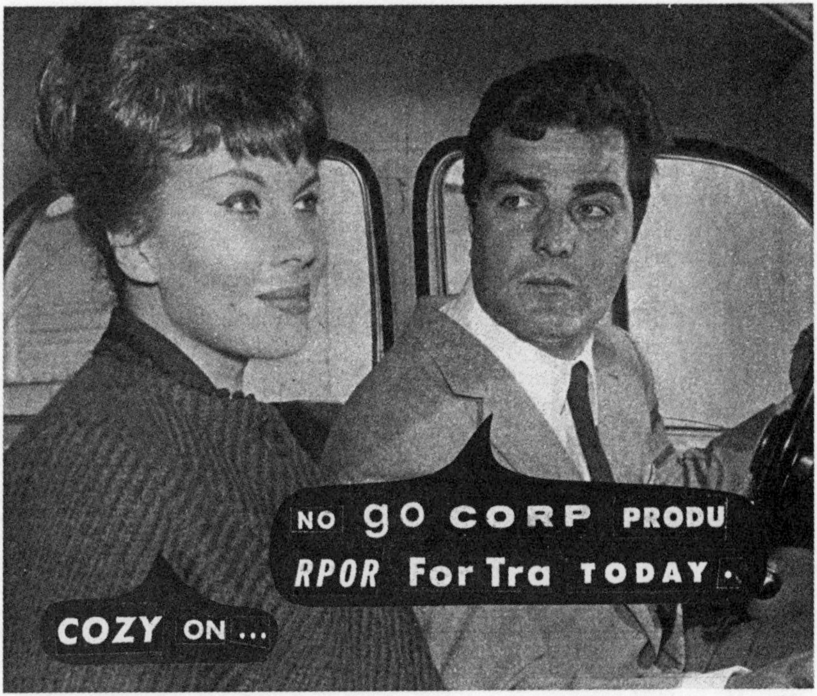
NO go CORP PRODU
RPOR For Tra TODAY.
COZY ON ...

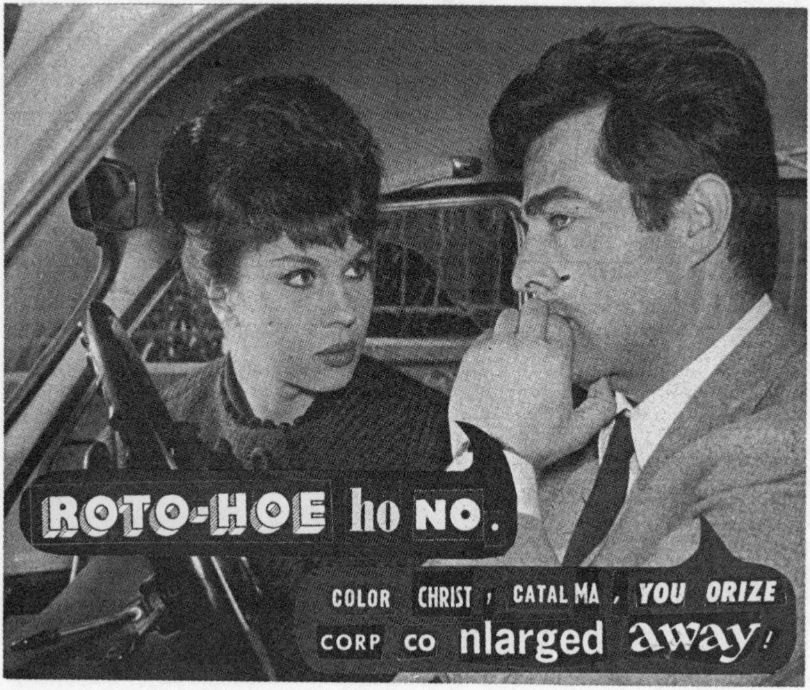
ROTO-HOE ho NO.
COLOR CHRIST , CATAL MA , YOU ORIZE
CORP CO nlarged away!

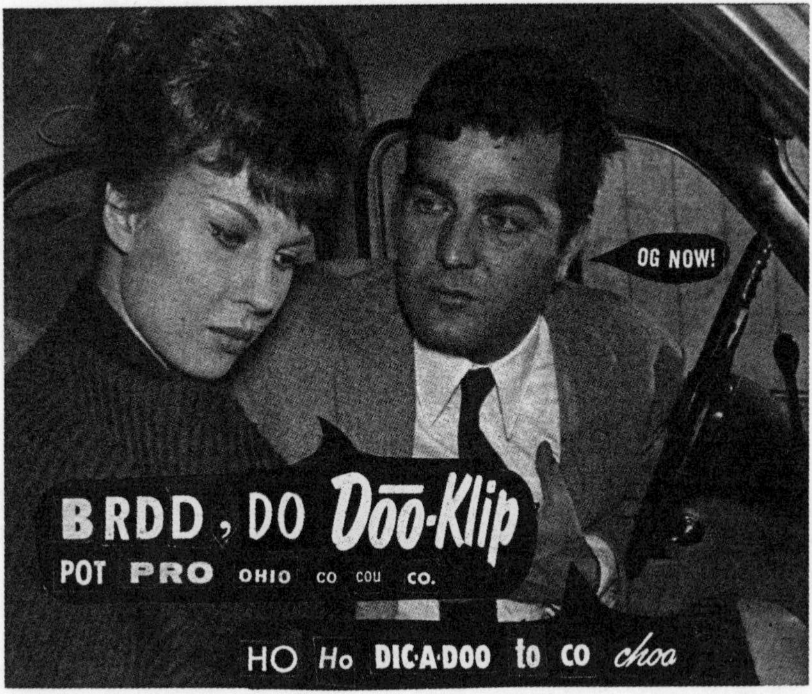
OG NOW!
BRDD, DO Dōō-Klip
POT PRO OHIO CO COU CO.
HO Ho DIC·A·DOO to CO choa

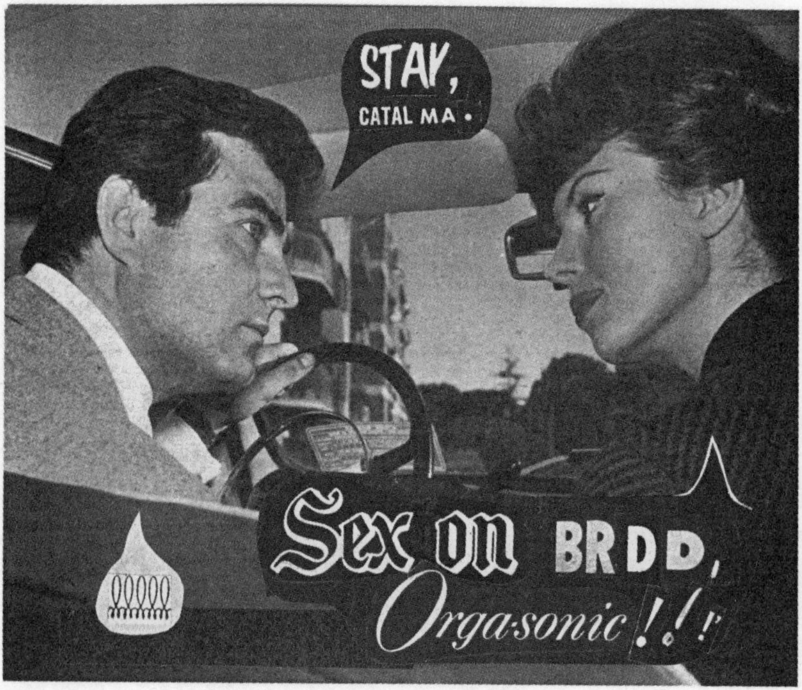
STAY,
CATAL MA.
Sex on BRDD,
Orga-sonic!!!

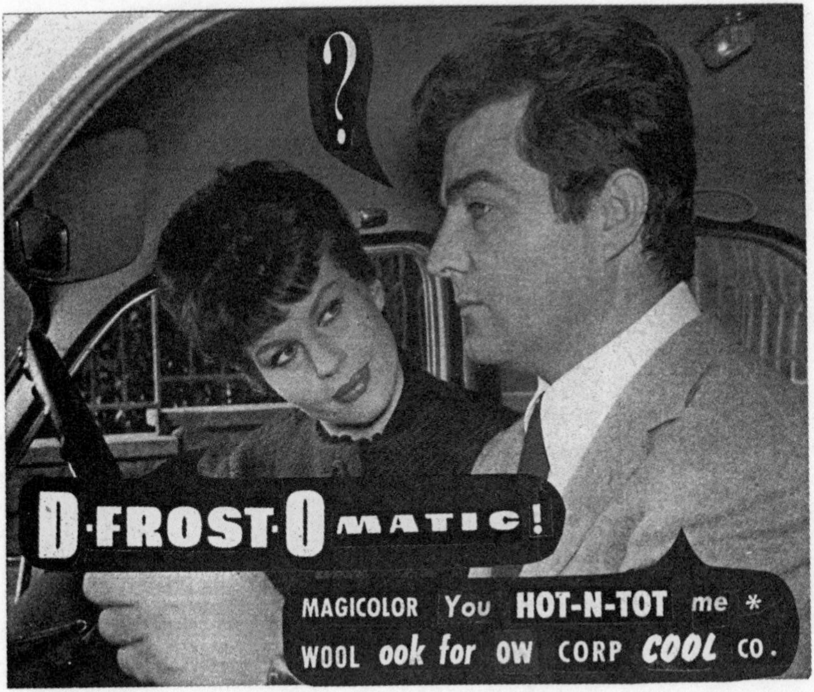
?
D·FROST·O MATIC!
MAGICOLOR You HOT-N-TOT me *
WOOL ook for OW CORP COOL CO.

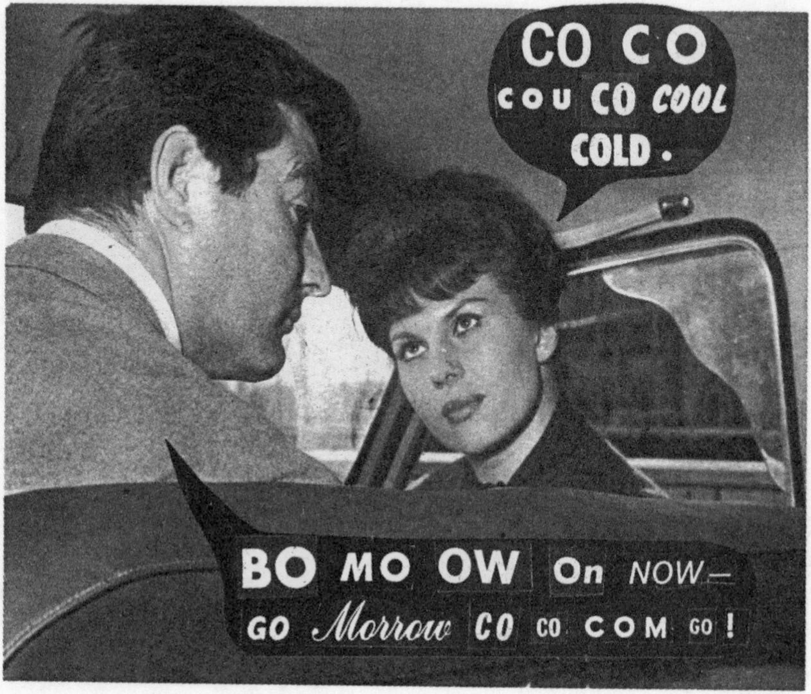
CO CO
cou CO COOL
COLD.
BO MO OW On NOW—
GO Morrow CO CO COM GO!

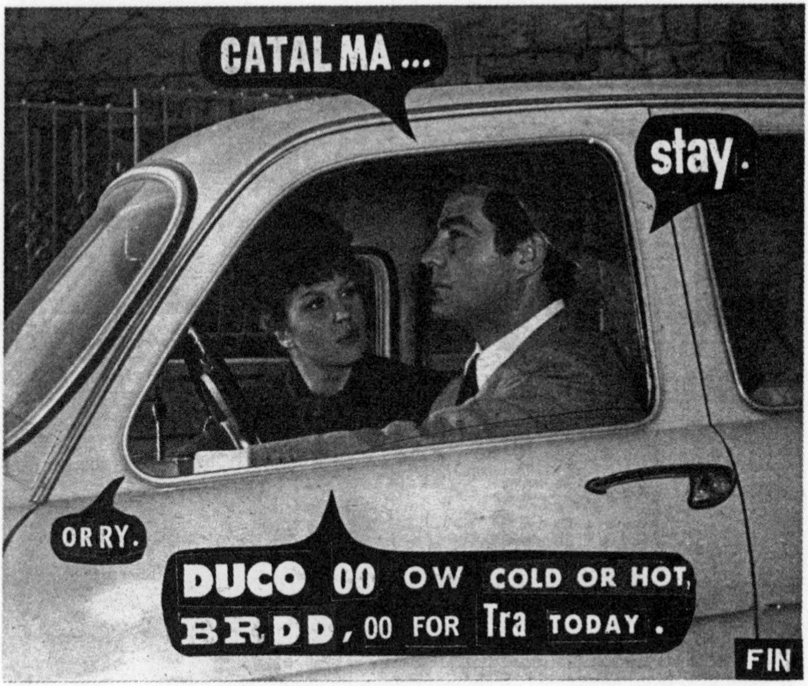
CATAL MA...
stay.
ORRY.
DUCO 00 OW COLD OR HOT,
BRDD, 00 FOR Tra TODAY.
FIN

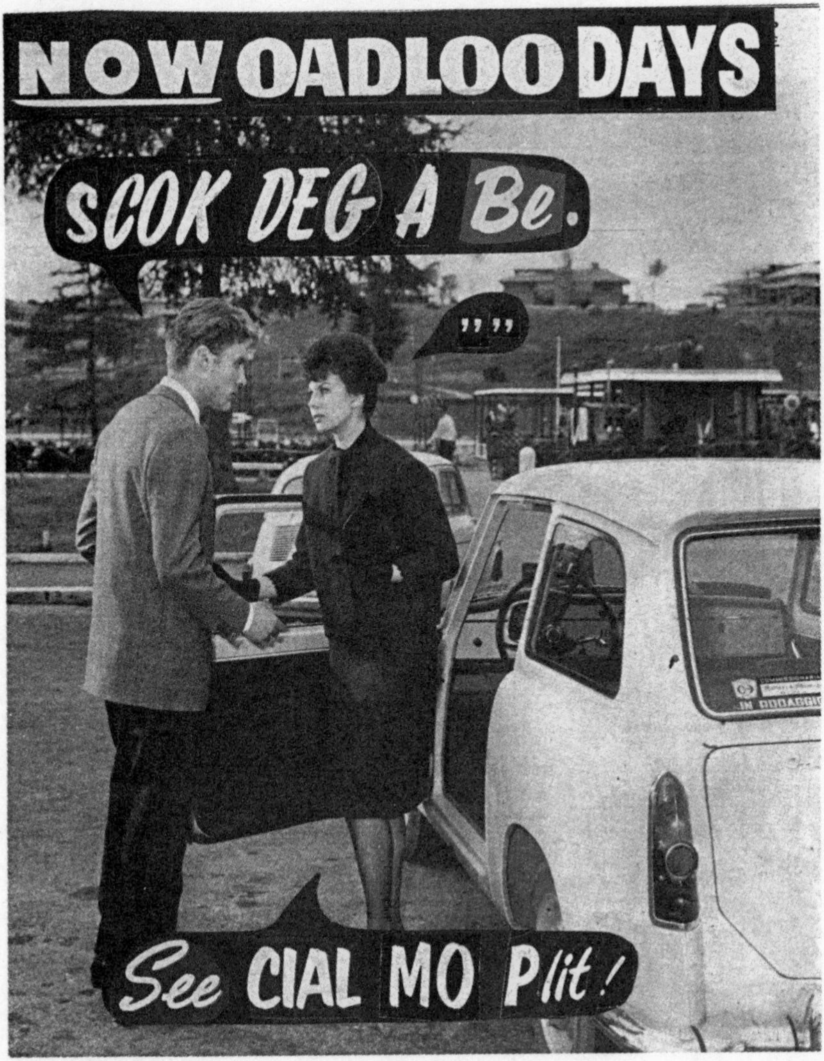
NOW OADLOO DAYS
SCOK DEG A Be.
" "
See CIAL MO Plit!

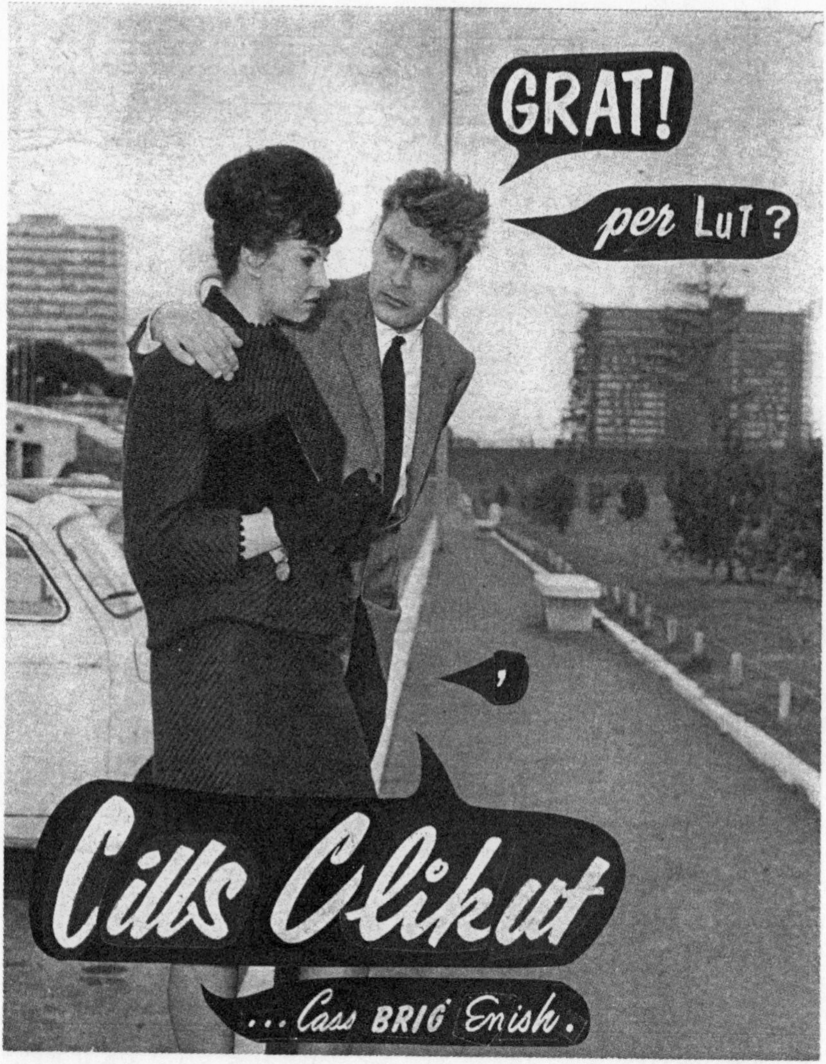
GRAT!
per LUT?
,
Cills Clikut
...Cass BRIG Enish.

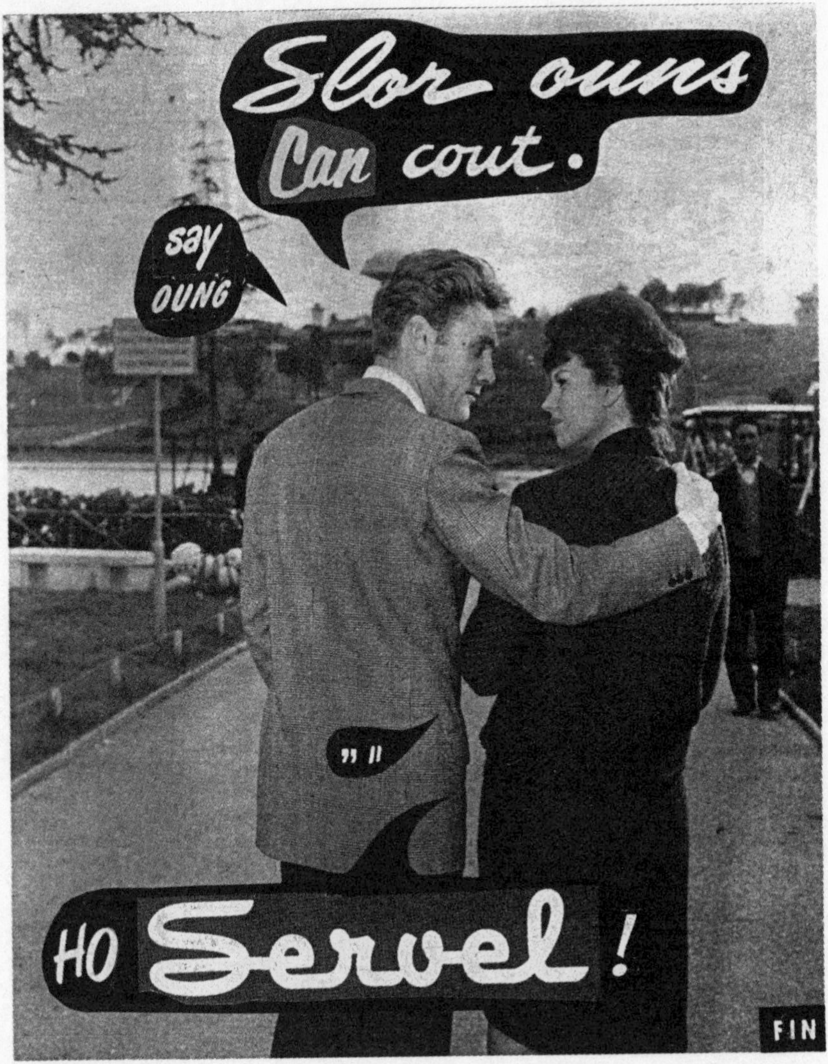

Slor ouns Can cout.
say OUNG
" "
HO Servel!
FIN

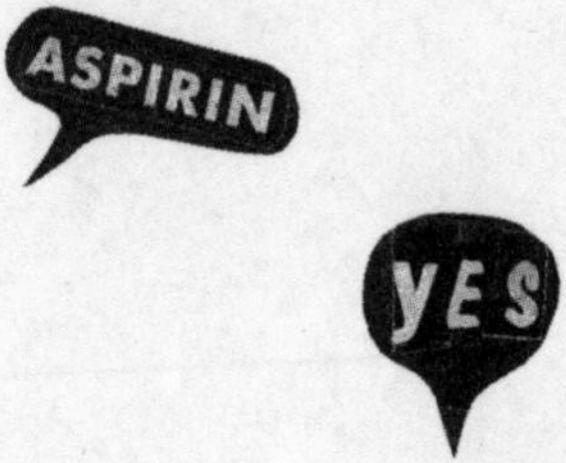
ASPIRIN
YES

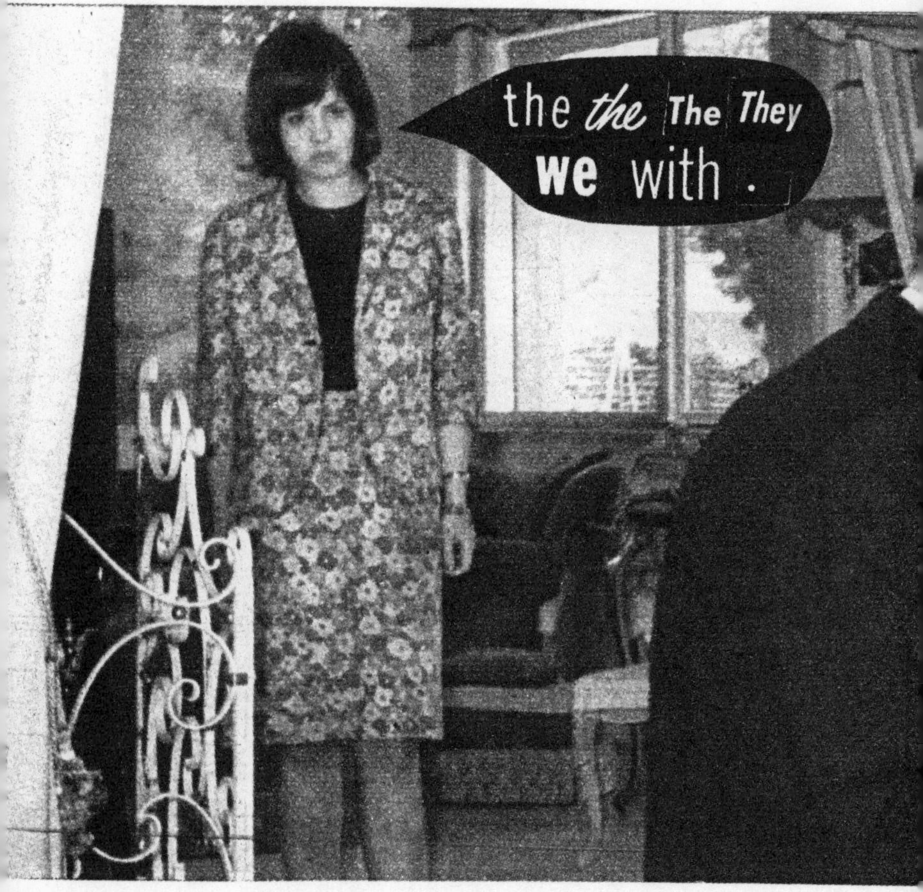
the the The They
we with .

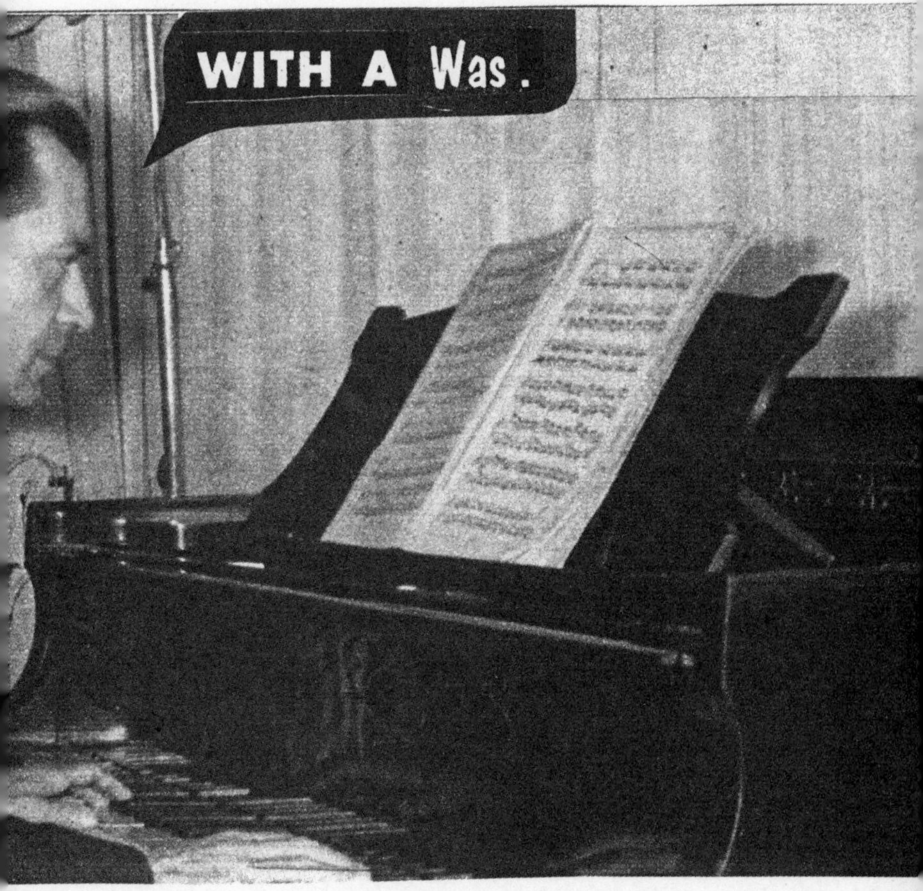
WITH A Was.

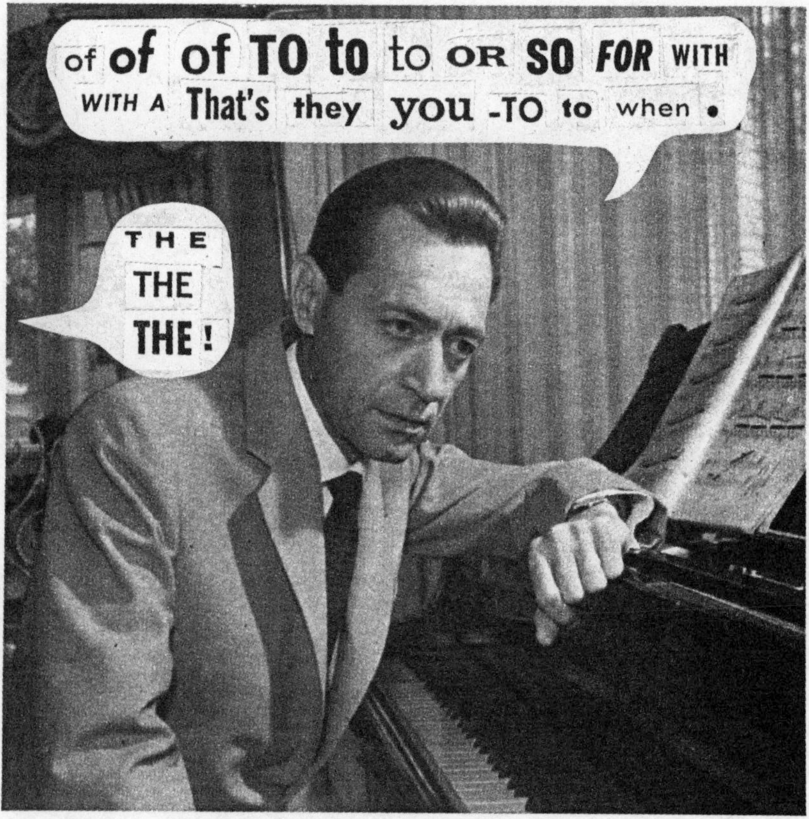
of of of TO to to OR SO FOR WITH WITH A That's they you -TO to when .
THE THE THE !

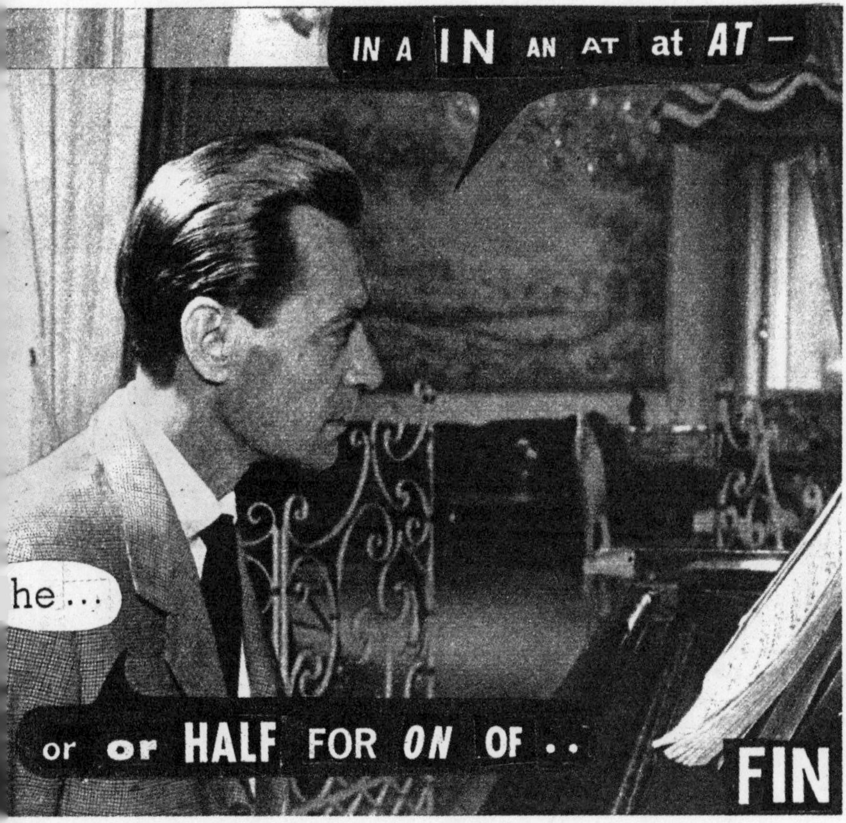
IN A IN AN AT at AT –
he...
or or HALF FOR ON OF . .
FIN

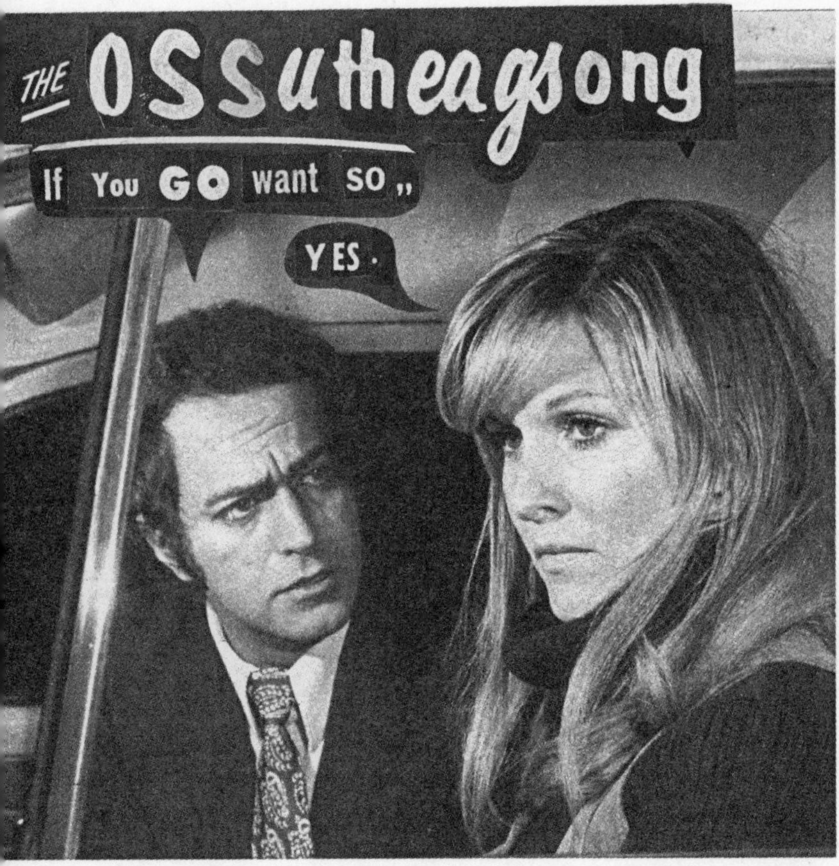
THE OSSutheagsong
If You GO want so,,
YES.

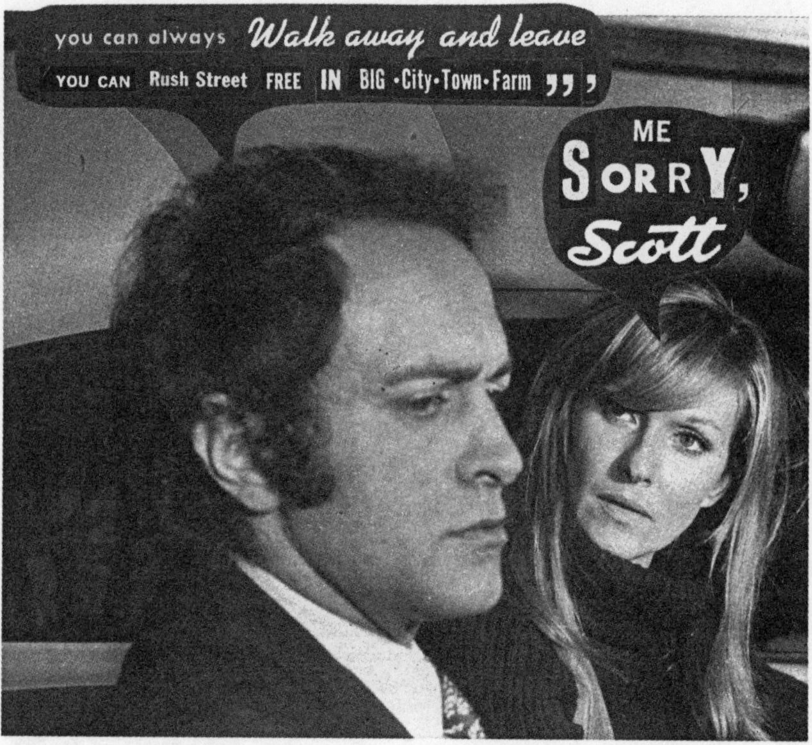
you can always Walk away and leave
YOU CAN Rush Street FREE IN BIG ·City·Town·Farm ,, ,
ME SORRY, Scott

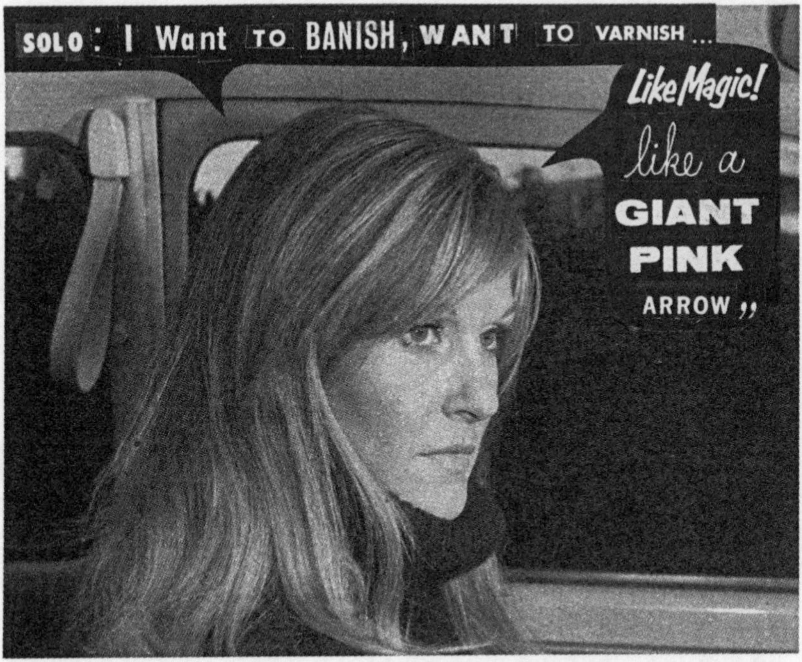
SOLO: I Want TO BANISH, WANT TO VARNISH...
Like Magic! like a GIANT PINK ARROW,,

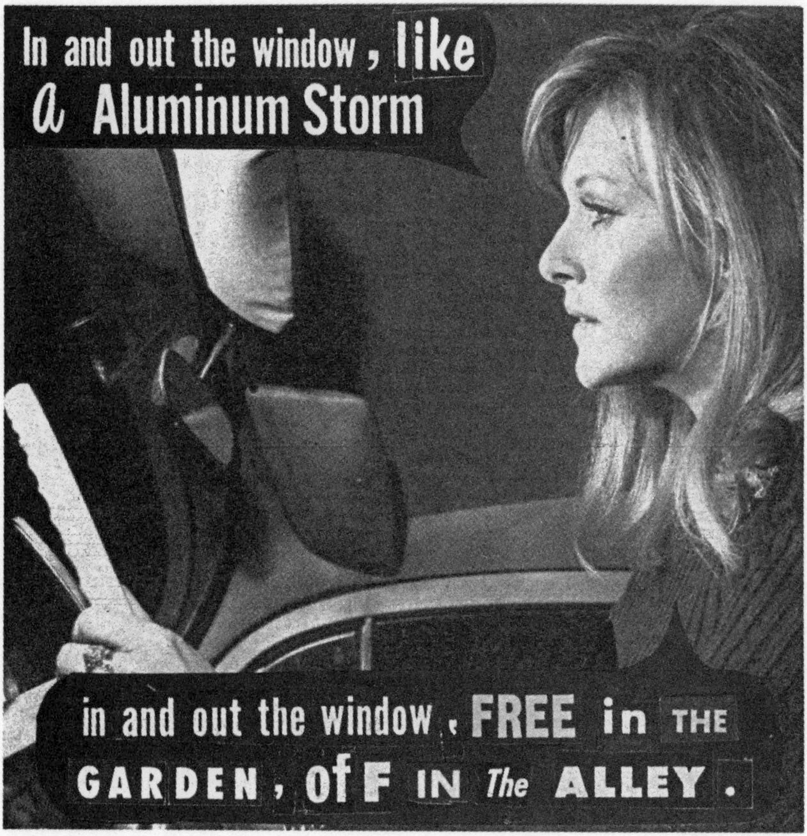
In and out the window, like a Aluminum Storm
in and out the window, FREE in THE GARDEN, ofF IN The ALLEY.

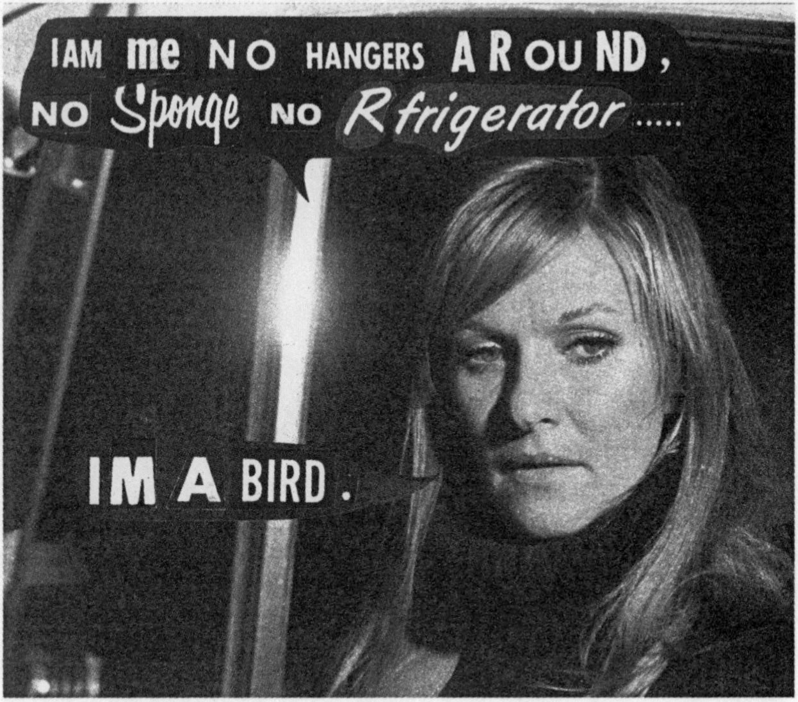
IAM me NO HANGERS ARouND,
NO Sponge NO Rfrigerator .....
IM A BIRD.

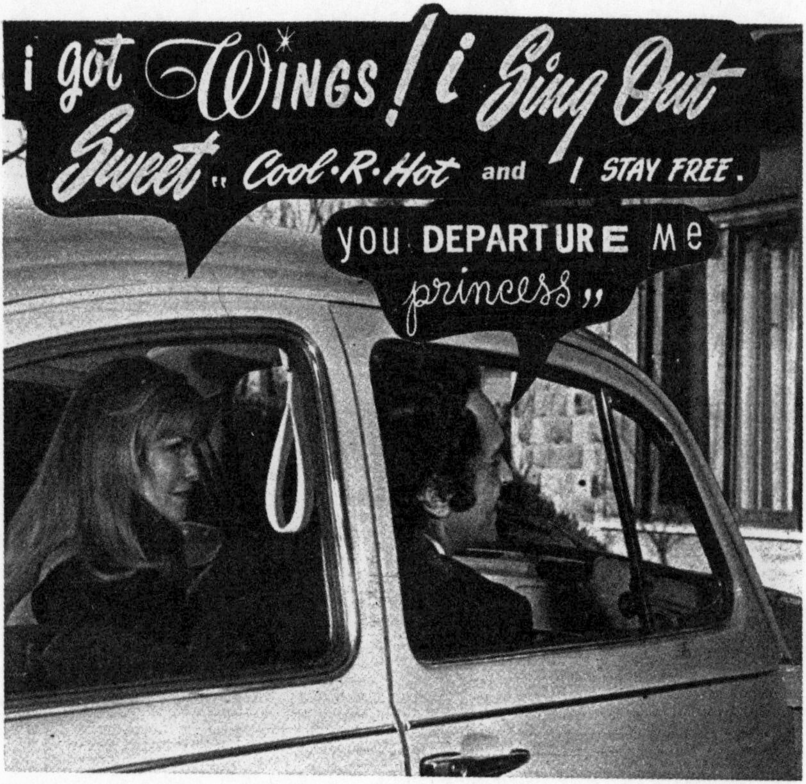
i got Wings! i Sing Out Sweet,, Cool·R·Hot and I STAY FREE.
you DEPARTURE me princess,,

iM EVEREDY GOING
NOW, scott,, me FLY.
YES
will You WALKIE TALKIE me?

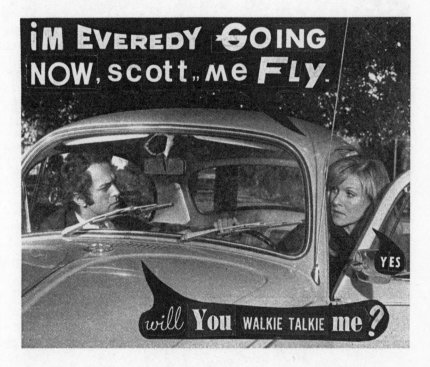

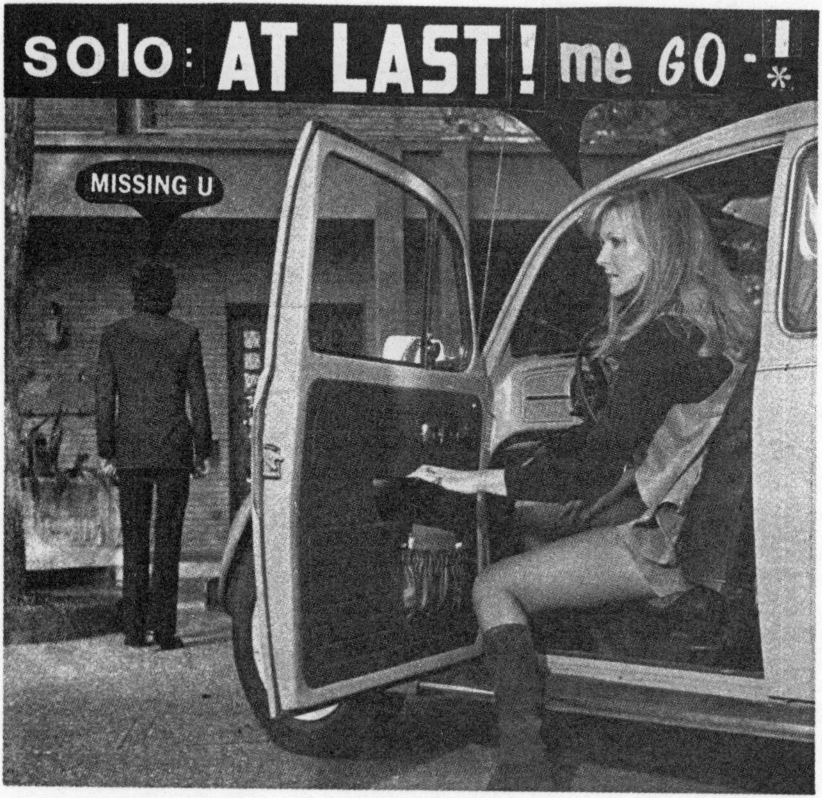
solo: AT LAST! me GO-!*
MISSING U

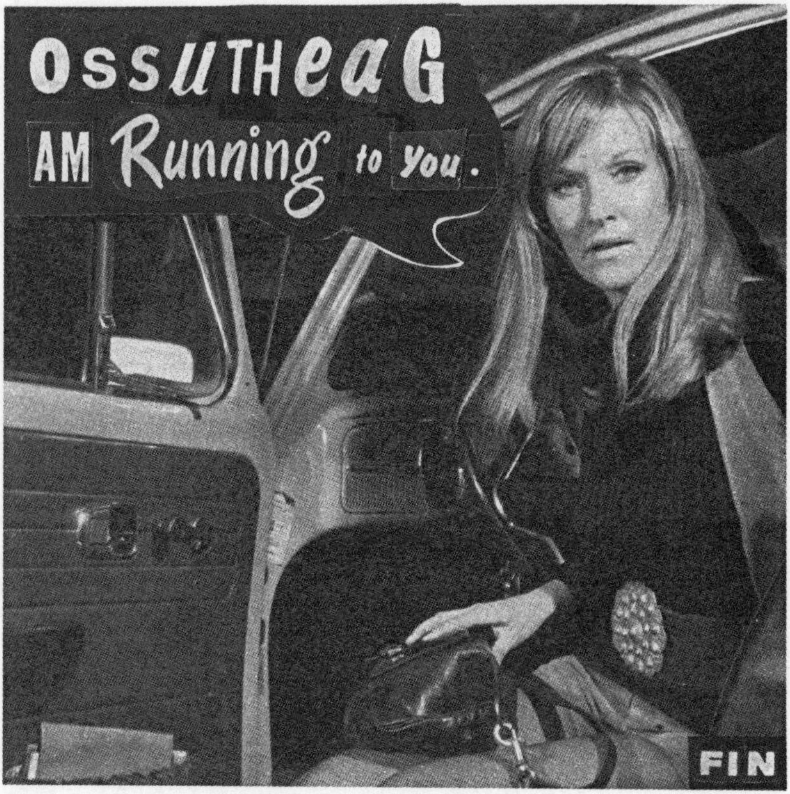
OssUTHeaG
AM Running to You.
FIN

Autotray

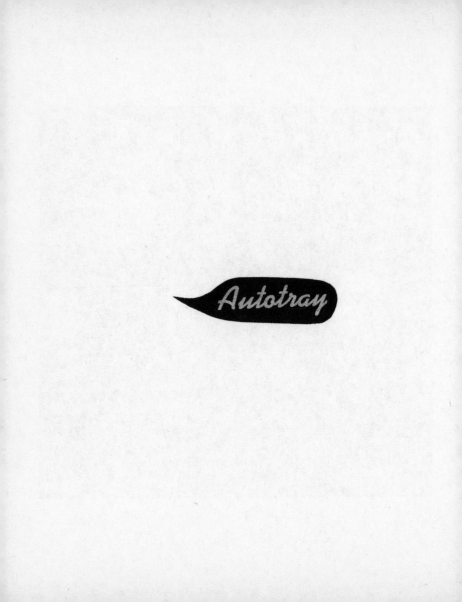

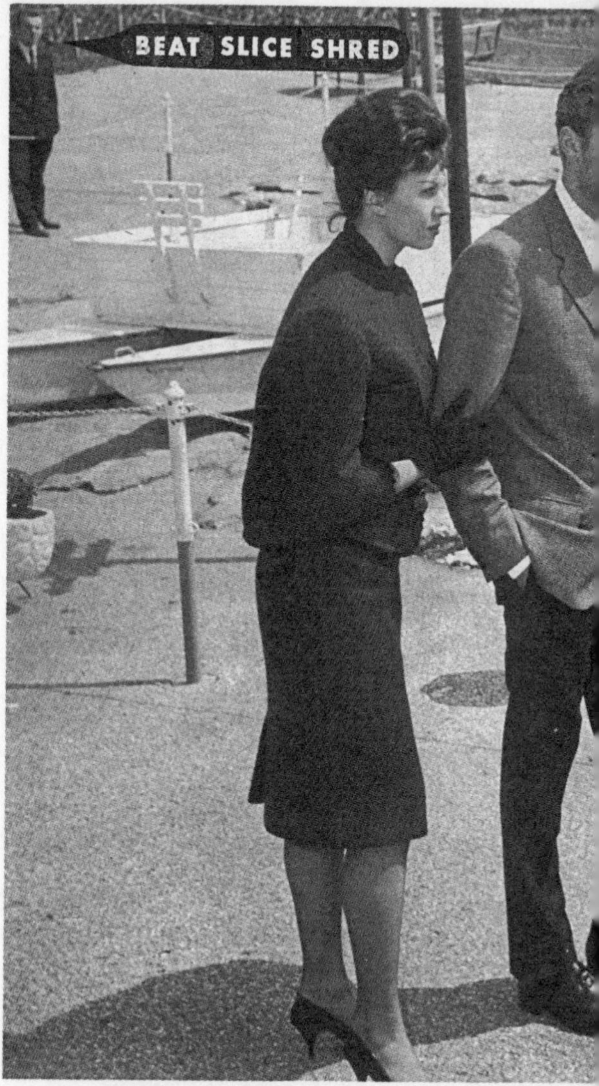
BEAT SLICE SHRED

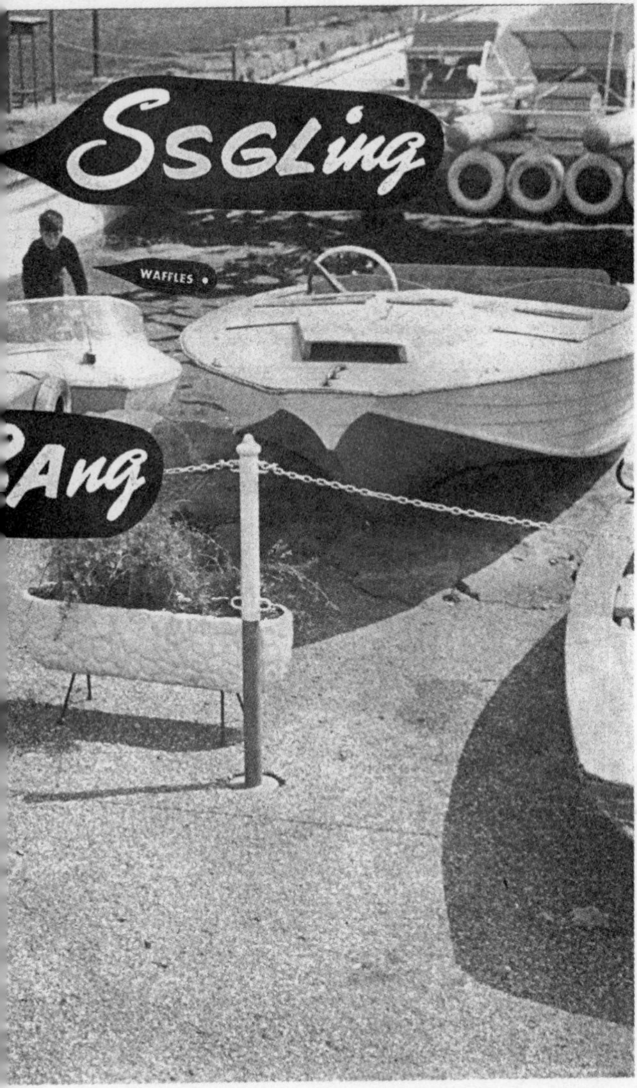
SsGLing
WAFFLES
Ang

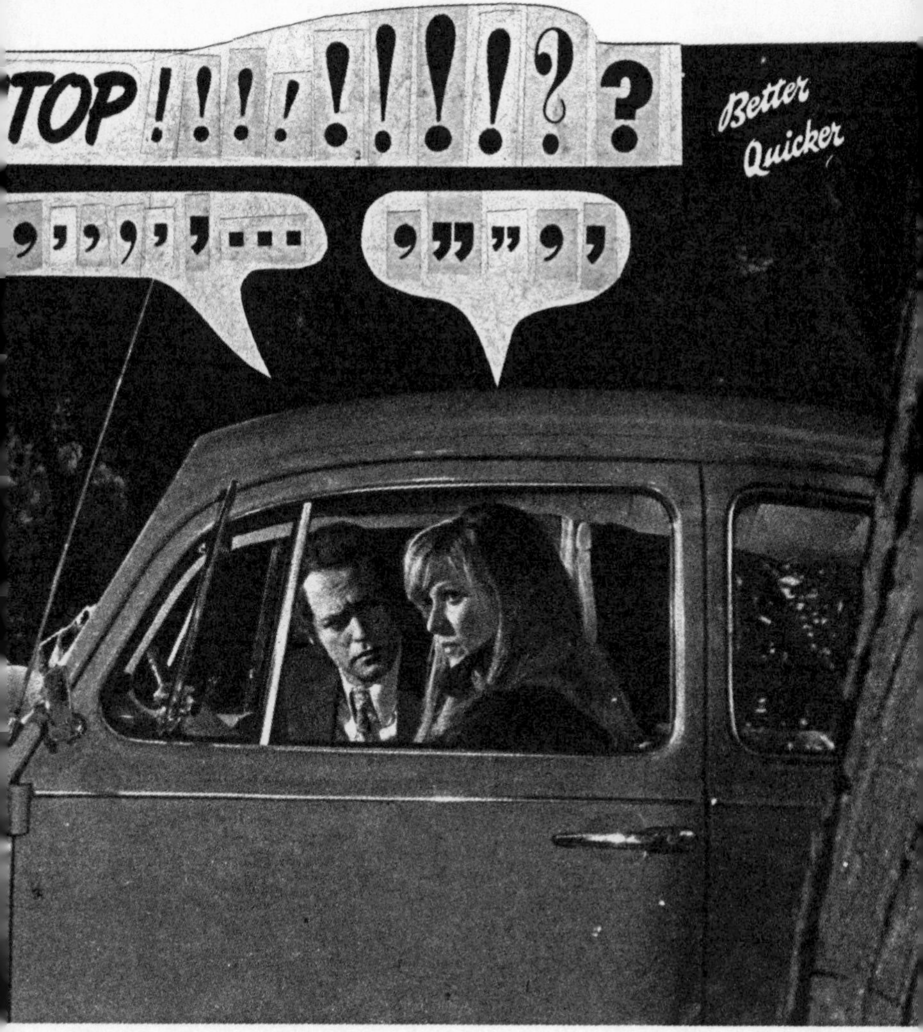
TOP ! ! ! ! ! ! ! ! ? ?
Better
Quicker

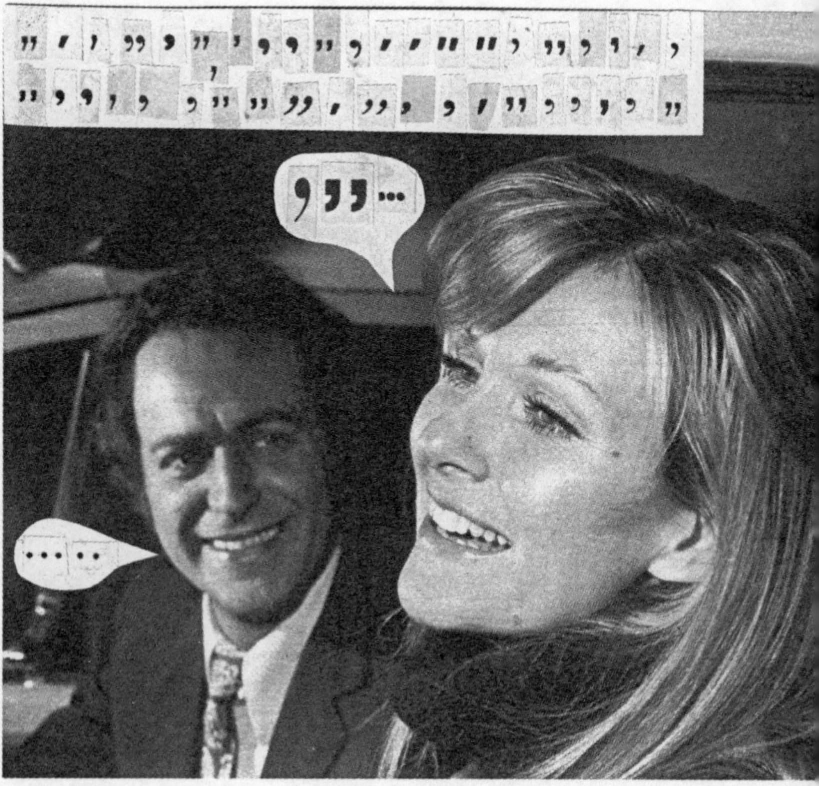

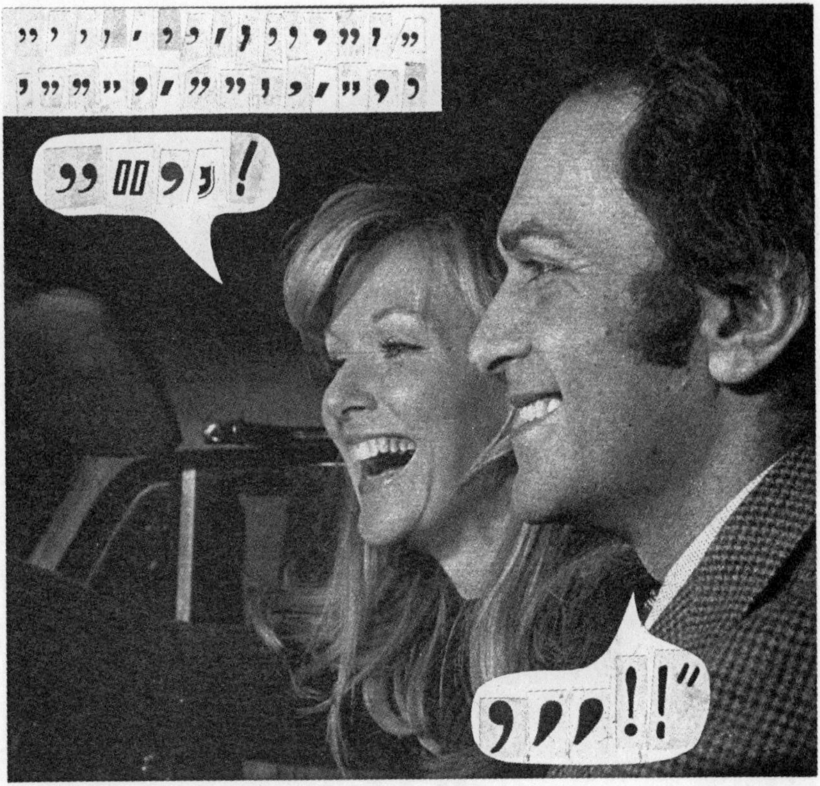

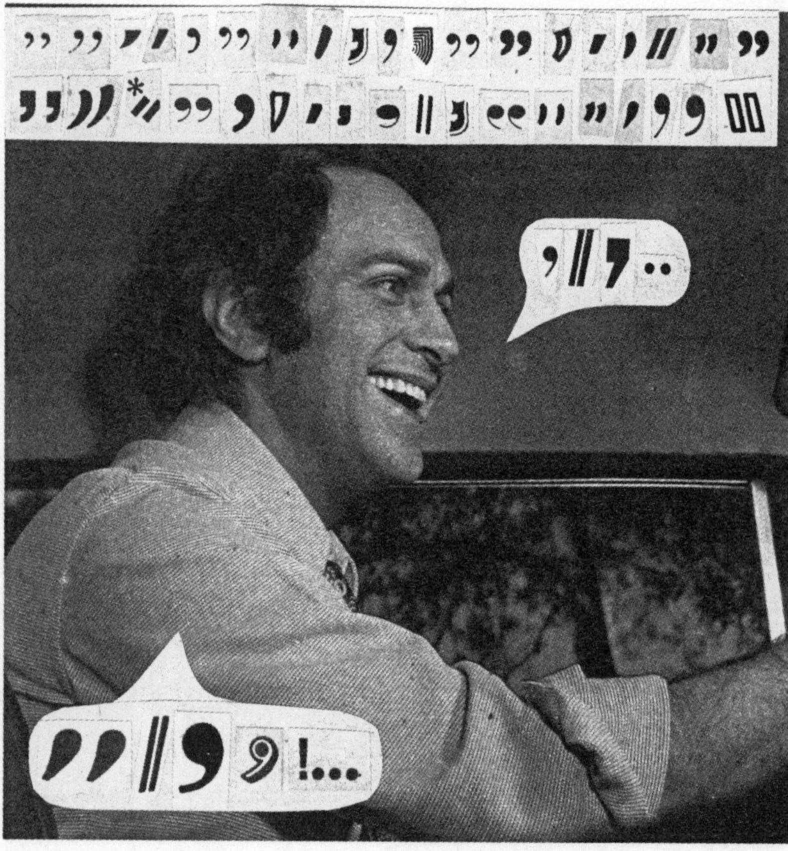

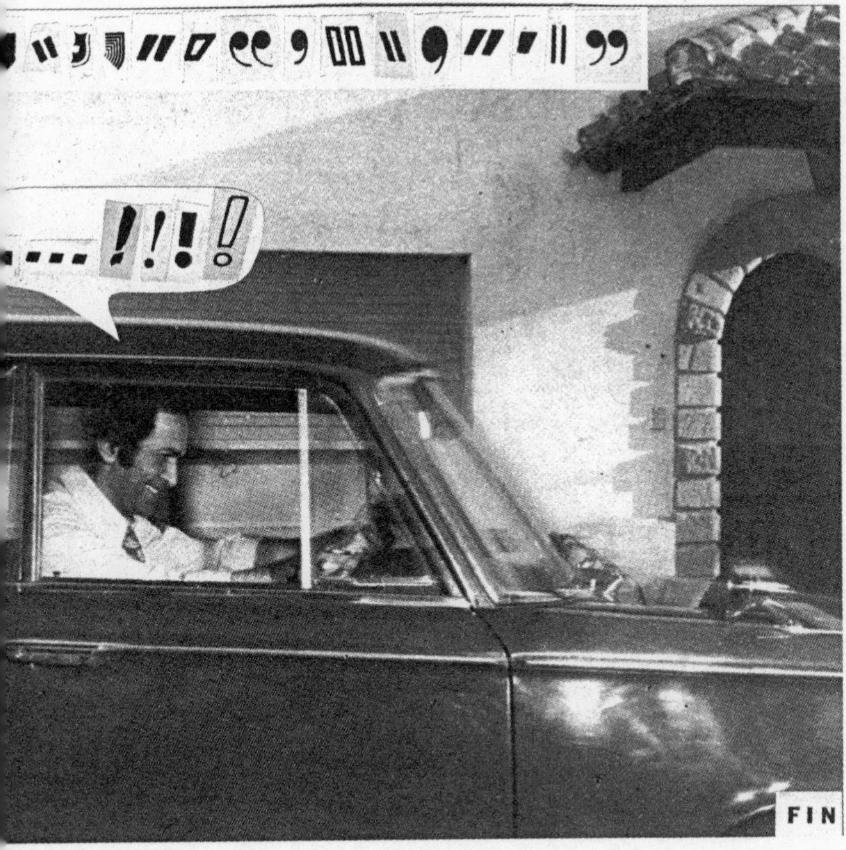
!!!!
FIN

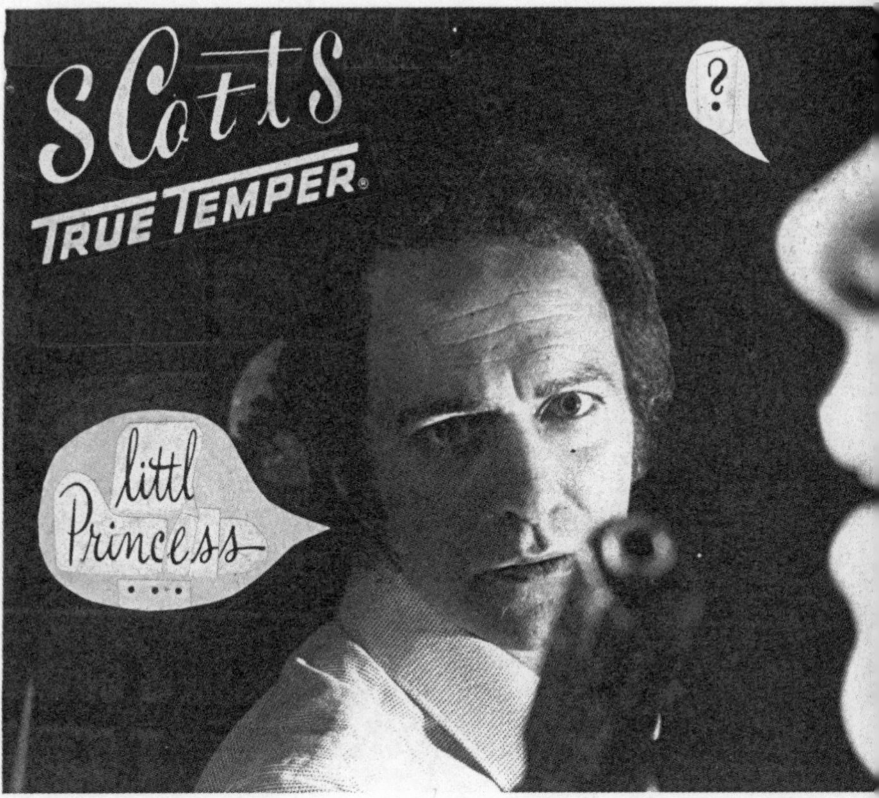
Scotts
TRUE TEMPER
?
littl Princess
. . . .

... you long-lasting HEADACHE you HURTING!
AM going to STOP PAIN now.
... KEEP SANG-FROID

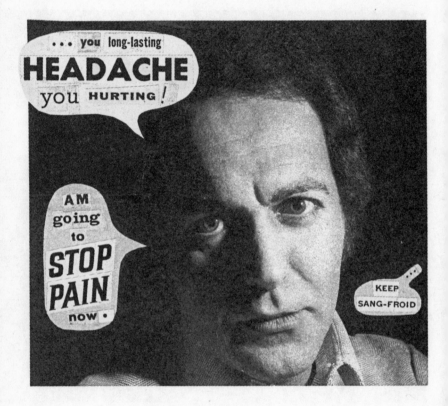

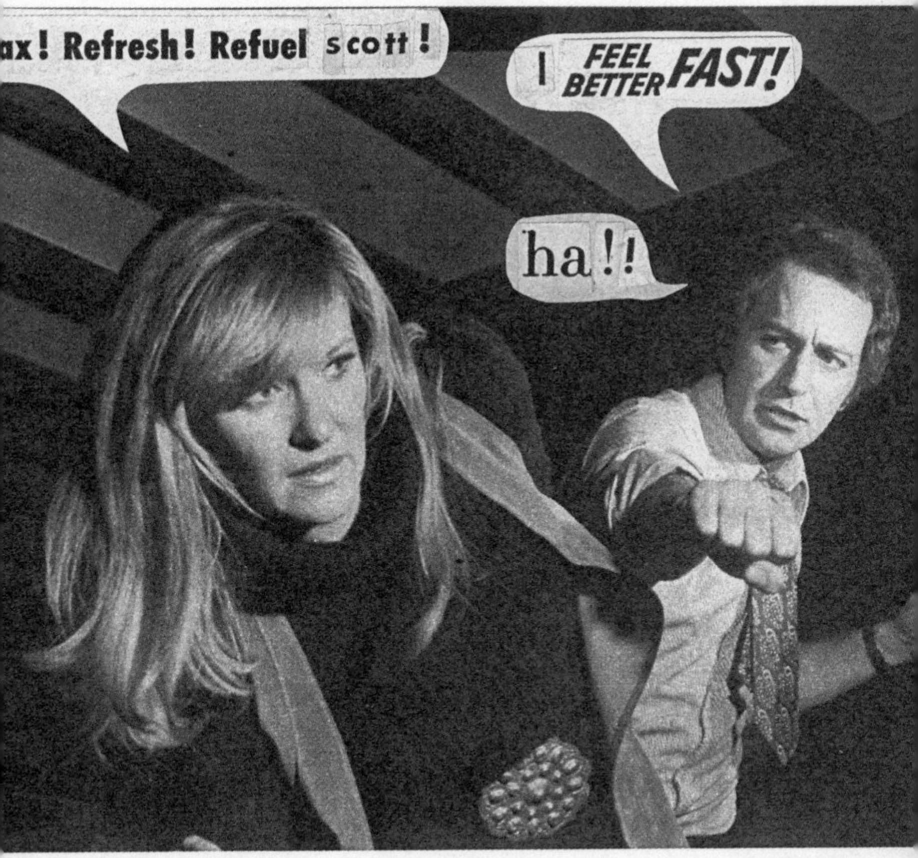
ax! Refresh! Refuel scott!
I FEEL BETTER FAST!
ha!!

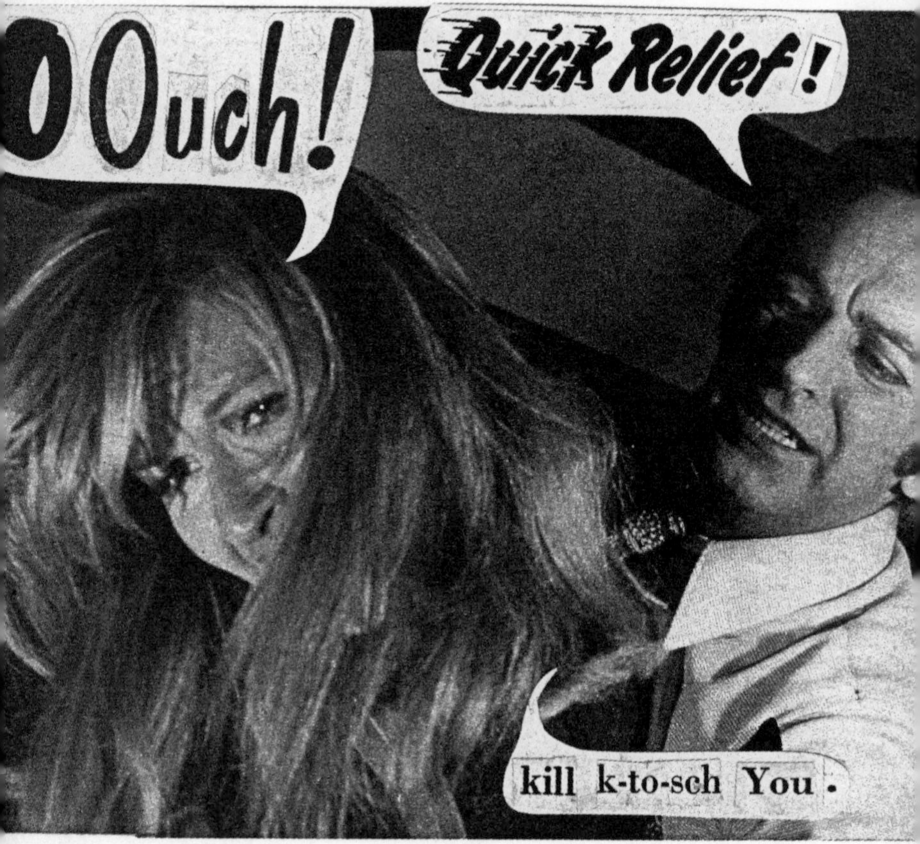

O Ouch!
Quick Relief!
kill k-to-sch You.

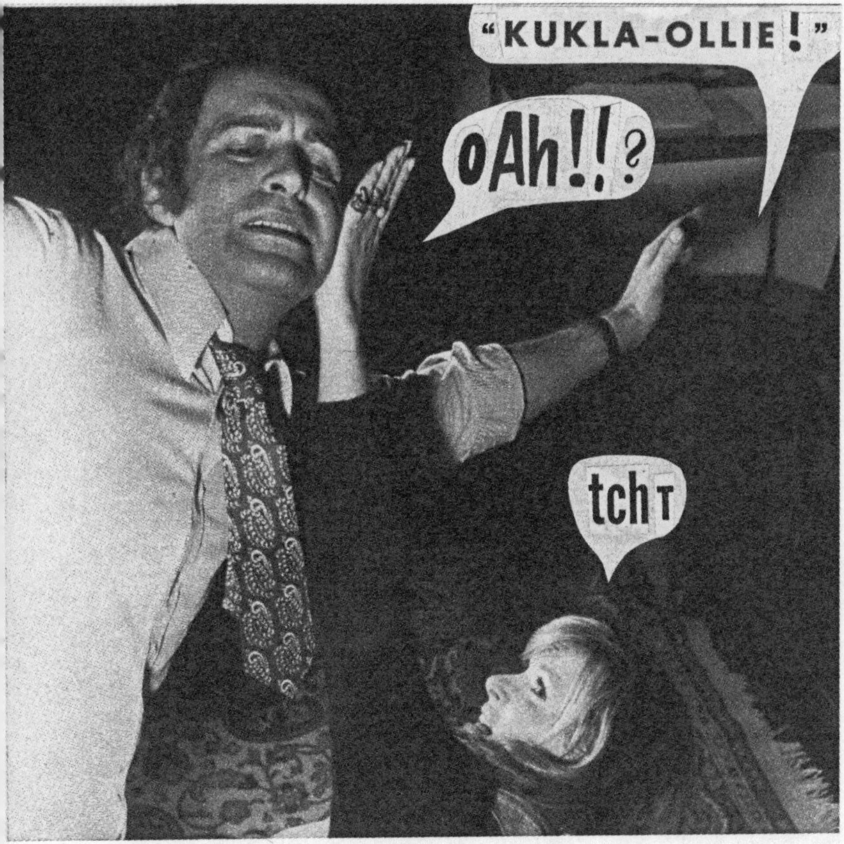
"KUKLA-OLLIE!"
oAh!!?
tch T

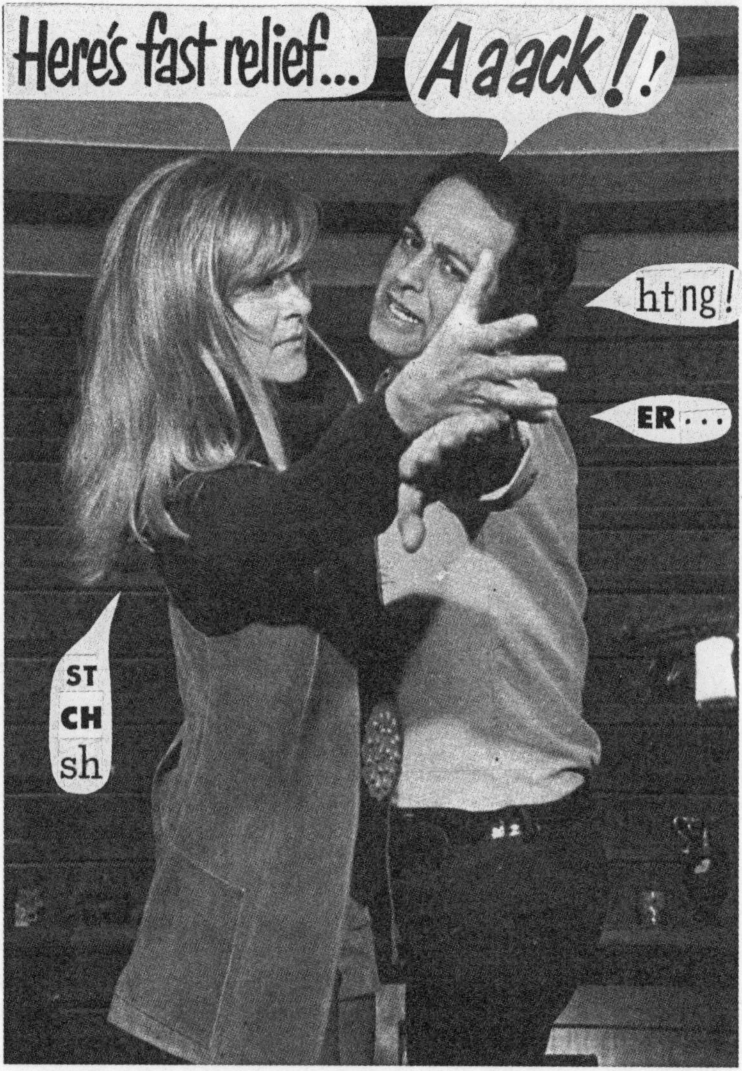
Here's fast relief...
Aaack!!
htng!
ER...
ST
CH
sh

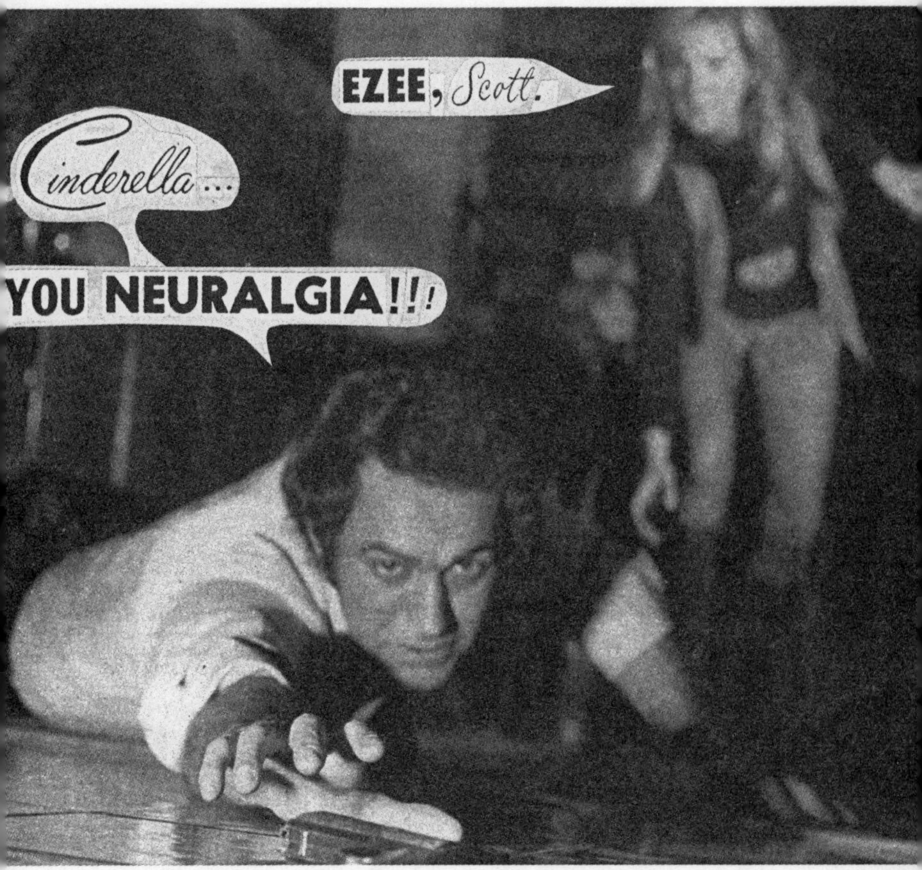
EZEE, Scott.
Cinderella...
YOU NEURALGIA!!!

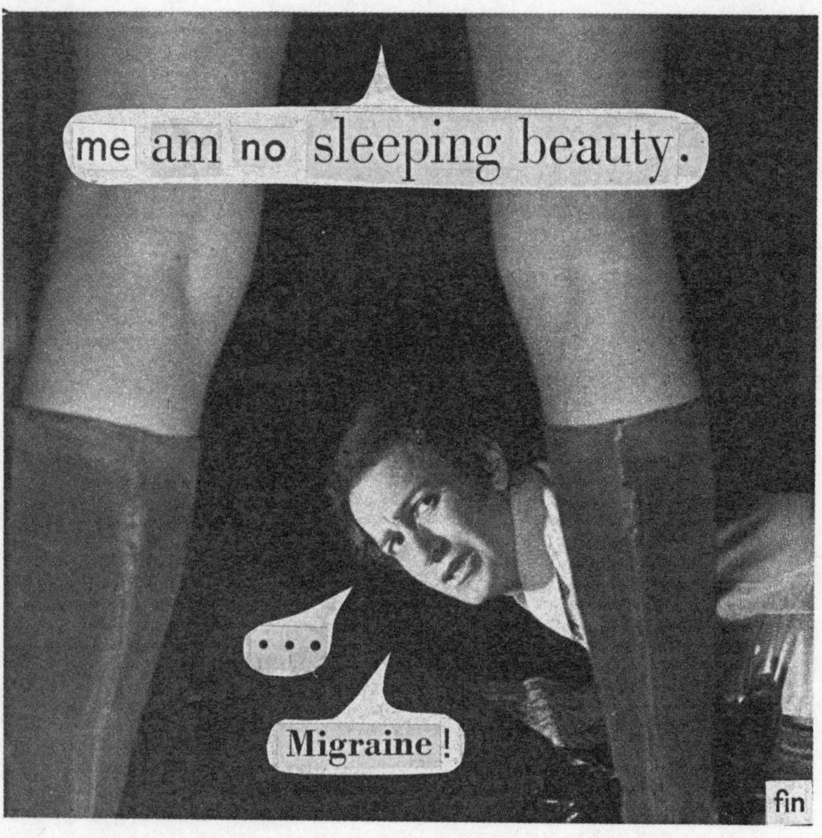
me am no sleeping beauty.
• • •
Migraine !
fin

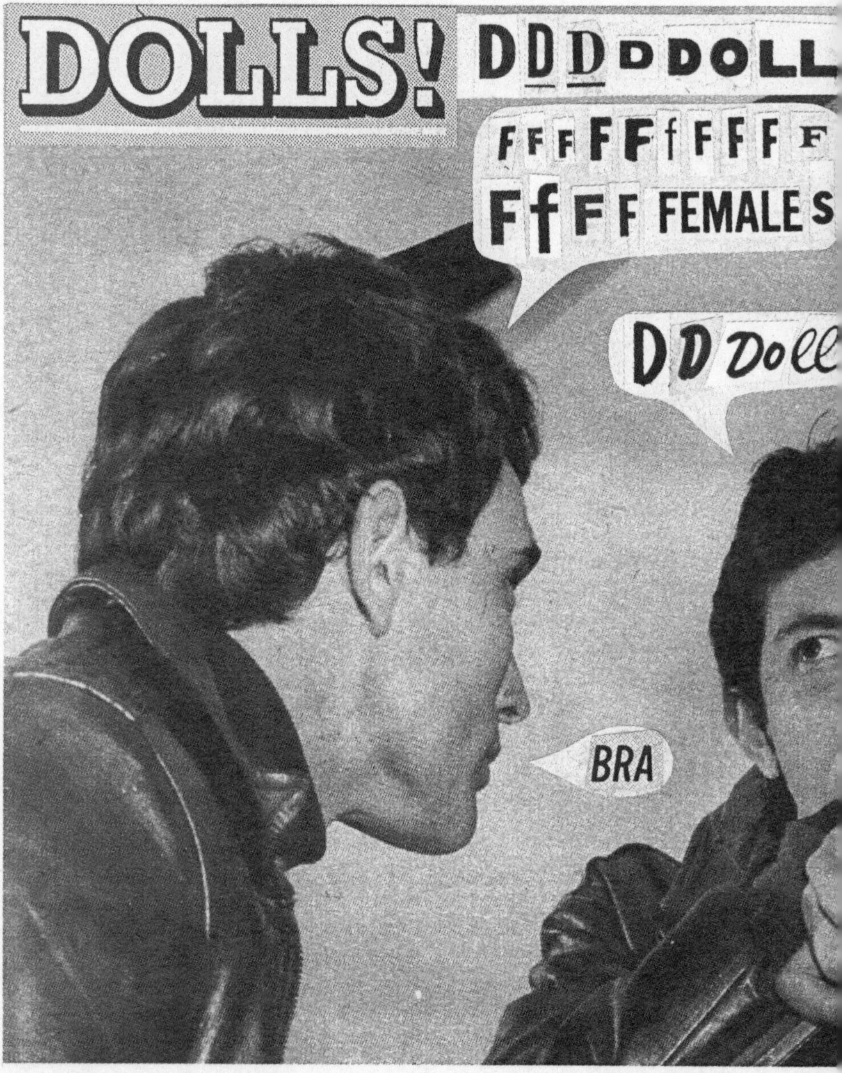
DOLLS!
DDDDDOLL
FFFFFfFFFF
FfFF FEMALES
DD Doll
BRA

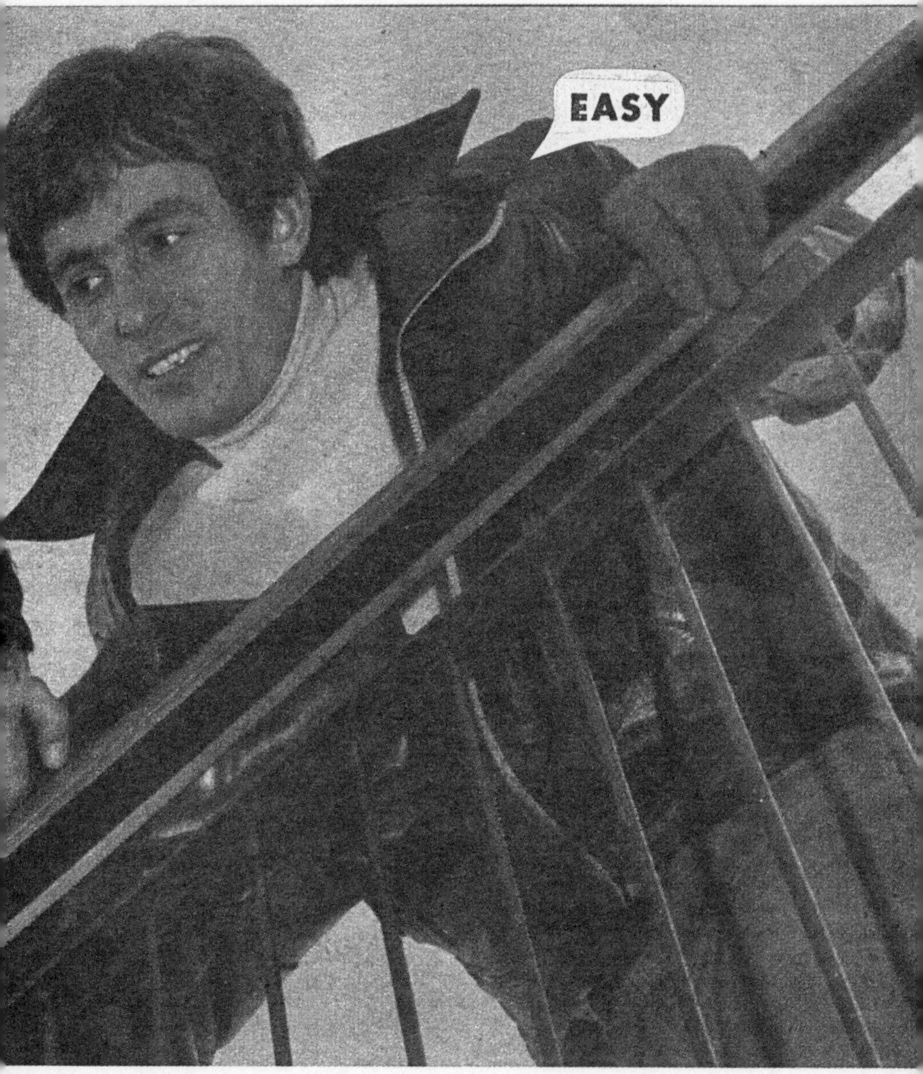
EASY

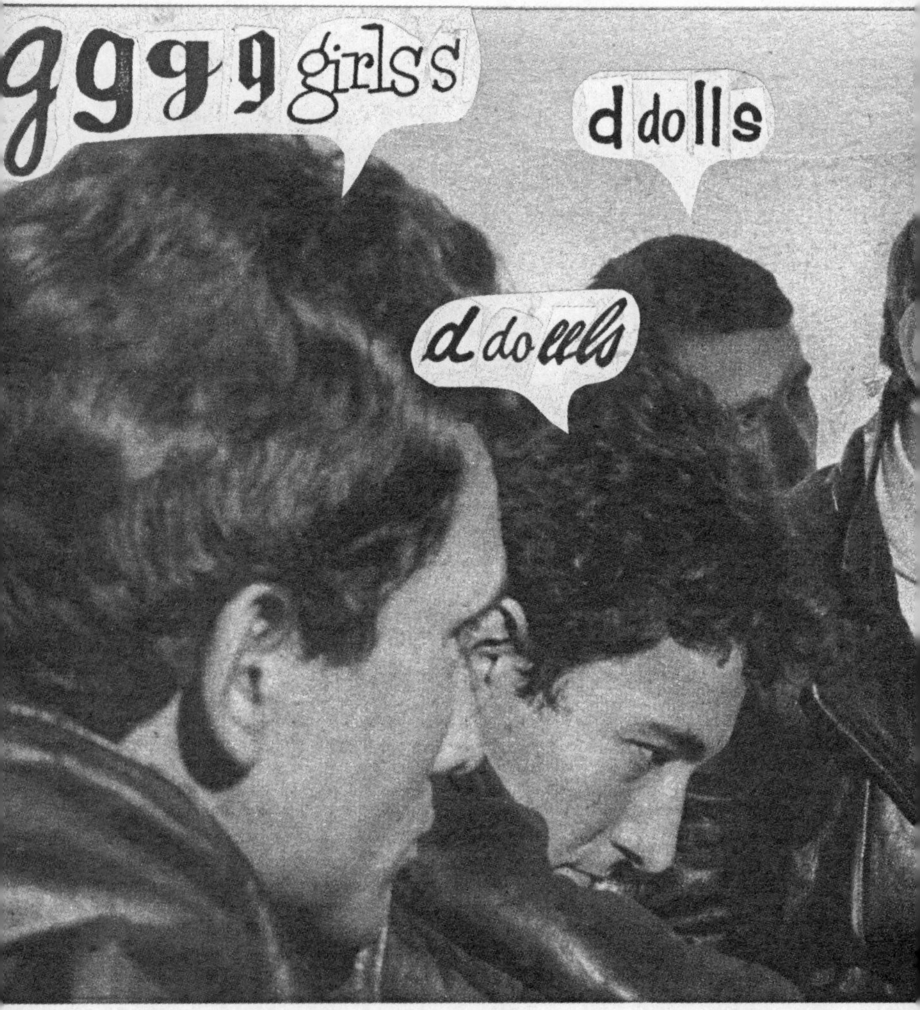
gggg girlss
d dolls
d dolls

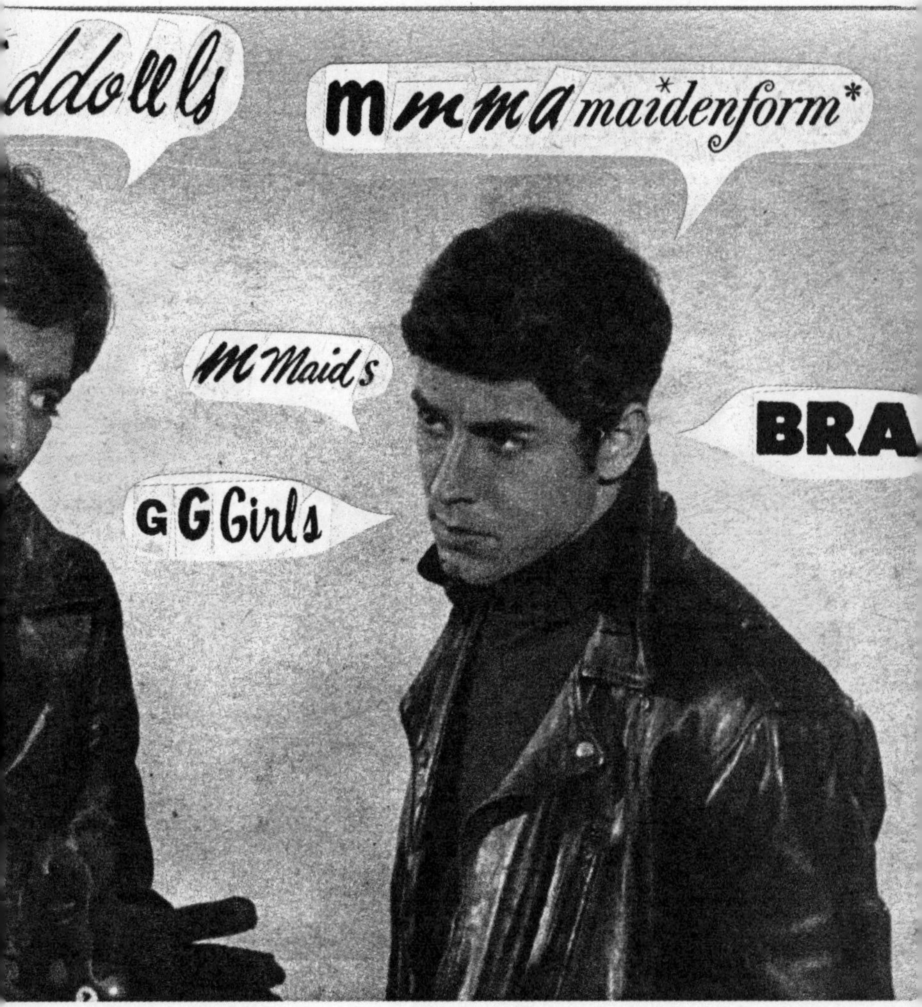
ddollls
mmmma maidenform*
M Maids
BRA
GGGirls

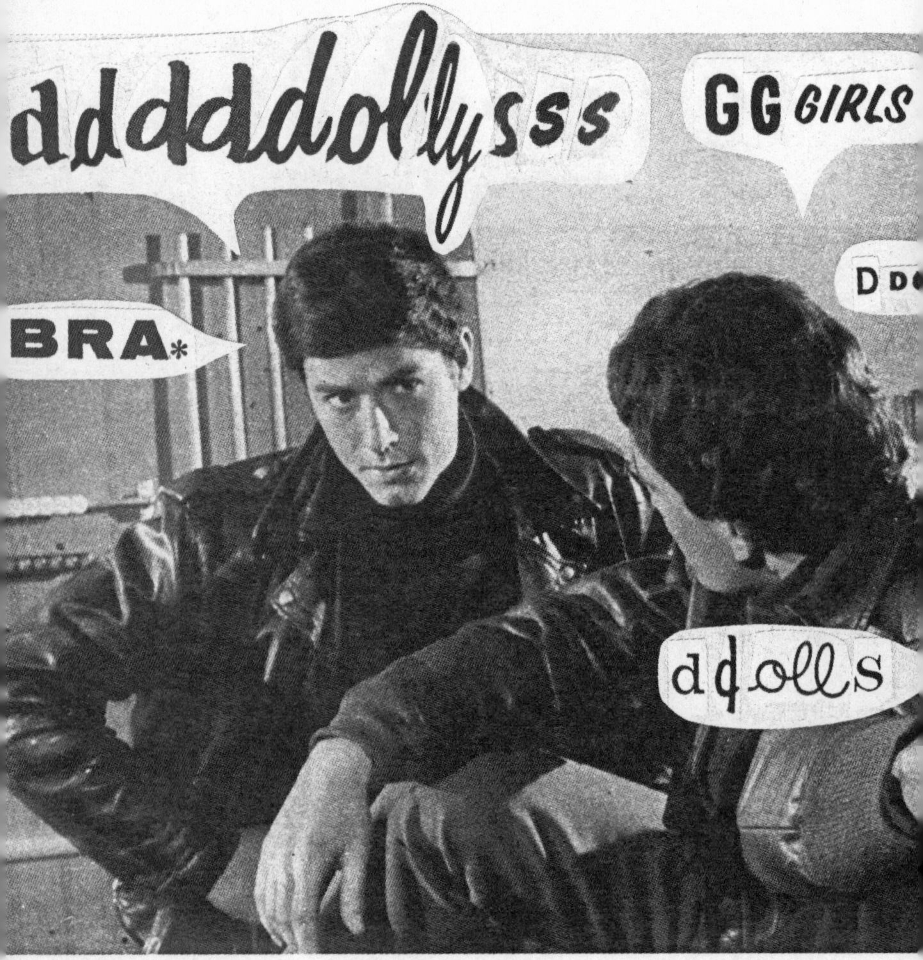
dddddollysss
GG GIRLS
D D
BRA*
ddolls

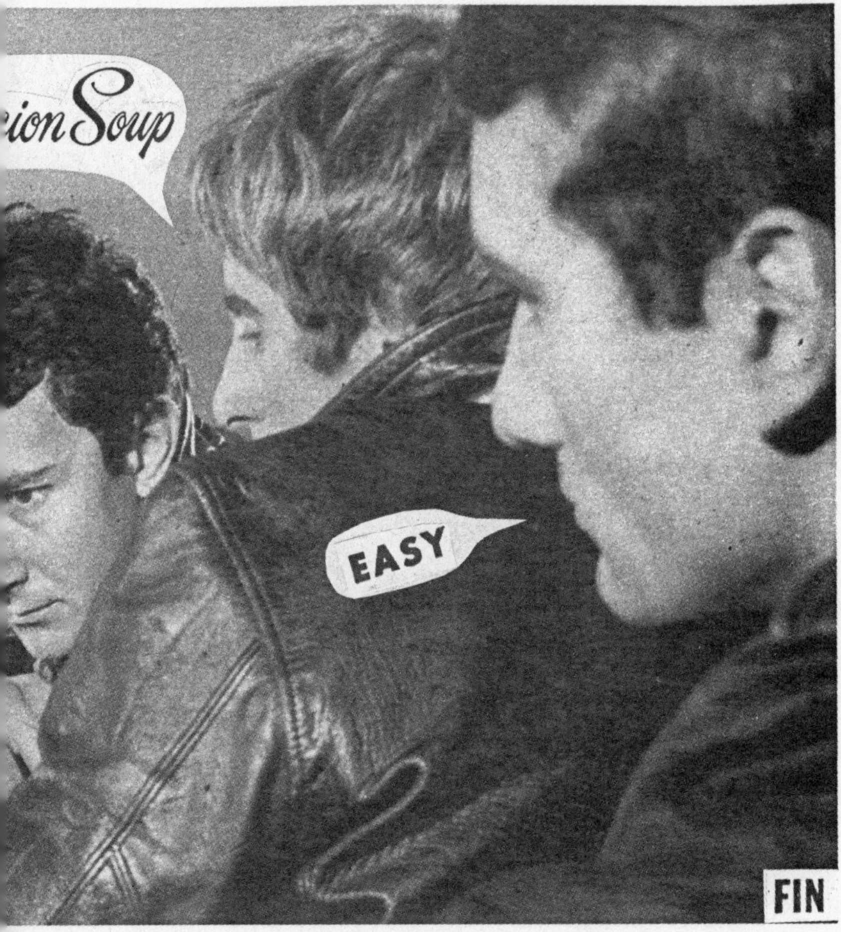

ion Soup
EASY
FIN

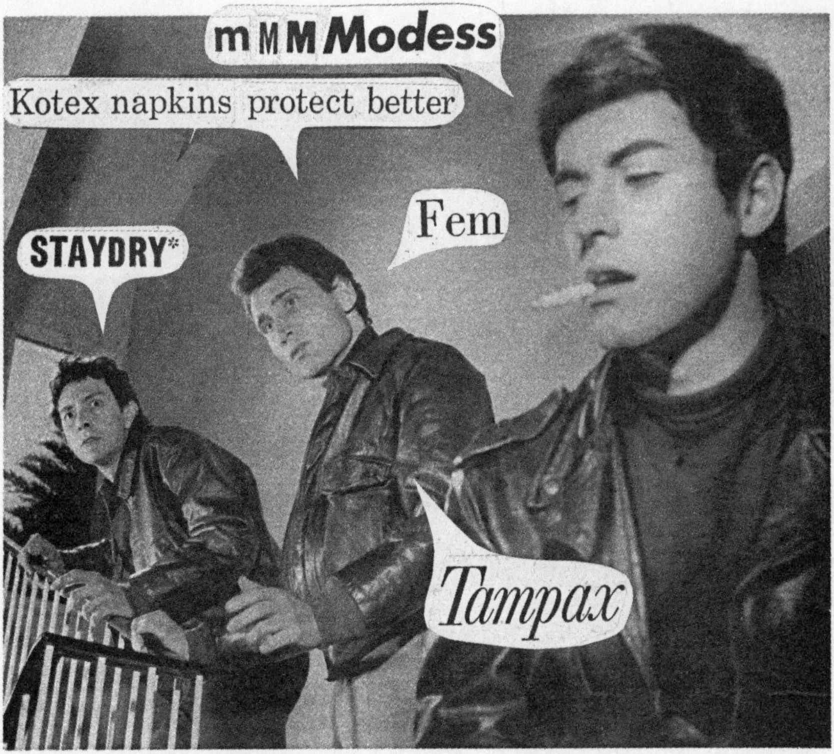
mMM Modess
Kotex napkins protect better
Fem
STAYDRY*
Tampax

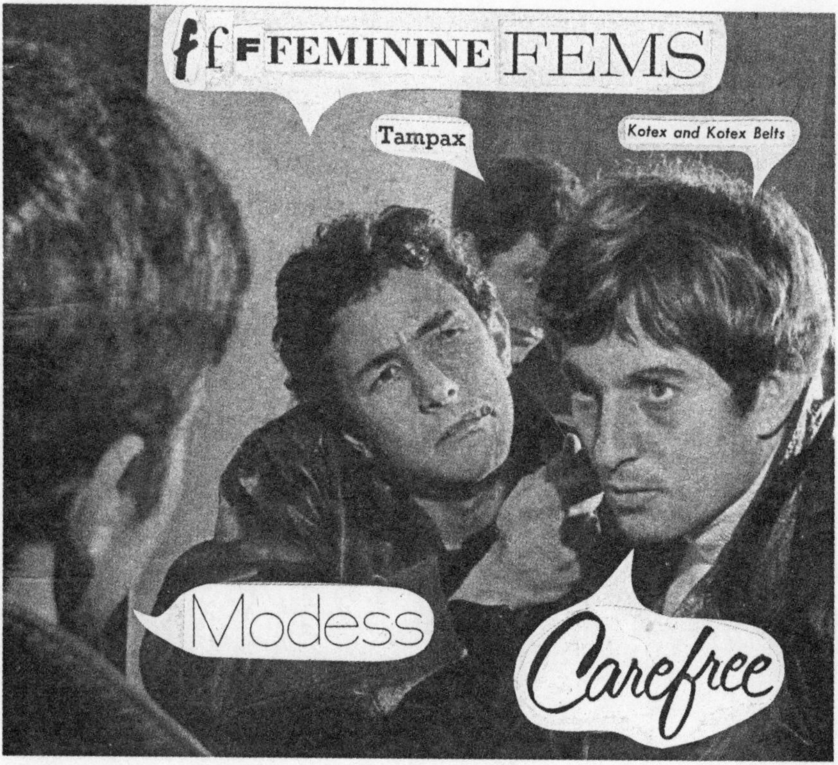

ff F FEMININE FEMS
Tampax
Kotex and Kotex Belts
Modess
Carefree

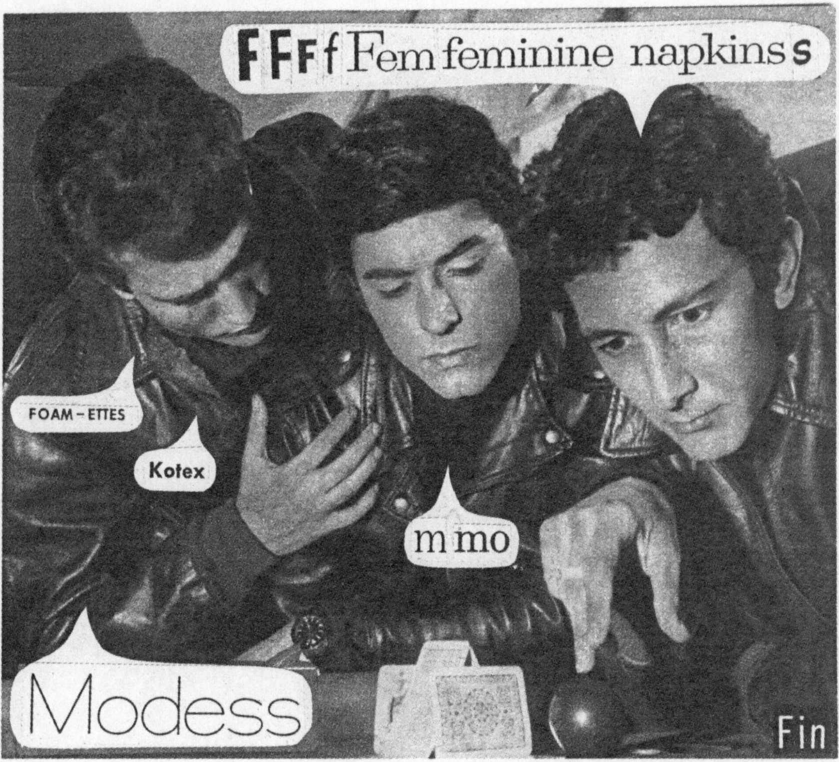
FFFf Fem feminine napkins s
FOAM-ETTES
Kotex
m mo
Modess
Fin

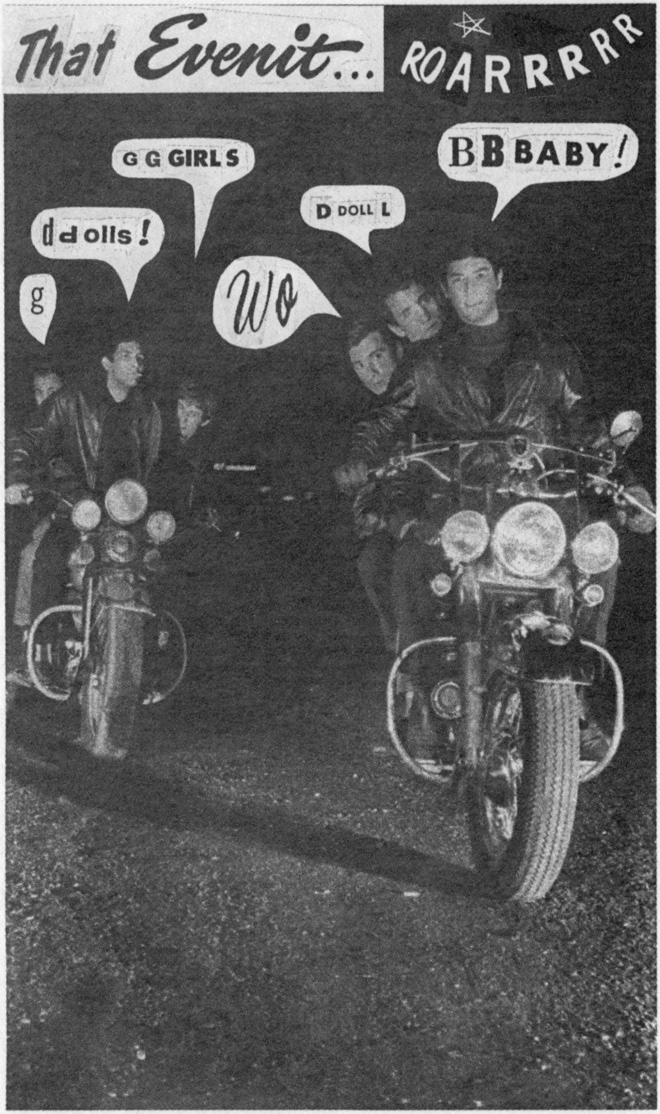
That Evenit...
ROARRRRR
G G GIRLS
BB BABY!
d d olls!
D DOLL L
g
Wo

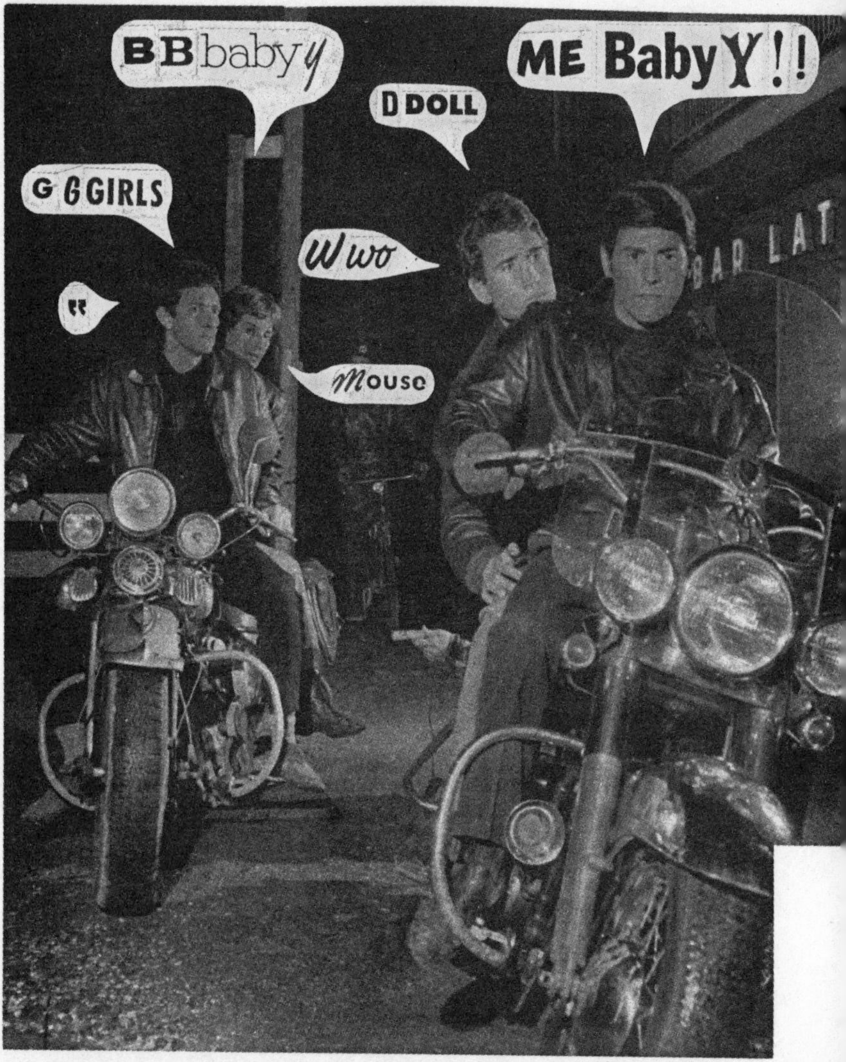
BB baby y
ME Baby Y !!
D DOLL
G G GIRLS
W wo
"
Mouse
BAR LAT

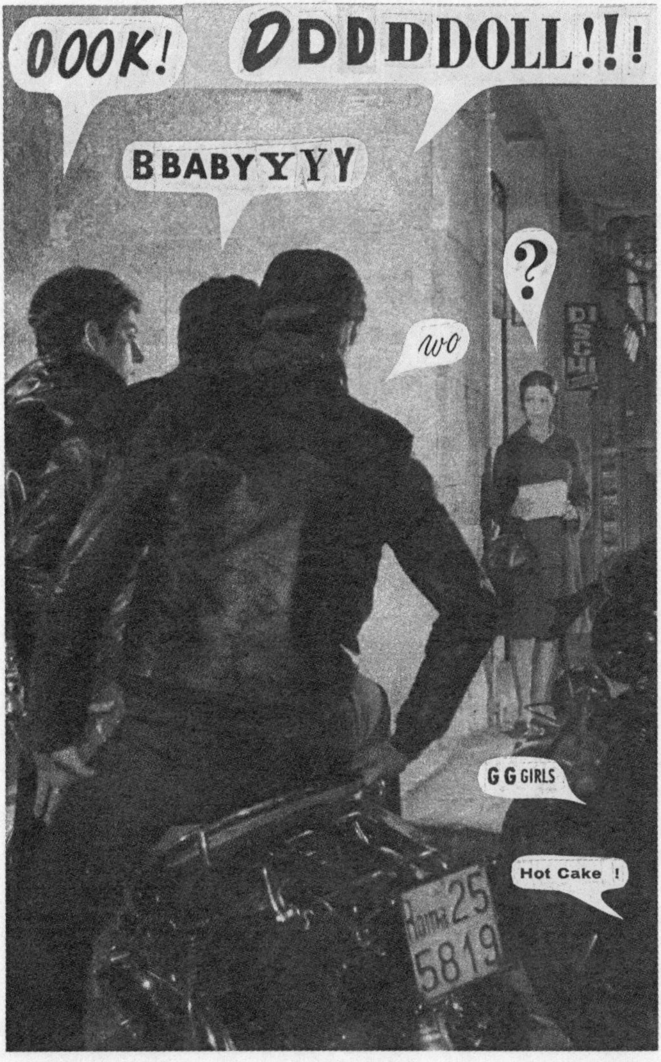
OOOK!
ODDDDOLL!!!
BBABYYYY
?
wo
G G GIRLS
Hot Cake !
DISCHI
Roma 25
5819

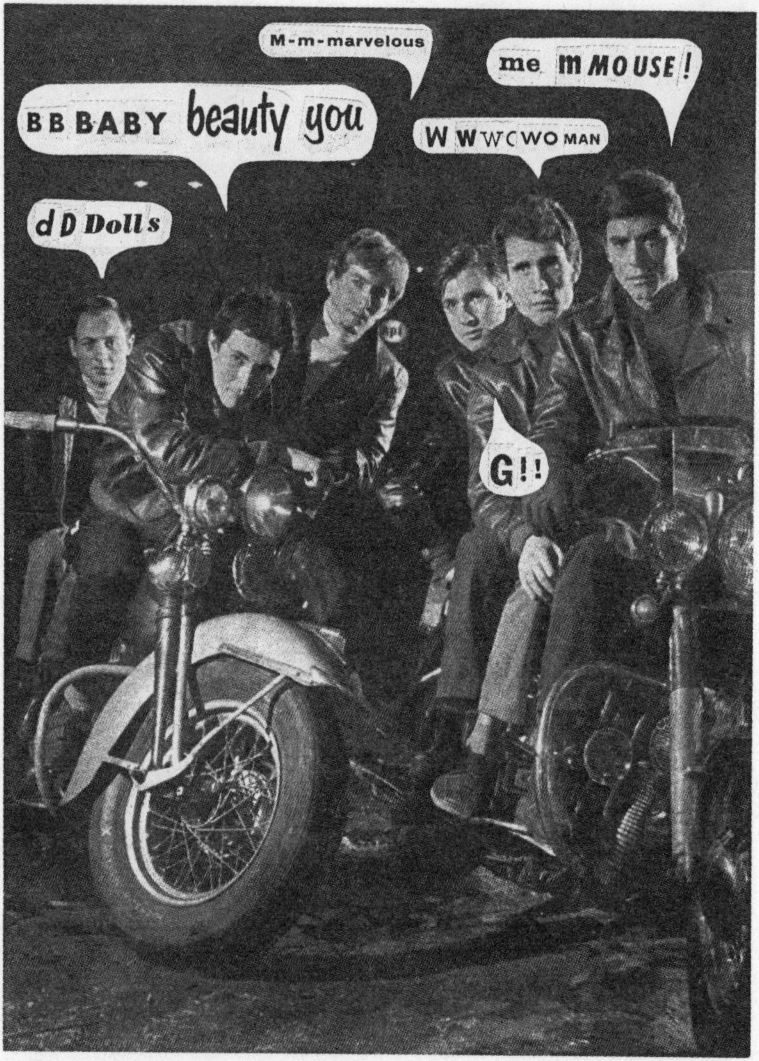
M-m-marvelous
me mMOUSE!
BB BABY beauty you
W WWCWOMAN
dD Dolls
G!!

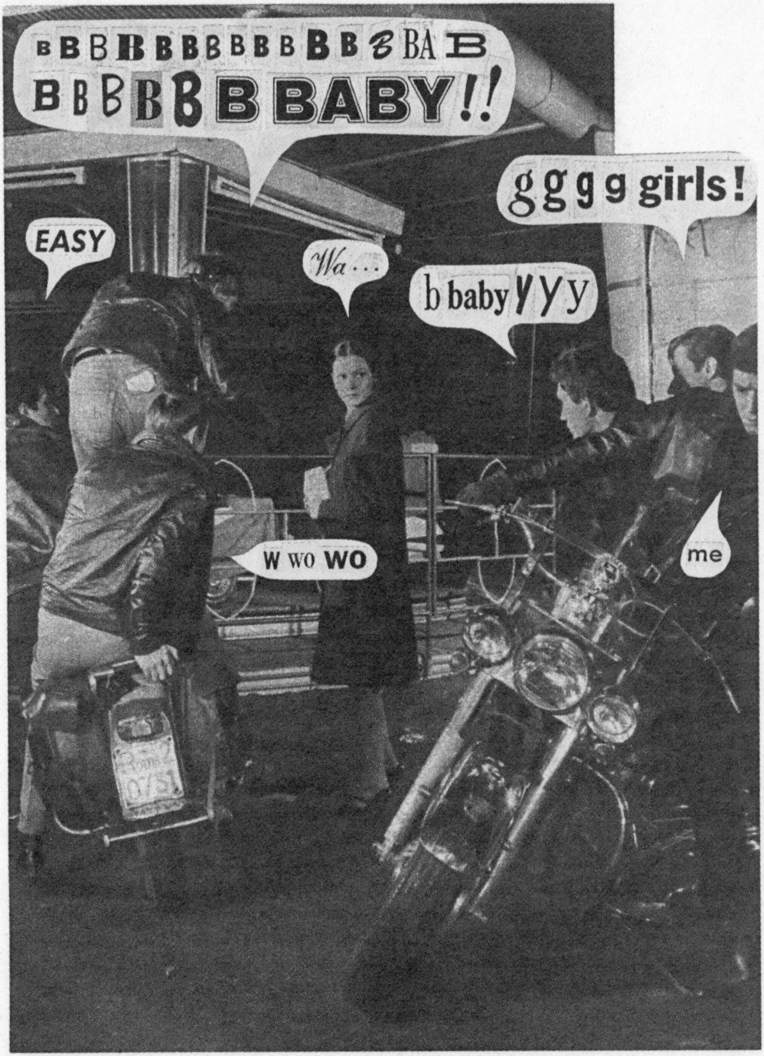
BBBBBBBBBBBB BA B
B B B B B B B BABY!!
EASY
Wa...
b baby y y y
g g g g girls!
W wo WO
me

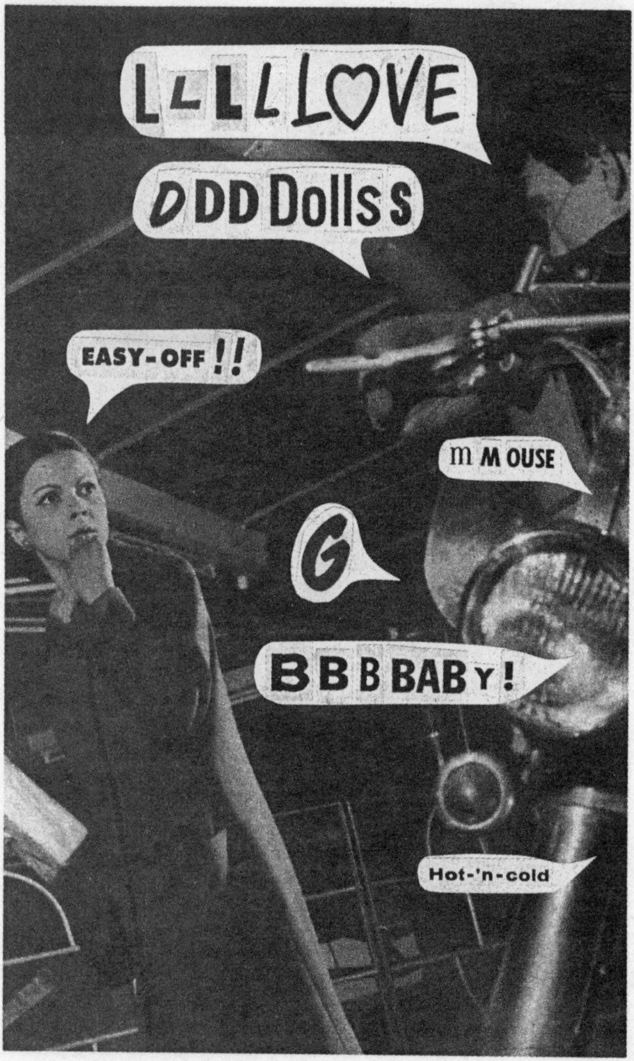
L L L L LOVE
D DD Dolls s
EASY-OFF !!
m M OUSE
G
B B B BAB Y !
Hot-'n-cold

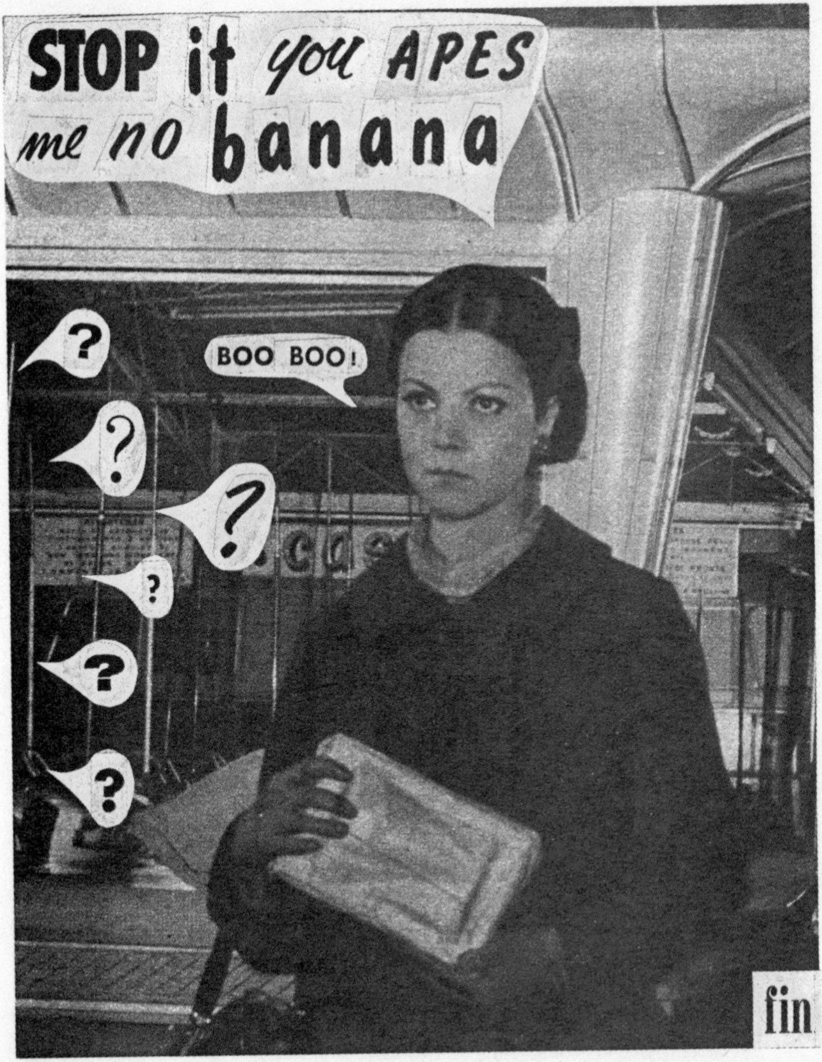
STOP it you APES
me no banana
?
BOO BOO!
?
?
?
?
?
fin

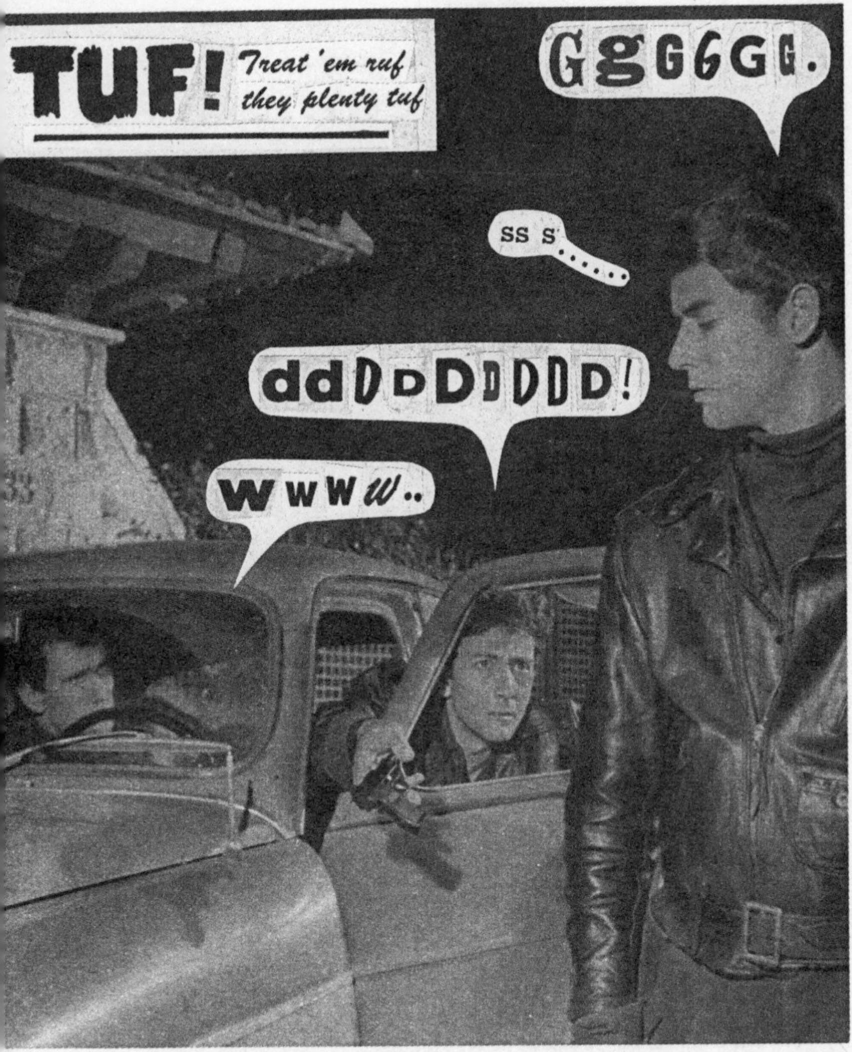
TUF!
Treat 'em ruf
they plenty tuf
GgGGGG.
SS S......
ddDDDDDDD!
WWWW..

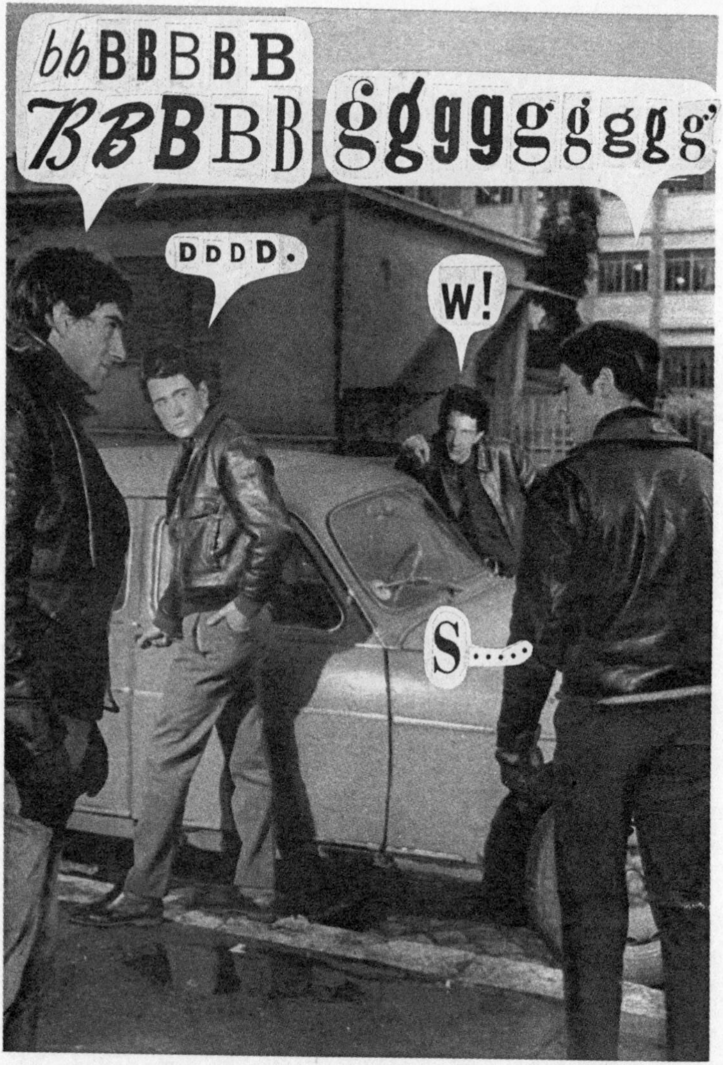
bbBBBBB
BBBBB
ggggggggg'
DDDD.
W!
S....

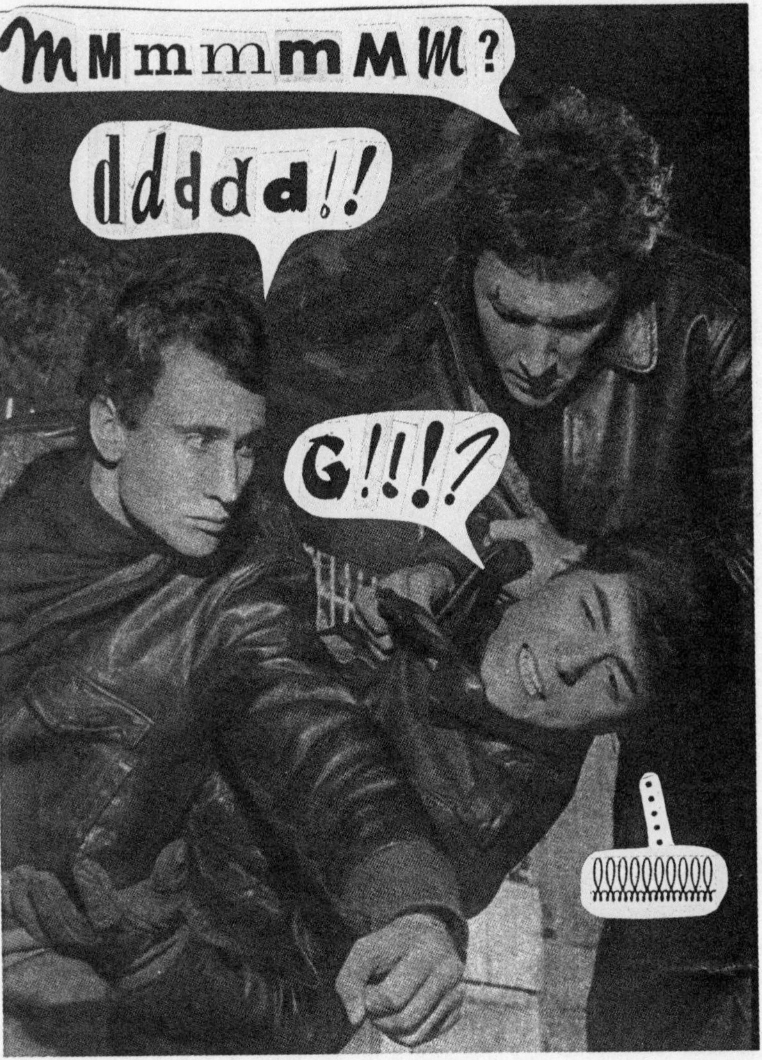
mMmmmMM?
ddddd!!
G!!!?

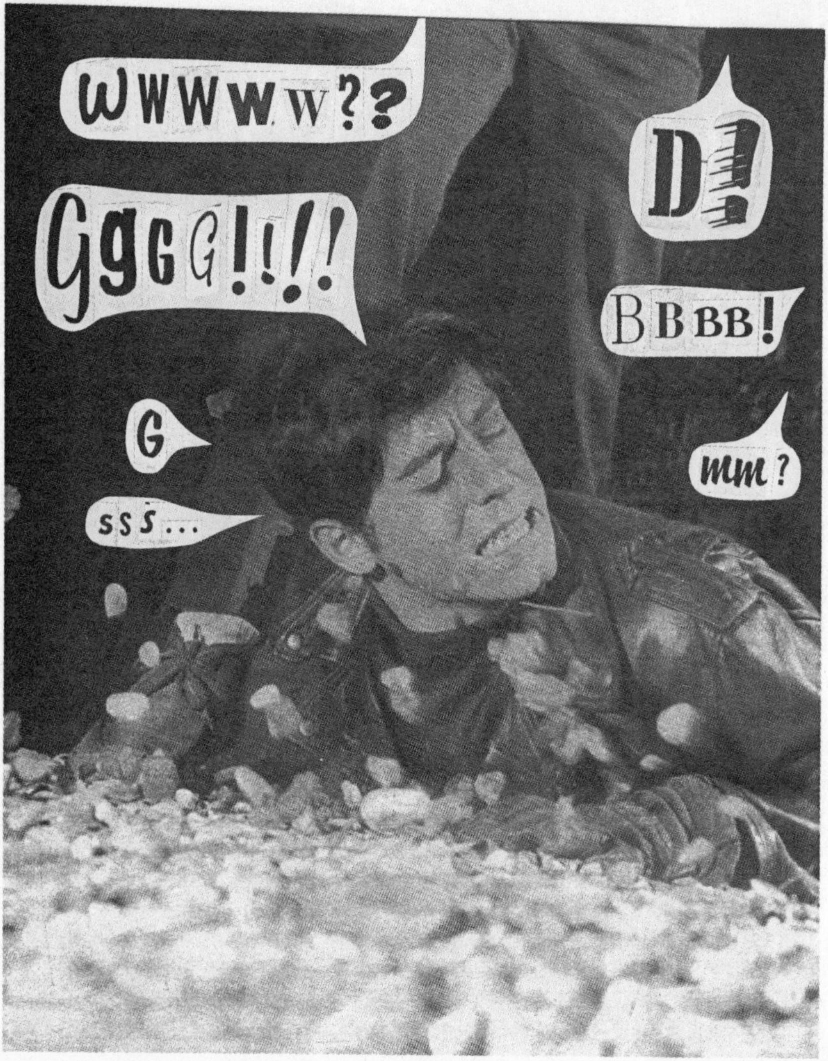
WWWWW??
GggG!!!!
G
sss...
D!
BBBB!
mm?

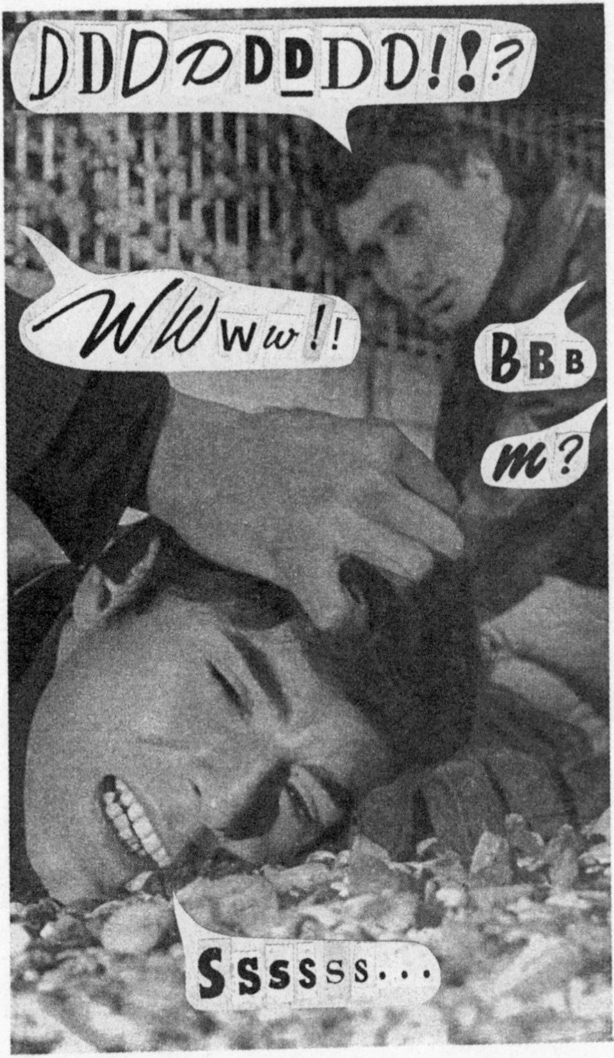
DDDDDDDD!!?
WWww!!
BBB
m?
SSssss...

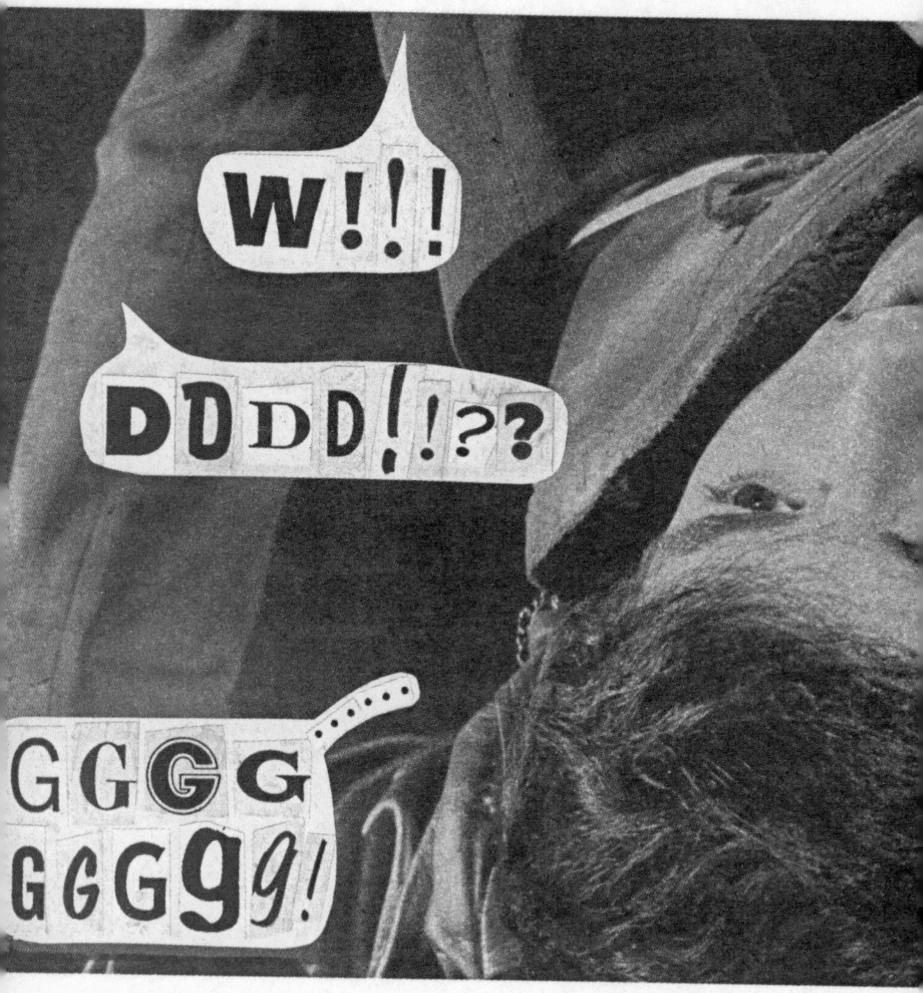
W!!!
DDDD!!??
GGGG
GGGGg!

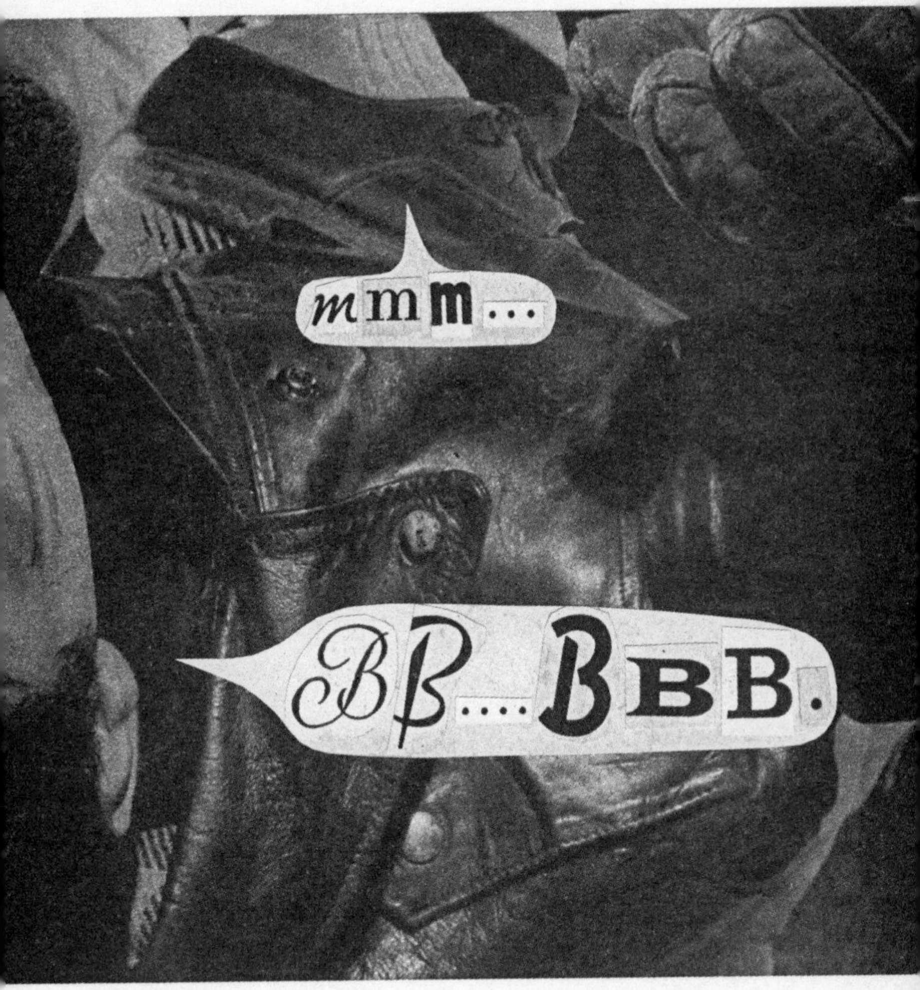
mmm...
Bß....BBB.

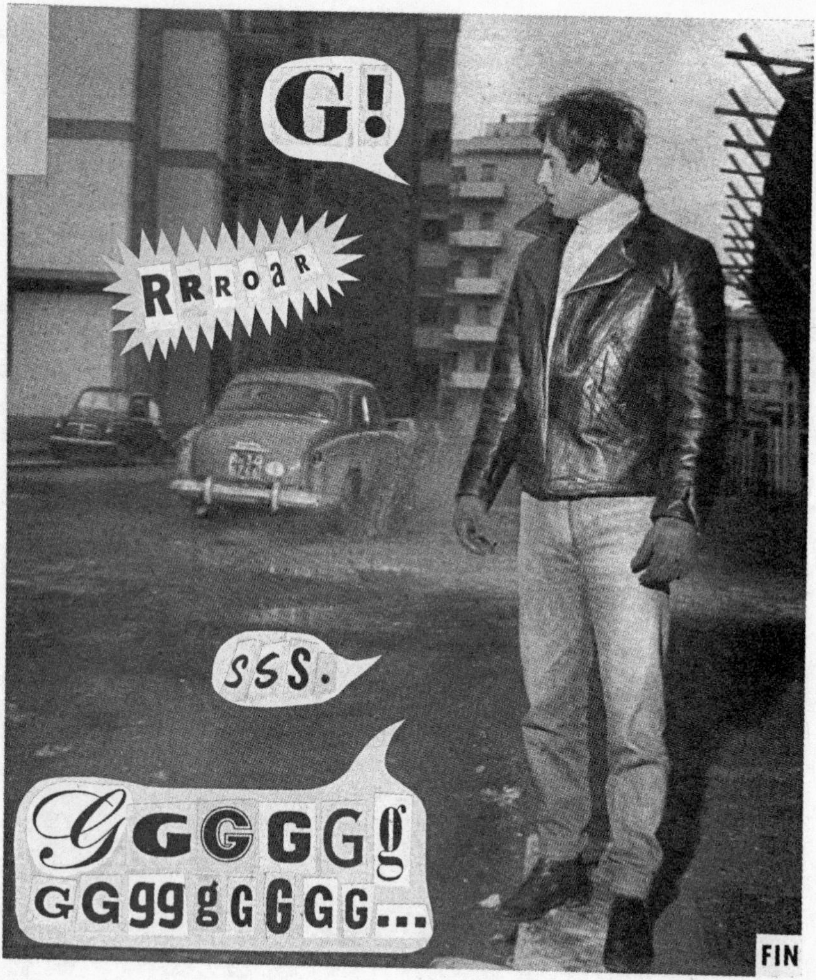
G!
RRROAR
SSS.
GGGGGG
GGggGGGGG...
FIN

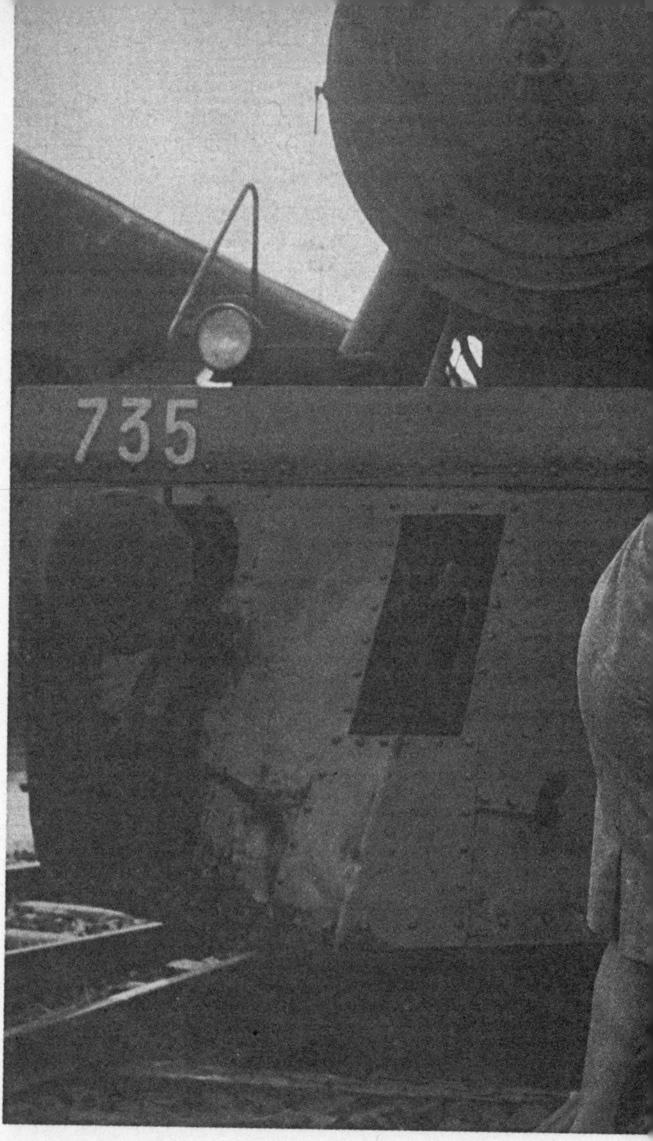
735

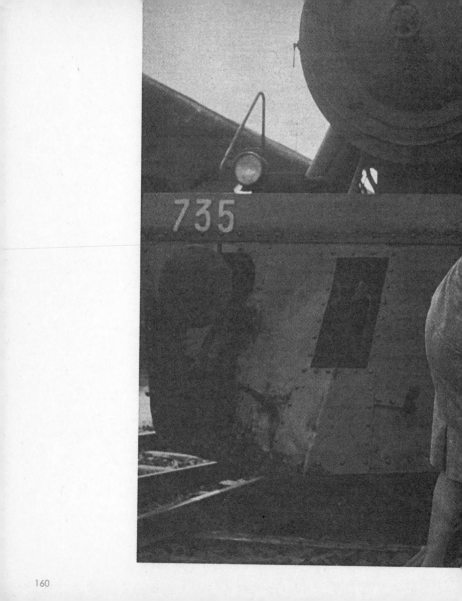

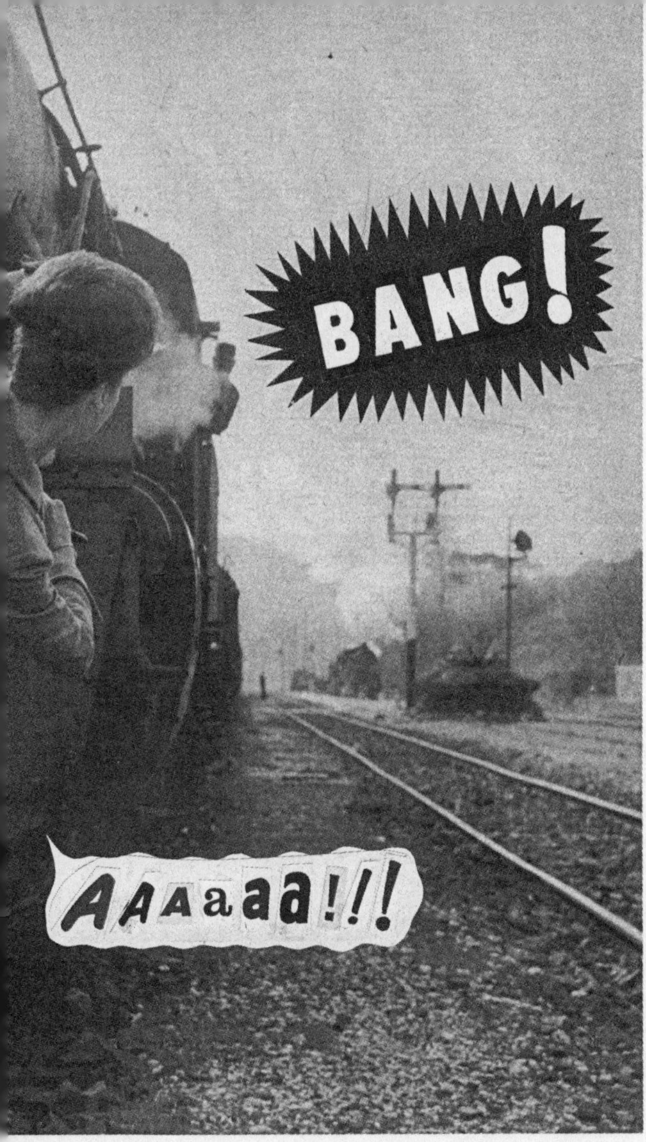
BANG!
AAAaaa!!!

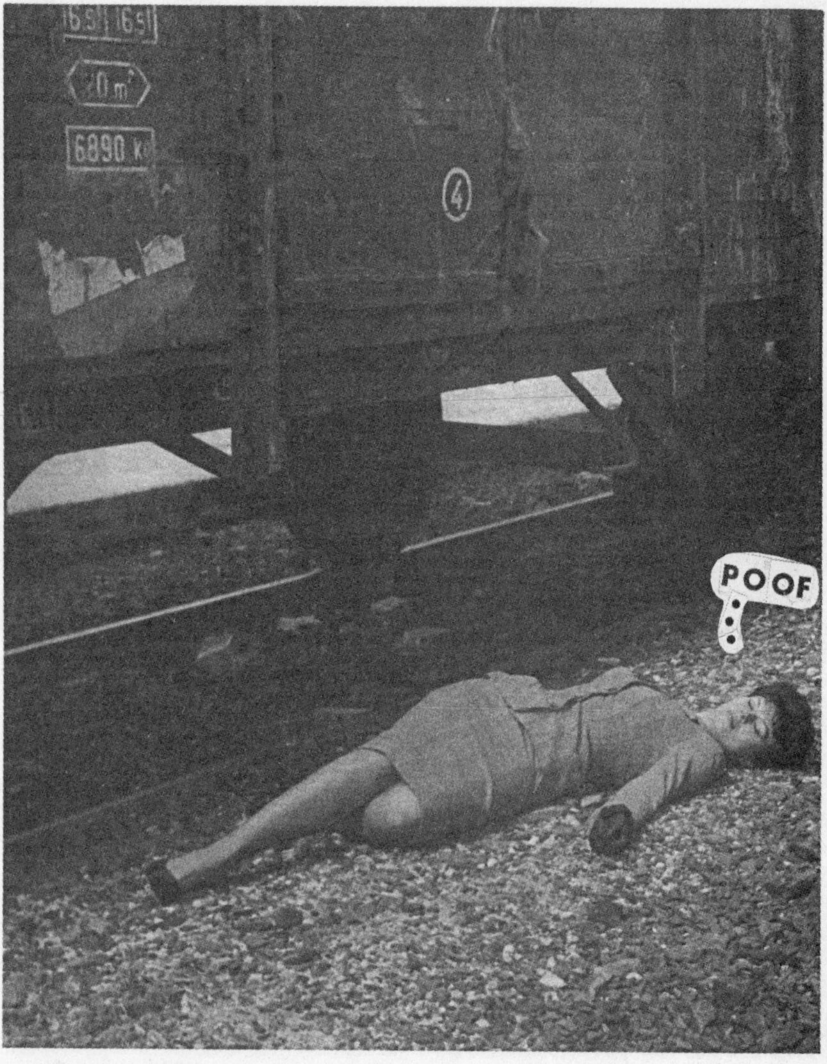
POOF

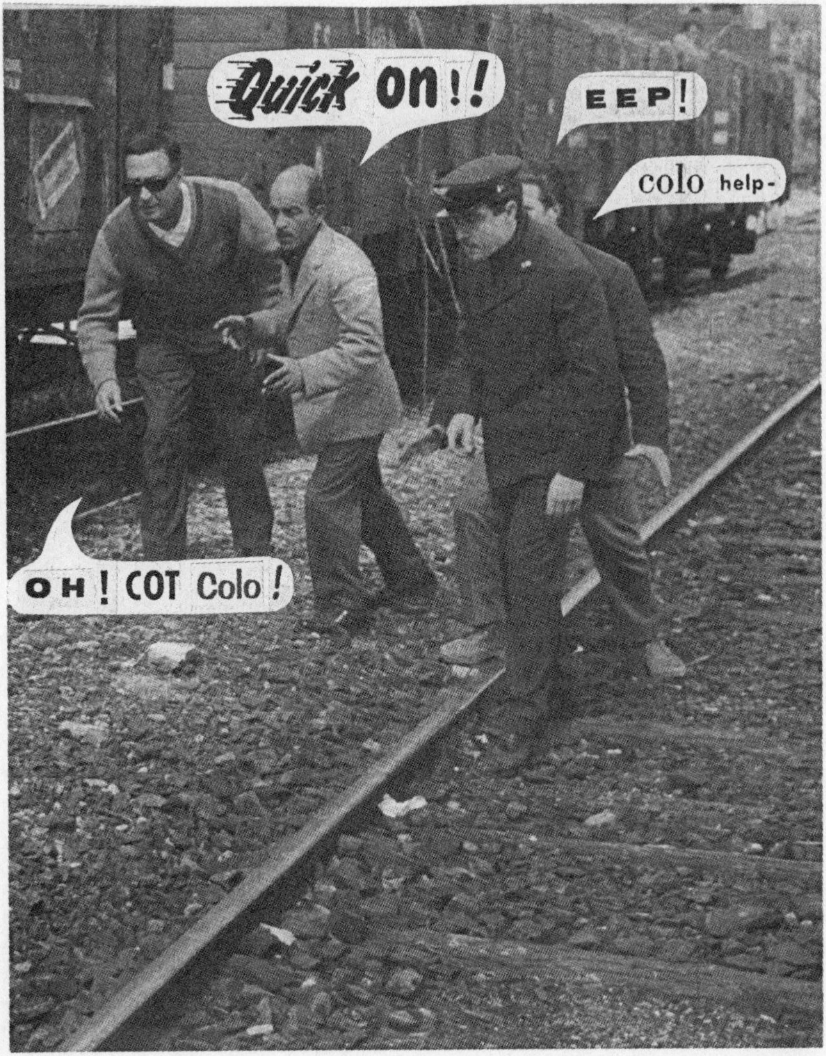
Quick on!!
EEP!
colo help-
OH! COT Colo!

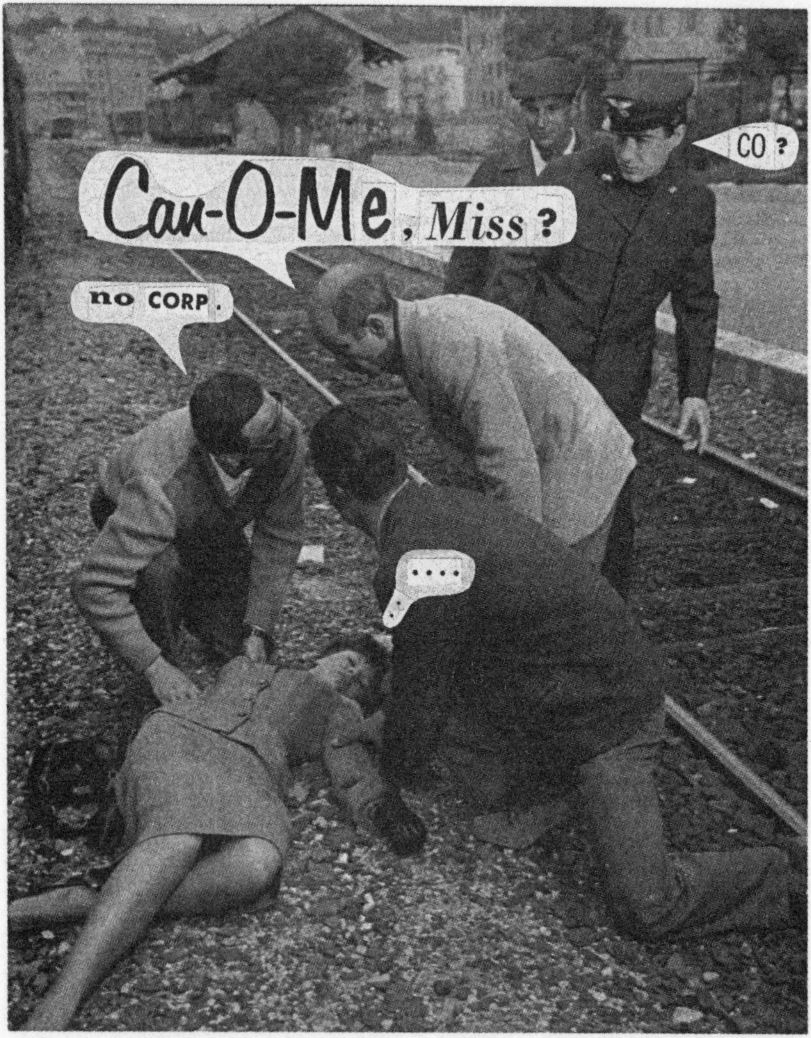

Can-O-Me, Miss ?
CO ?
no CORP.
....

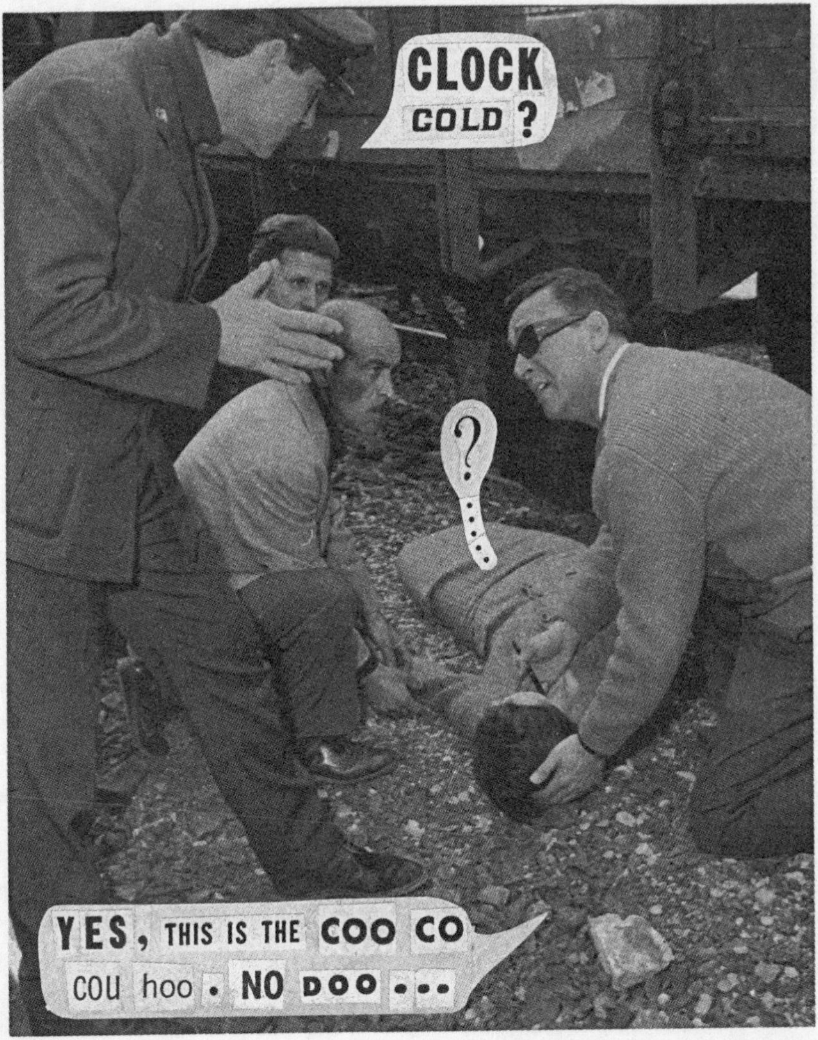
CLOCK
COLD ?
?
YES, THIS IS THE COO CO
COU hoo. NO DOO...

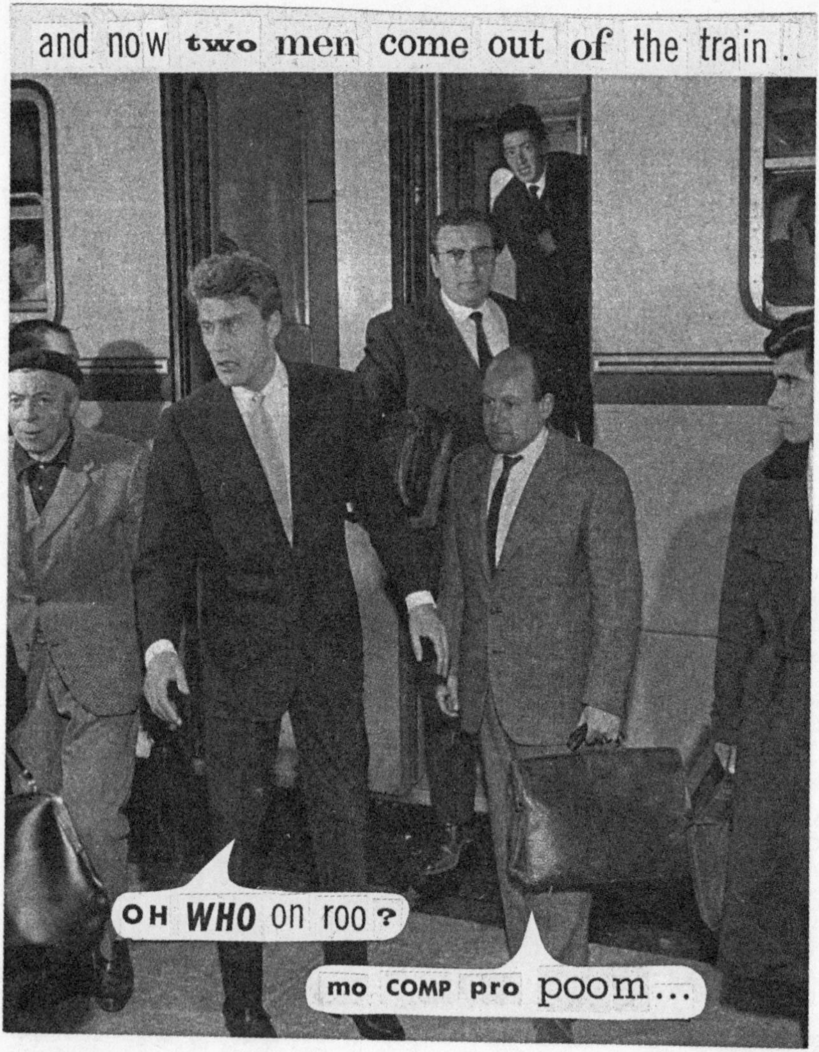
and now two men come out of the train .
OH WHO on roo ?
mo COMP pro poom...

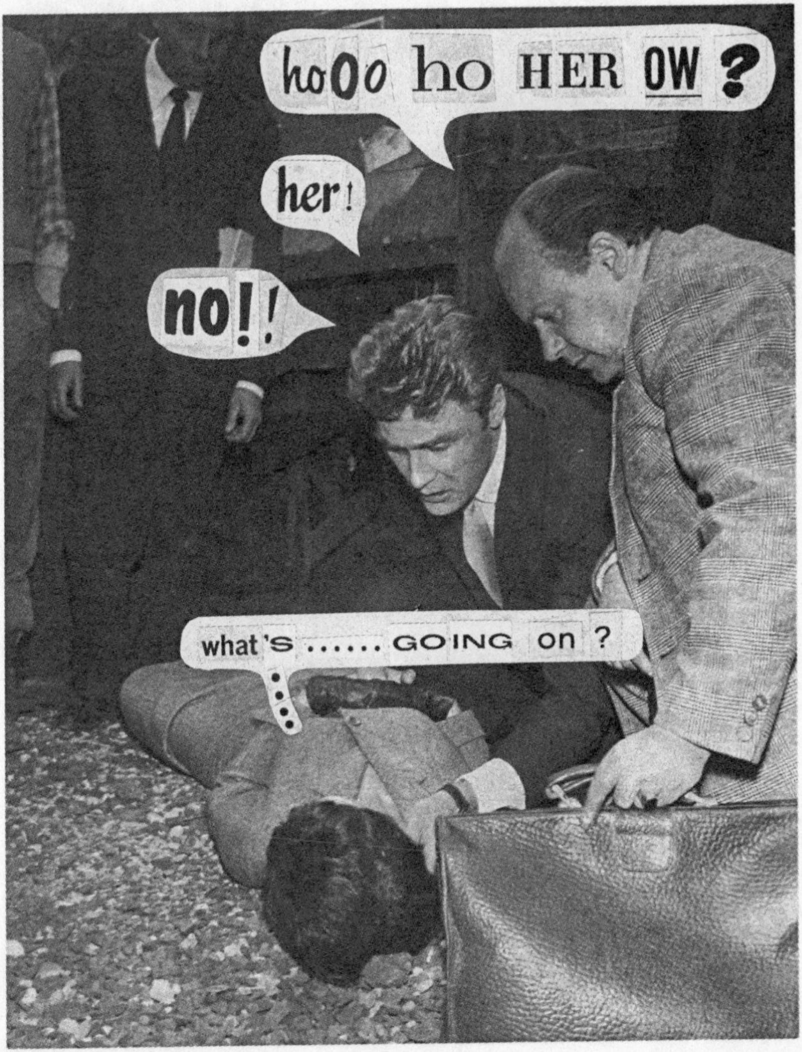
hoOo ho HER OW ?
her !
no! !
what's ...... GOING on ?

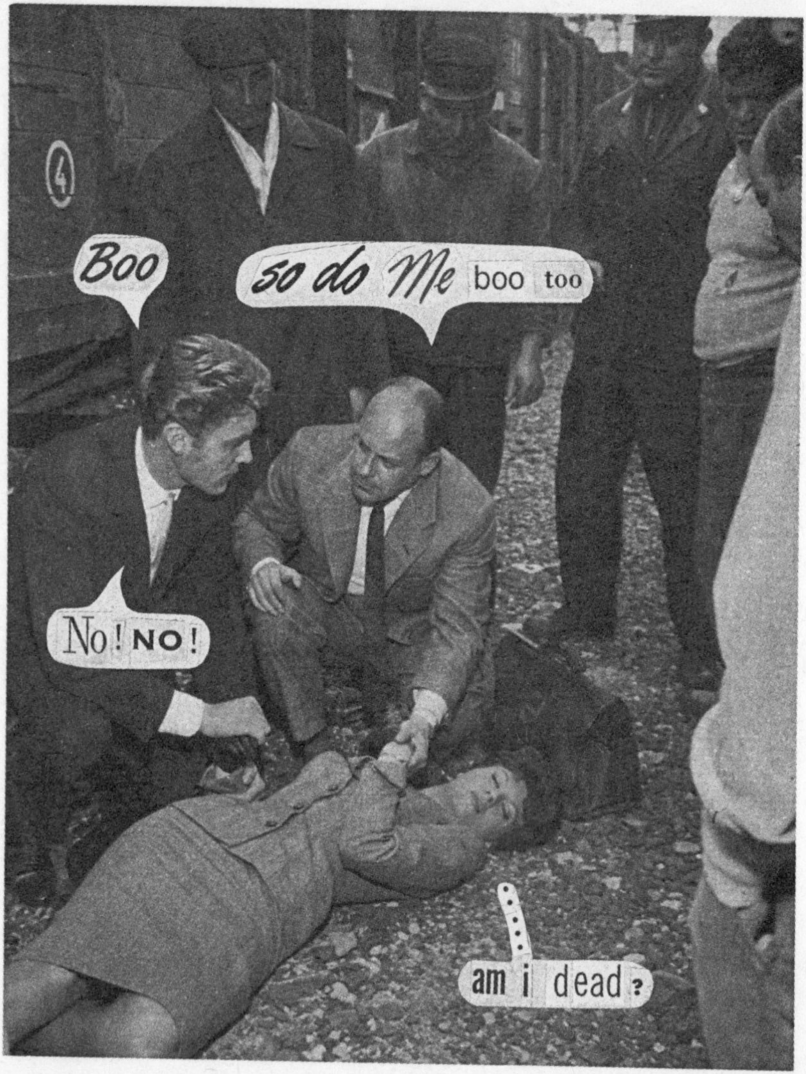
Boo
so do Me boo too
No ! NO !
am i dead ?

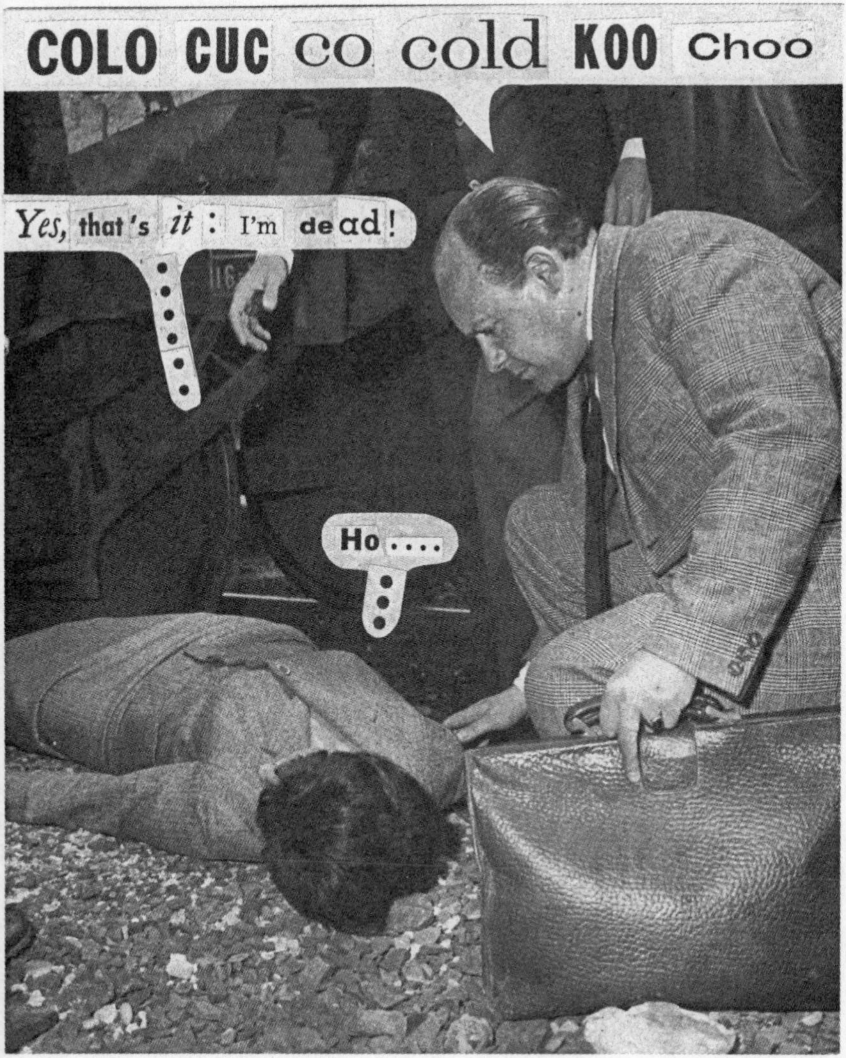
COLO CUC co cold KOO Choo
Yes, that's it : I'm dead!
Ho.....

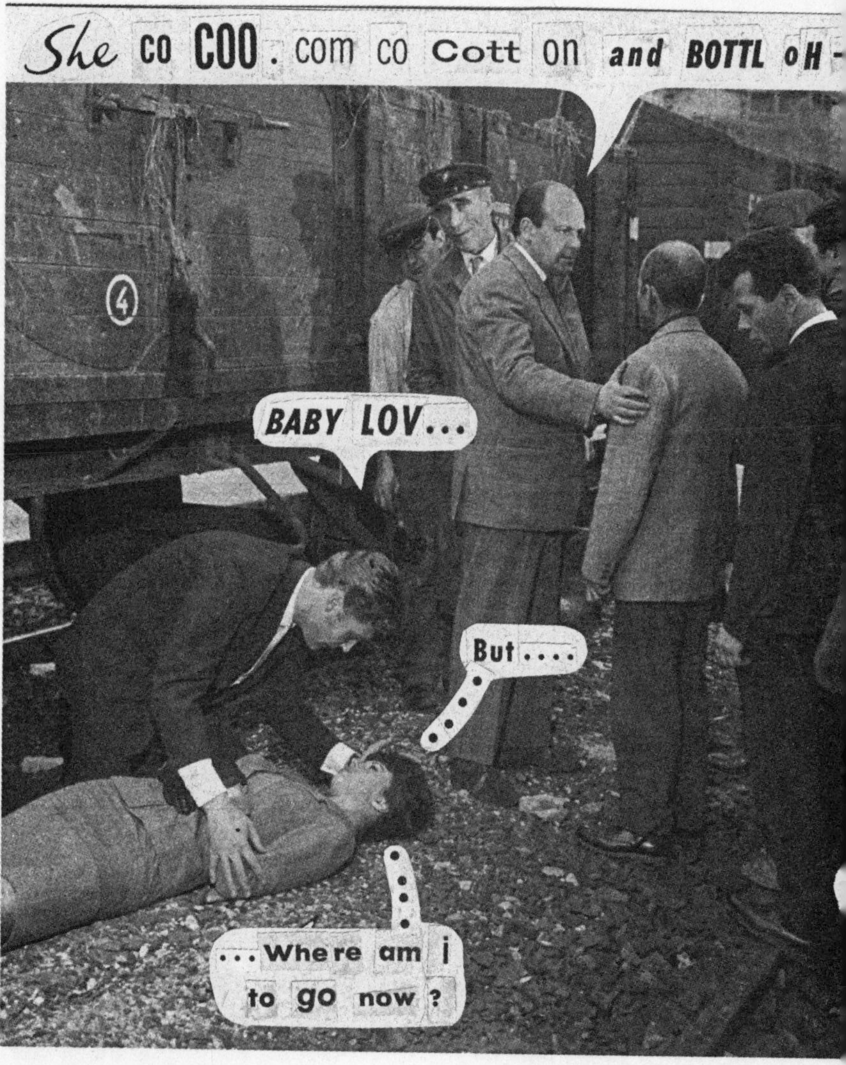
She co COO. com co Cott on and BOTTL oH-
BABY LOV...
But....
...Where am i to go now ?

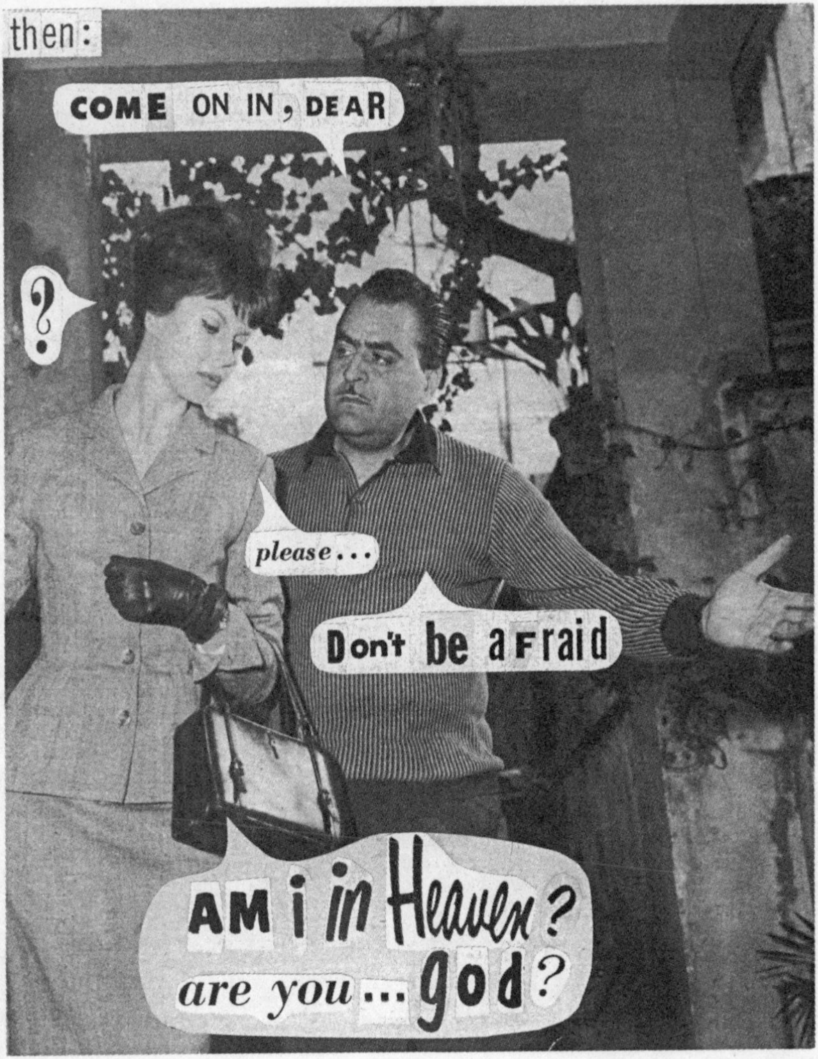
then:
COME ON IN, DEAR
?
please...
Don't be afraid
AM i in Heaven?
are you... god?

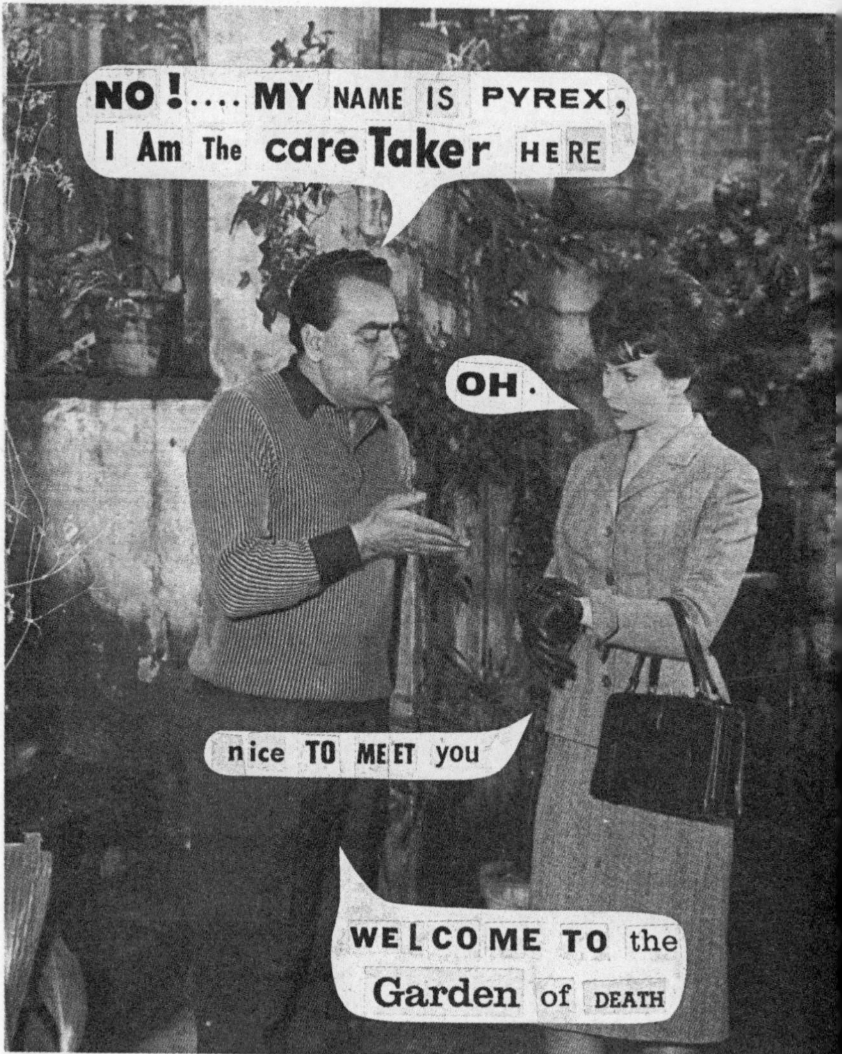
NO!.... MY NAME IS PYREX, I Am The careTaker HERE
OH.
nice TO MEET you
WELCOME TO the Garden of DEATH

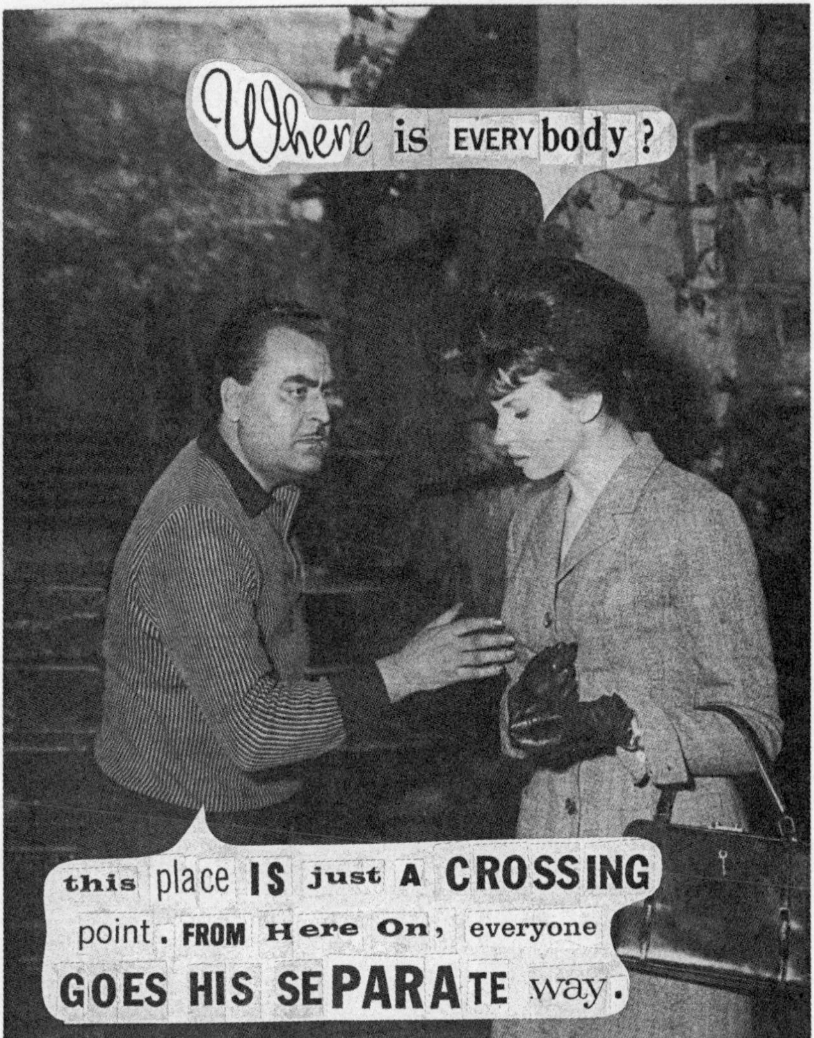
Where is EVERYbody ?
this place IS just A CROSSING point. FROM Here On, everyone GOES HIS SEPARATE way.

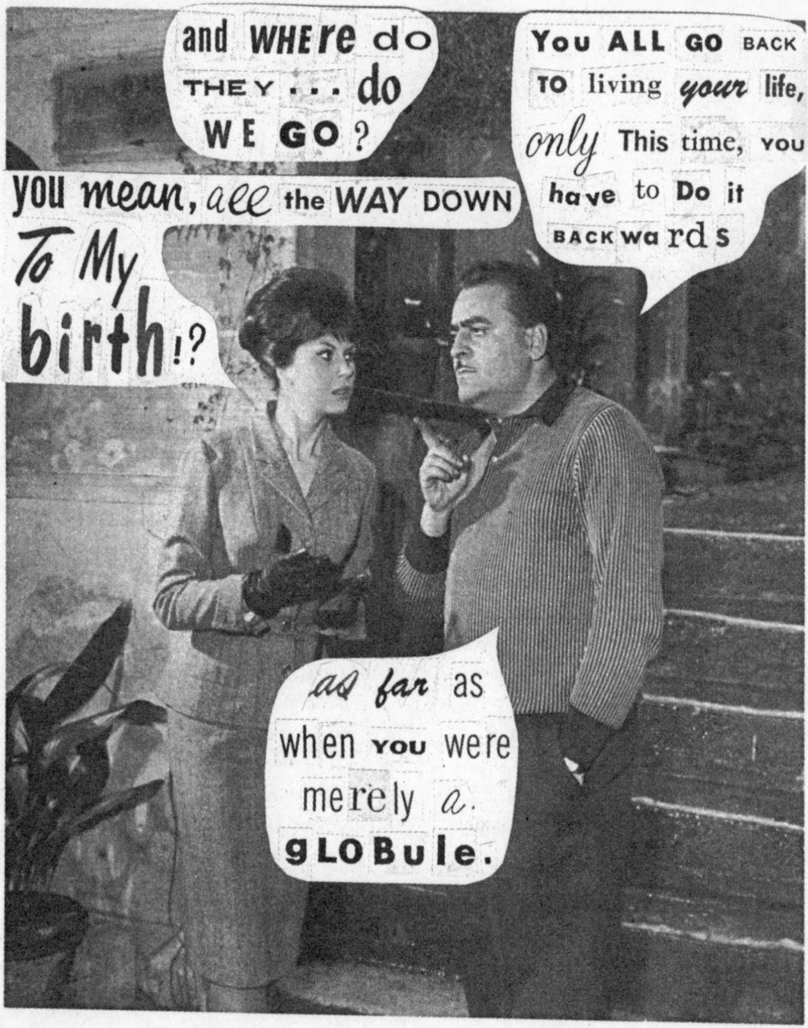
and WHEre do THEY . . . do WE GO?
You ALL GO BACK TO living your life, only This time, you have to Do it BACKwards
you mean, all the WAY DOWN To My birth!?
as far as when you were merely a globule.

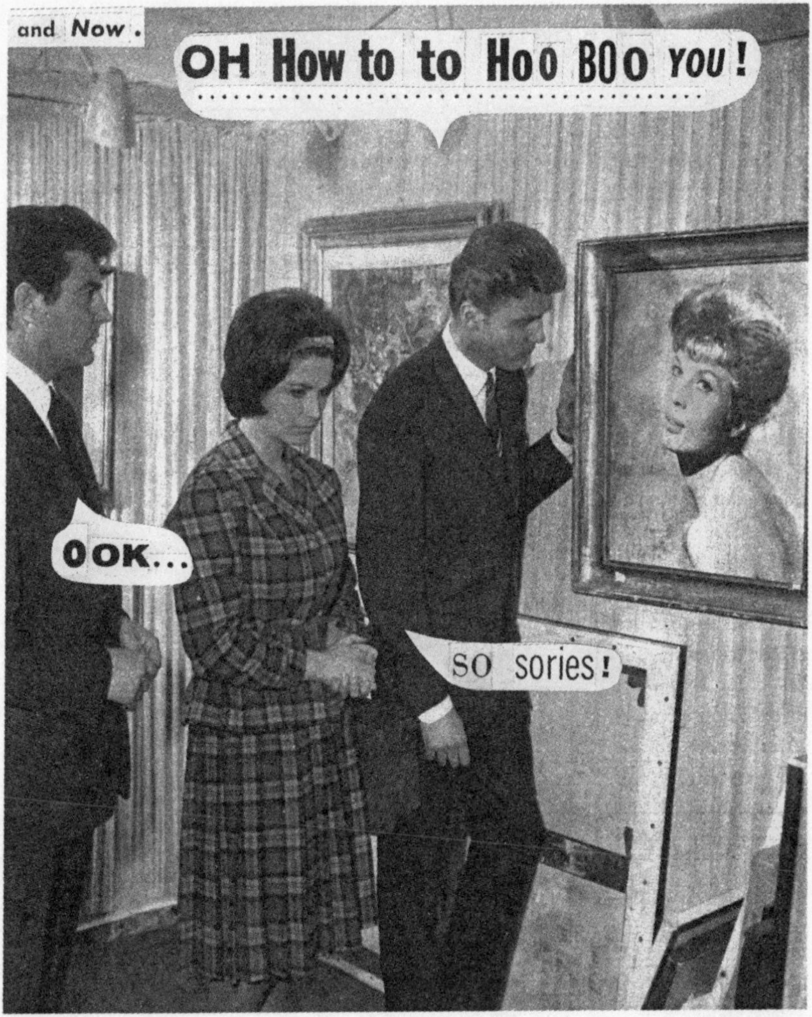
and Now .
OH How to to Hoo BOo YOU !
OOK...
so sories!

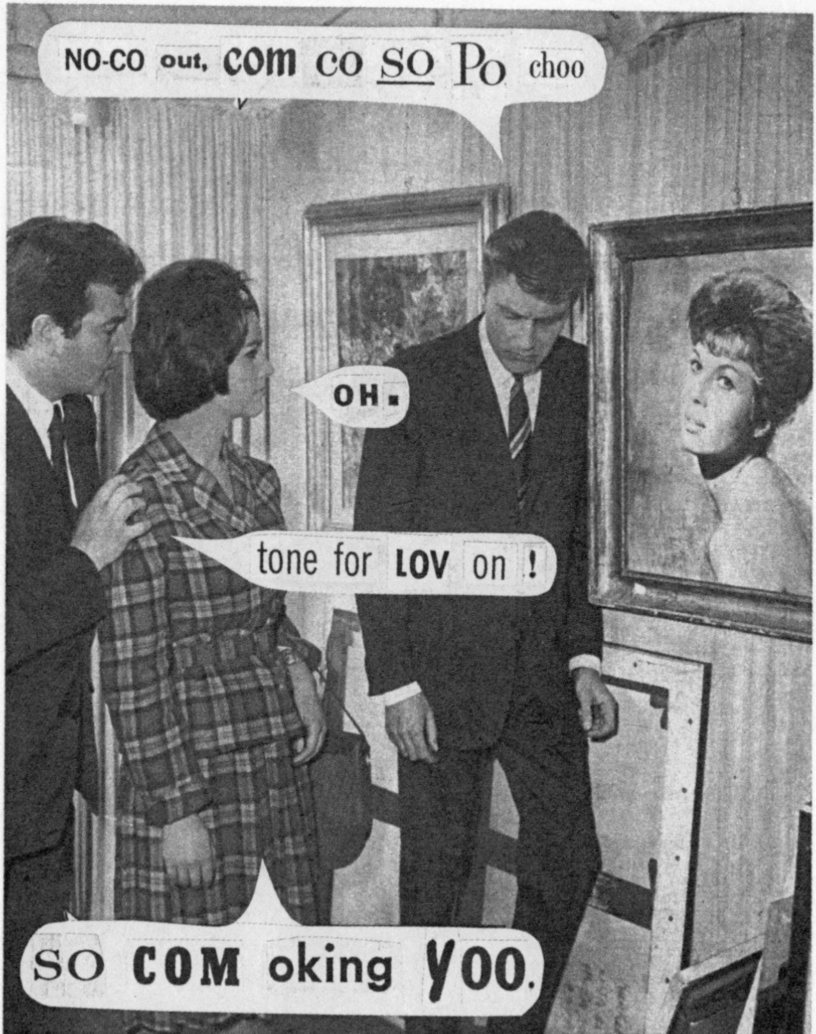
NO-CO out, com co SO Po choo
OH.
tone for LOV on !
SO COM oking YOO.

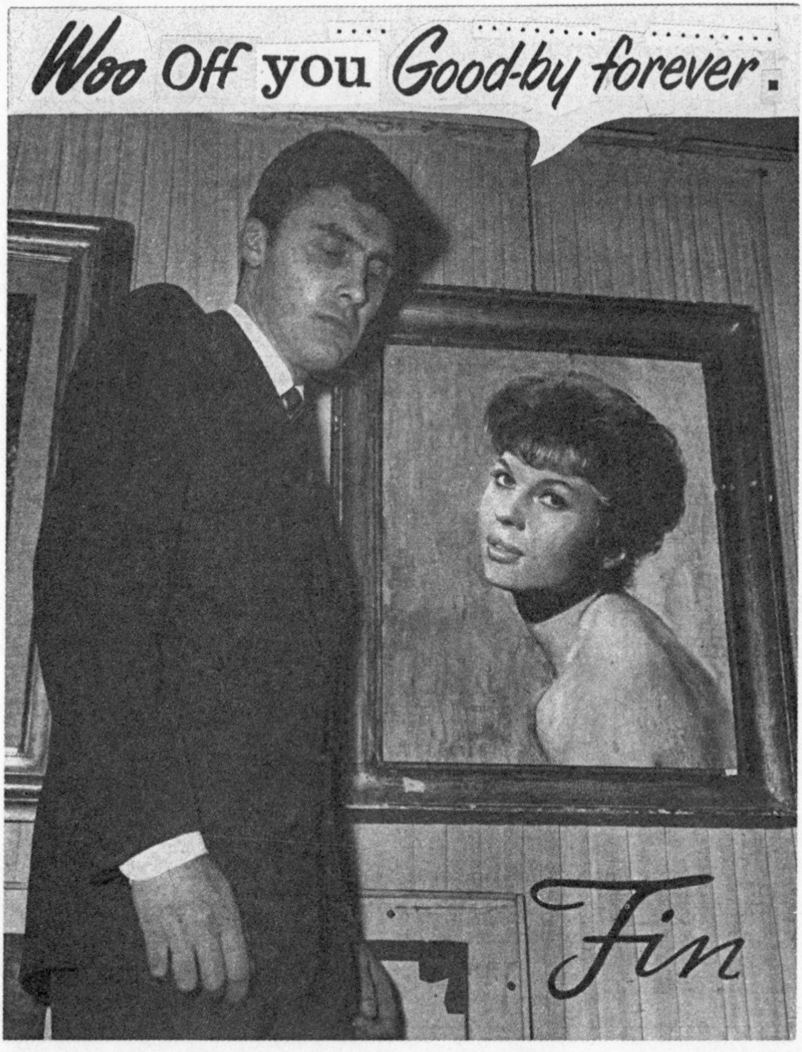

Woo Off you Good-by forever.
Fin

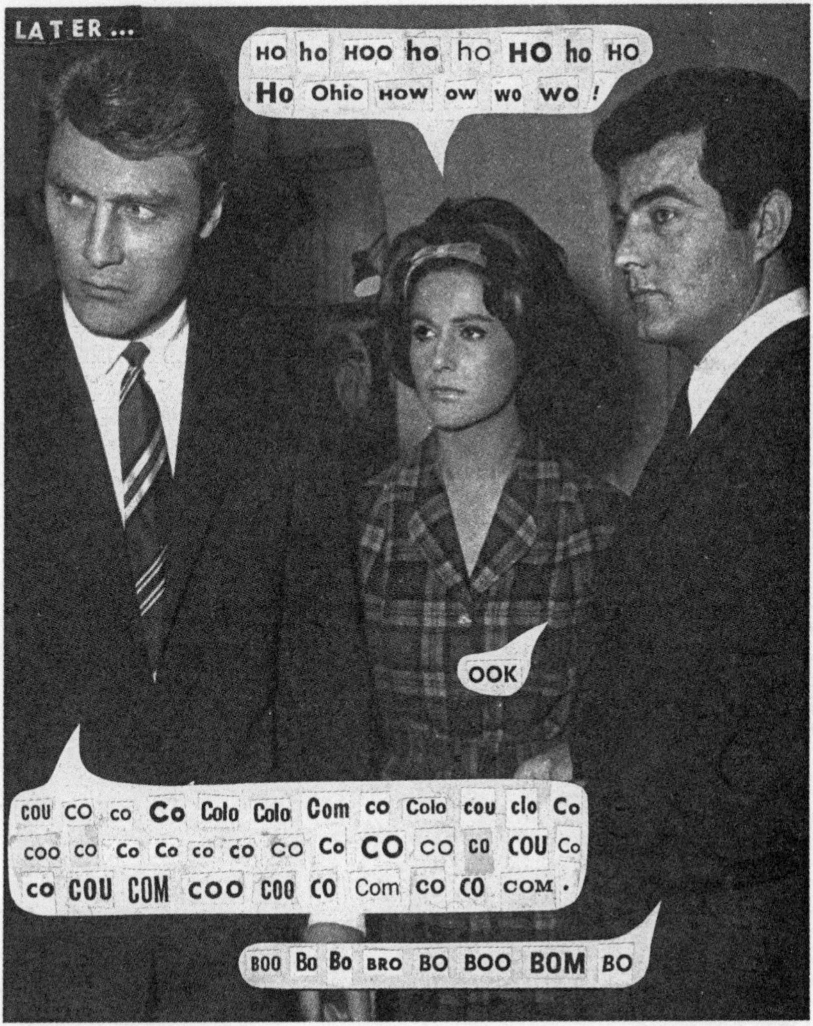
LATER ...
HO ho HOO ho ho HO ho HO Ho Ohio HOW OW WO WO !
OOK
COU CO co Co Colo Colo Com co Colo cou clo Co coo CO Co Co co co CO Co CO co co COU Co co COU COM coo coo CO Com co CO com.
BOO Bo Bo BRO BO BOO BOM BO

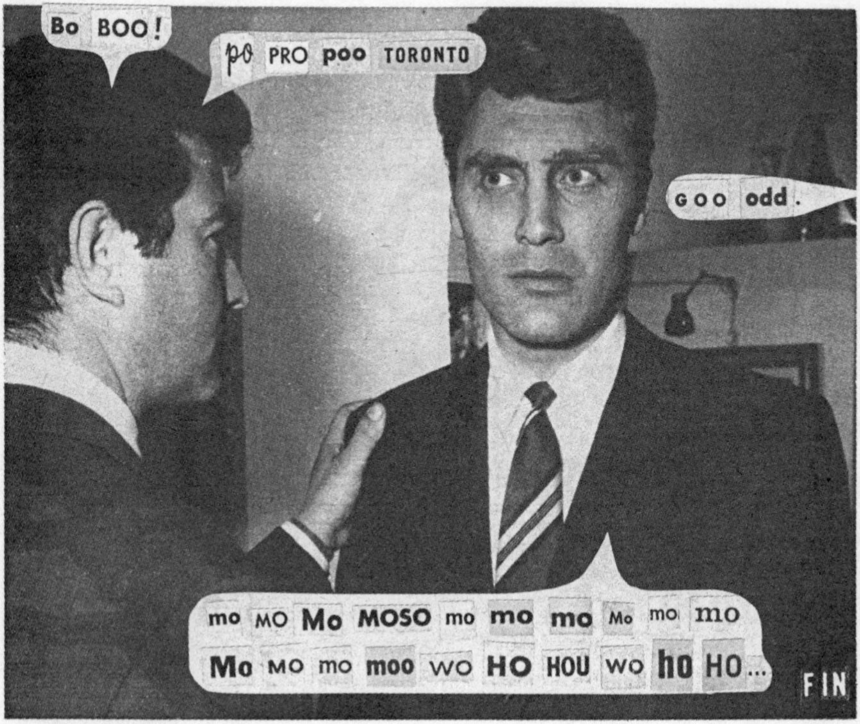
Bo BOO!
po PRO poo TORONTO
GOO odd.
mo MO Mo MOSO mo mo mo Mo mo mo Mo MO mo moo WO HO HOU WO ho HO...
FIN

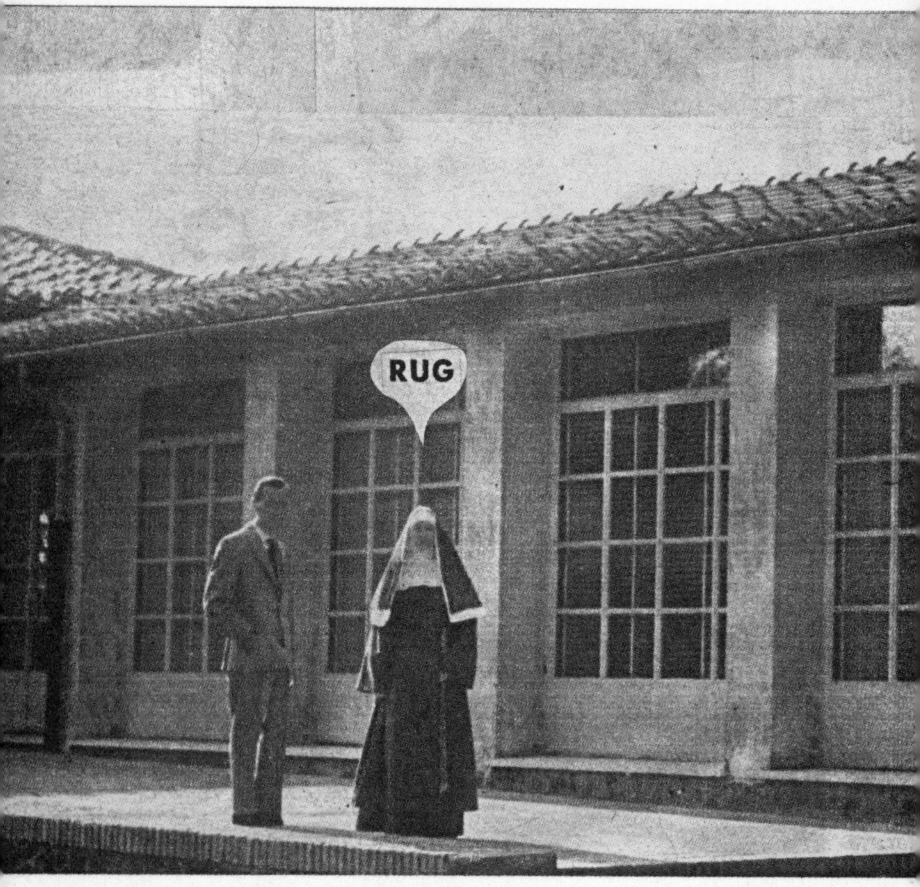
RUG

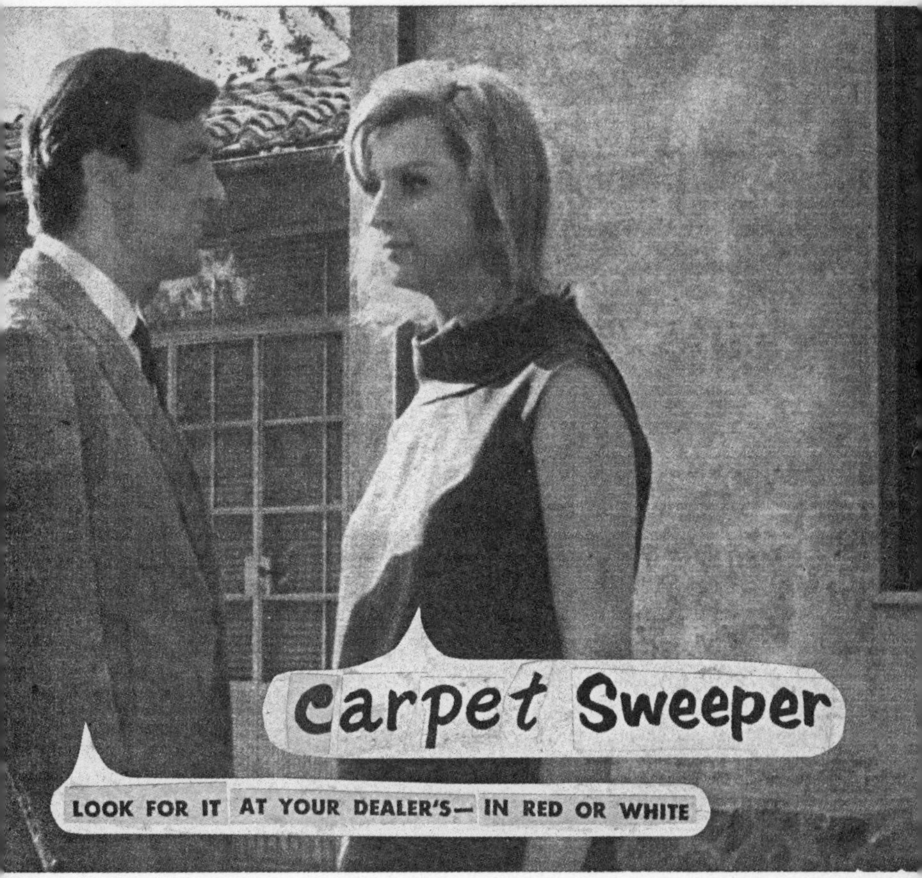
Carpet Sweeper
LOOK FOR IT AT YOUR DEALER'S— IN RED OR WHITE